Reaching the Unreached

Reaching the Unreached
An Introductory Study
on Developing an Overall Strategy
for World Evangelization

by Edward C. Pentecost

William Carey Library

533 HERMOSA STREET • SOUTH PASADENA, CALIF. 91030 • TEL. 213-682-2047

Copyright © 1974 by the William Carey Library

All rights reserved. No part of this book may be used or reproduced in any manner whatsoever without written permission, except in the case of brief quotations embodied in critical articles or reviews. For information address the William Carey Library, 305 Pasadena Ave., S. Pasadena Calif., 91030, Telephone 218-799-4559.

Library of Congress Catalog Card Number 74-11270
International Standard Book Number 0-87808-418-5

In accord with some of the most recent thinking in the academic press, the William Carey Library is pleased to present this scholarly book which has been prepared from an author-edited and author-prepared camera-ready manuscript.

PRINTED IN THE UNITED STATES OF AMERICA

Dedication

This book is dedicated to God, the Holy Spirit, on behalf of the unreached peoples of this world. My prayer is that God will use it to cause Christians to recognize distinct units of unreached peoples, and to consider what they can do to reach them.

Table of Contents

	Page
TABLE OF GRAPHICS	v
PREFACE	vii
ACKNOWLEDGMENTS	ix
GLOSSARY	xi

Chapter 1	INTRODUCTION	1
	The Challenge	1
	The Scope	2
	The Detail	6
	The Occasion	8
	The Historical Perspective	11
	The Present Trend	16
	The Ultimate Purpose	18

PART ONE

	THE IDENTIFICATION OF THE UNREACHED	21
Chapter 2	THE IMPORTANCE OF SEEING THE WORLD IN HOMOGENEOUS UNITS	23
	Definition Of Terms	29
	Scriptural Validity	31
	The Obstacles Of Magnitude And Complexity	32
	The Prominence Of People Consciousness	35
	The Diversity Of Expression	38

		Page
Chapter 3	BASIC TYPES OF HOMOGENEOUS UNITS	43
	Ethnic	44
	Linguistic	45
	Religious	46
	Socio-economic	47
	Urban	50
	Rural	50

PART TWO

THE EVANGELIZATION OF UNITS — 55

Chapter 4	UNDERSTANDING SCRIPTURAL EVANGELISM	57
	Proclamation	58
	Response	58
	Message	59
	Witness	60
Chapter 5	EFFECTIVE COMMUNICATION FOR EVANGELISM	62
	Comprehensible Communication	62
	Cultural Relevance	64
	The Reception Of The Message	67
	The Channel Of Communication Of The Message	70

PART THREE

THE EVIDENCES OF RESPONSIVENESS — 77

Chapter 6	USE OF INDICATORS TO DETERMINE READINESS TO RESPOND	79
	Validity Of Indicators	80
	Limitations In The Use Of Indicators	83
	Examples Of The Use Of Indicators	84

		Page
Chapter 7	PROPOSED INDICATORS	91
	Dissatisfaction	91
	Culture Change	93
	Kinship Structures	97
	Communication Channels	98
	Political Change	98
	Economic Change	100
	Migration	102
	Linguistic Change	105
	Religious Change	106
	Prototype	107
	Degree Of Christian Influence	109
Chapter 8	PRAGMATICS	112
	High-Low Scale Pattern	112
	Venn Diagram Pattern	116
	Communication Pattern	118

PART FOUR

THE POTENTIAL AMBASSADORS   121

Chapter 9	PEOPLE FROM ALL THE WORLD	123
	Missions Not A Western Monopoly	125
	Effective Communication	125
	Acceptable Prototype	126
	Gifted Of The Spirit	127
	Increasing Influence	129

	Page
BIBLIOGRAPHY	135
INDEX	145
APPENDIX	151

PART I

COUNTRY GRAPHICS - PERCENTAGE CHRISTIAN BY ETHNIC GROUPS 151

PART II

Section A - Professing Christianity 196

Section B - Questionnaire 200
Unreached Peoples List 206

Section C - Status of Christianity
Country Profile BURMA 215
Status of Christianity
Profile Series 223

Section D - Summary People Profiles 224

Section E - Empirical Data 230

Table of Graphics

		Page
Graphic 1	THE VISIBLE CHURCH	3
Graphic 2	THE VISIBLE CHURCH (b)	4
Graphic 3	WORLD POPULATION GROWTH DURING THE "CHRISTIAN CENTURY"	5
Graphic 4	INDONESIA - ESTIMATED CHRISTIAN POPULATION BY ETHNIC GROUPS	7
Graphic 5	INDIA - ESTIMATED CHRISTIAN POPULATION BY ETHNIC GROUPS	25
Graphic 6	NIGERIA - ESTIMATED RELIGIOUS PROFESSIONS BY ETHNIC GROUPS	37
Graphic 7	RACE AND CLASS IN BRAZIL	49
Graphic 8	RURAL COMMUNITY STRUCTURE	52
Graphic 9	RURAL VILLAGE STRUCTURE	53
Graphic 10	CITY STRUCTURE	54
Graphic 11	COMMUNICATION BARRIERS	75
Graphic 12	VENN DIAGRAM	89
Graphic 13	WATTS RIOT	90
Graphic 14	WALLACE DIAGRAM	92
Graphic 15	LAOS - ESTIMATED CHRISTIAN POPULATION BY ETHNIC GROUPS	104
Graphic 16	READY RESPONSE AREA	117
Graphic 17	COMMUNICATION PATTERN	118

Preface

To express personal gratitude to all who gave assistance and encouragement toward the compilation of this project would be impossible. I can mention only a few of those who deserve special recognition. My first expression of gratitude is to the Lord Himself who so miraculously worked out all the details. Within days of having the field of study approved, I was asked to serve as Research Coordinator for the International Congress on World Evangelization which afforded a base from which to conduct the research.

My sincerest appreciation is expressed to Mr. Paul E. Little, Associate Director for Program of ICOWE and his part in providing the opportunity for the research; to Mr. Edward R. Dayton, Director of Missions Advanced Research and Communications Center, for his constant oversight in management of the entire project; to Mr. William L. Needham, Associate Director of MARC, for his meticulous care and wise judgment in every aspect of the research; to all of the personnel of MARC who assisted with correspondence and handling of information that was accumulated, as well as with all of the many details of the operation.

Special recognition must be given to all of those in various countries who provided information and input to the research endeavor. Without their cooperation the whole project would have been a failure.

Mr. Leslie Brierley of the Worldwide Evangelization Crusade was especially helpful in the accomplishment of this task, making available valuable information which he sent from England from his own personal files.

The entire faculty of the School of World Mission of Fuller Theological Seminary became my counselors in the administering and carrying out of the duties incumbent upon such an undertaking. They formed an important part in the whole program, as well as serving in capacity of academic oversignt and encouragement.

The Research Associates of the School of World Mission also assisted by providing information from their rich and assorted backgrounds.

Special recognition must be given to Dr. Ralph D. Winter who willingly served as Mentor for the writing of this document, and constantly gave wise counsel and encouragement in the preparation of it.

Recognition must be given to Dr. Arthur F. Glasser, Dean of the School of World Mission of Fuller Theological Seminary, and to Mr. C. Peter Wagner, both of whom served on the Examining Committee and gave most helpful suggestions and constant encouragement.

Finally, I am most grateful to my wife and family who daily supported me with their prayers and endured with patience all the long hours of work and time taken from family activities that otherwise would have been ours. Without their support this work never would have been done.

To all, I express my deepest appreciation.

The author
May, 1974

Acknowledgments

Grateful acknowledgment is given to the following publishers and authors for permission to reprint copyright material from the titles listed below:

Christianity Today, for permission to quote from the article "Existing Churches: Ends or Means?" by Ralph D. Winter in the January 19, 1973 issue.

Creation House, Carol Stream, Ill., for permission to quote from *Look Out! The Pentecostals Are Coming* by C. Peter Wagner, © 1973.

Wm. B. Eerdmans Publishing Co., Grand Rapids, Michigan, for permission to quote from *Understanding Church Growth* by Donald McGavran, © 1970.

Harper & Row Publishers, New York, N.Y., for permission to quote from *Religion Across Cultures,* by Eugene A. Nida, © 1968.

International Review of Missions, for permission to quote from the article, "Bangkok, the New Opportunity" by Emilio Castro in the October issue, 1973.

Macmillan Publishing Co., Inc., New York, N.Y., for permission to quote from *Communication of Innovations: A Cross-Cultural Approach,* by Everett M. Rogers, © 1971.

McGraw-Hill Book Co., New York, N.Y., for permission to quote from *Innovation: The Basis of Culture Change,* by Homer G. Barnett, © 1953.

Missions Advanced Research & Communications Center, Monrovia, Cal., for permission to quote from *Brazil 1980: The Protestant Handbook,* by William R. Read and Frank Ineson, © 1973.

Missiology, for permission to quote from the article, "Dynamic Equivalence Churches" by Charles H. Kraft, January, © 1973.

Prentice-Hall, Inc., Englewood Cliffs, New Jersey, for permission to quote from *Spatial Organization: The Geographer's View of the World*, by Ronald Abler, John S. Adams, and Peter Gould, © 1971.

C. Peter Wagner, Pasadena, Cal., for permission to quote from *Frontiers in Missionary Strategy*, © 1971.

William Carey Library, South Pasadena, Cal., for permission to quote from *The Gospel and Frontier Peoples*, by R. Pierce Beaver, ed., © 1973.

World Wide Publications, Minneapolis, Minn., for permission to quote from *One Race, One Gospel, One Task*, by Carl F. H. Henry and W. Stanley Mooneyham, © 1967.

Yale University Press, New Haven, Conn., for permission to quote from *World Handbook of Political and Social Indicators*, by Bruce Russett, © 1962, and *The Dynamics of Culture Change*, by Bronislaw Malinawski © 1949.

Glossary

ADVOCATE - One who speaks in favor of something, usually something new. i.e., a proponent of something new as a missionary or evangelist who proposes Christianity to a people or group who have not previously accepted the gospel message.

ANTHROPOLOGY - The study of man within his cultural characteristics, customs, and social relationships.

CHRISTIAN - One who professes belief in Jesus as the Christ, and becomes His follower.

COMMUNICATIONS - The science of the art of giving or exchanging information or ideas.

ECLECTICISM - The developing of a system by selection from various systems, doctrines, or sources.

ETHNO-LINGUISTIC - Related to racial and language characteristics. i.e., one is of a certain homogeneous unit, characterized by being of the same race and language as another, bringing both into the same group.

EVANGELIZED - To have had a real chance to intelligently decide to become responsible members of Christ's Church.

[The terms "Evangelized" and "Reached" are interpreted differently. To some, a person is "Evangelized" when he receives the Gospel, "Reached" when he hears the Gospel whether he responds or not. To others the inverse is true; when a person has been "Reached" his heart has been touched so that he responds to the Gospel, and he may be "Evangelized" without responding.

The difference seems to be entirely one of understanding and definition of the individual. For the purpose of this document there is no differentiation made between "Evangelized" and "Reached."]

FRONTIERS - Those areas where one group of people comes into face to face contact with another. i.e., the "Frontier" in Brazil where the indians of the Amazon jungle come into face to face contact with Christianity.

GOSPEL - The "good news" of salvation in Jesus Christ, by which one who believes is made a child of God, with sins forgiven and redemption received. It is the message of the death of Christ, His burial and resurrection in substitution for mankind.

HOMOGENEOUS UNITS - Groups of people that have characteristics, interests, or elements that are similar or identical. i.e., people that speak the same dialect are homogeneous as defined by identical language. People of the same race are homogeneous as defined by similar racial characteristics.

INNOVATOR - One who introduces something new, being within the group to which it is being introduced, thus the first within a unit to accept a new method, custom, device. i.e., the first to accept the gospel message within a homogeneous unit.

PARAGON - A model of perfection or excellence. To set as an example.

PEOPLE-CONSCIOUSNESS - The recognition of self identity, or personal worth as a group.

REACHED - To have been evangelized.

RECEPTIVE - Ready to listen to the presentation of the gospel message, usually implying a subsequent response to it when it is understood.

PROTOTYPE - A standard of reference. An ideal, concept, or mental image which one has in his mind by which he judges. i.e., the concept an individual has concerning Christianity determines whether he wants to follow it or not.

RESISTANT - Unready to accept the gospel message and become responsible members of the Church of Jesus Christ, usually implying a lack of willingness to respond when the message is understood.

RESPONSIVE - Ready to react to suggestion or appeal to accept the gospel message and become responsible members of the Church of Jesus Christ.

SELF-IDENTITY - A recognition of worth, distinctives, and characteristics that lead to acceptance and appreciation. i.e., "Black is beautiful."

SOCIAL INDICATOR - Statistics, statistical series, and all other forms of evidence that enable us to assess where we stand and are going with respect to our values and goals, and to evaluate specific programs and determine their impact.

SOCIO-ECONOMIC - Related to class within society, and economic standards. i.e., one is of a certain socio-economic homogeneous unit, characterized by being of the same society, class, caste, and economic standard group.

SOCIOLOGY - The study of human relationships within which man moves, operates, and functions.

SUPRA-CULTURAL - That which is beyond human culture, usually implying divine characteristics.

SYNCRETISM - An attempt to correlate two different entities. i.e., to inter-mix practices and beliefs of two distinct religions. It may be Animism and Moslem practices, but usually refers to an attempt to mix Christian practices with animistic practices.

THEOLOGY - The study of God and the relationships between God, man, and the universe.

THIRD WORLD - The newly developing nations, usually considered as Asia, Africa, Latin America and Oceania. A term not appreciated by some, but generally used nevertheless.

TRANS-CULTURAL - That which is related to cross-cultural phenomena. That which pertains to various cultures, and may be transmitted or communicated from one to another.

UNEVANGELIZED - Not to have had a real chance to intelligently decide to become responsible members of Christ's Church.

UNREACHED - Not to have been evangelized. (See EVANGELIZED)

URBANIZATION - The developmental process by which cities are formed.

WORLD-VIEW - One's view of the world, and his understanding of his relationship to it and to the maker of it. Usually implies the religious position of one. The animist has one world view, in which he relates to the world around him and to his concept of the powers in the world to which he is in one way or another responsible or related, whether to fear or love, to sacrifice or prayer.

Chapter 1

Introduction

Out of the Berlin Congress on Evangelism in 1966 came the statement voiced by Ted W. Engstrom:

> The great challenge confronting the Church today is to identify and to locate every person in the world by the end of this century. There is no individual, no people, who cannot be reached with the Gospel if we set ourselves to this supreme task of the Church. We can truly go to "*every* creature" (Henry-Mooneyham, 1967:315).

In 1972 R. Pierce Beaver, recognized professor and author in the field of missionary studies, asked the question:

> Who and where are the presently unevangelized peoples? How can accurate, thoroughly reliable information be secured? ... How is the missionary mandate to be understood in the twentieth century, especially with respect to frontier tribal peoples? (Beaver, 1972:5).

THE CHALLENGE

In light of the command of our Lord "Go, and make disciples," the challenge that has been issued and the questions raised, we must seek to find answers. The purpose of this study is to accept the challenge and demonstrate a way by which the unreached can be identified, and discover a strategy by which they can be evangelized. By making use of research technology and modern scanning methods, the unevangelized peoples of our world can be located and identified. Statistical information can be compiled and made available to all who will heed the challenge of the unreached of the world. A strategy can be determined that will make the evangelization of the peoples of the world possible.

The Scope

   Graphics 1 and 2 demonstrate something of the scope of the task yet to be performed. According to estimates, about 28 percent of the people of the world are professing Christians. This includes Protestants, Anglicans, Roman Catholics, Orthodox, and any others who by their own profession accept Jesus Christ as Lord.
   The first graphic (Graphic 1) is a demonstration of the world population divided into the three major divisions, Protestant (including Anglican), Roman Catholic, and all other Christian professions. The second (Graphic 2) demonstrates the relative percentage of Christians in the major countries, showing the proportion of the population and the respective size of the Christian community within each country.
   The table given in the Appendix Part II is a compilation of some statistics gathered by Missions Advanced Research and Communications Center, giving the countries of the world with their reported percentages of Christian profession, from which the following graphics are composed.
   Further information is included also in Part II of the Appendix which demonstrates something of the scope of the evangelization of the world yet to be performed. The reader will do well to consider the implications of the data presented.

THE VISIBLE CHURCH

TOTAL WORLD POPULATION   3.5 BILLION

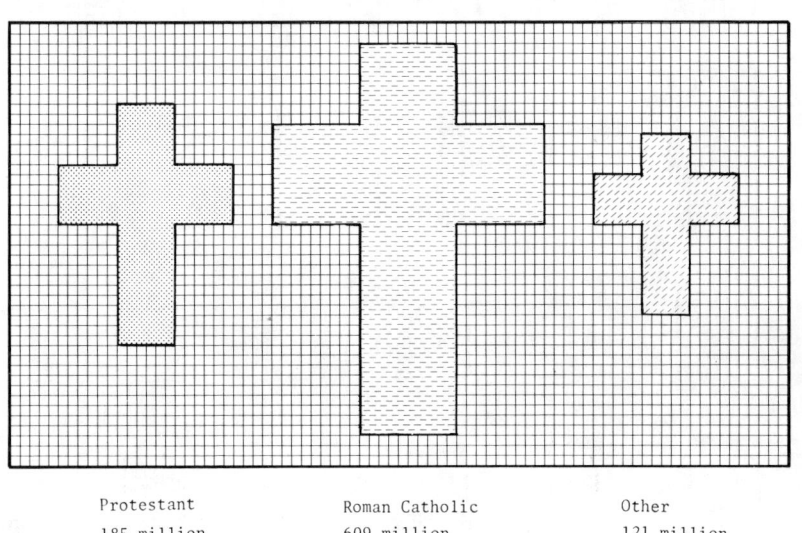

(Graphic 1)

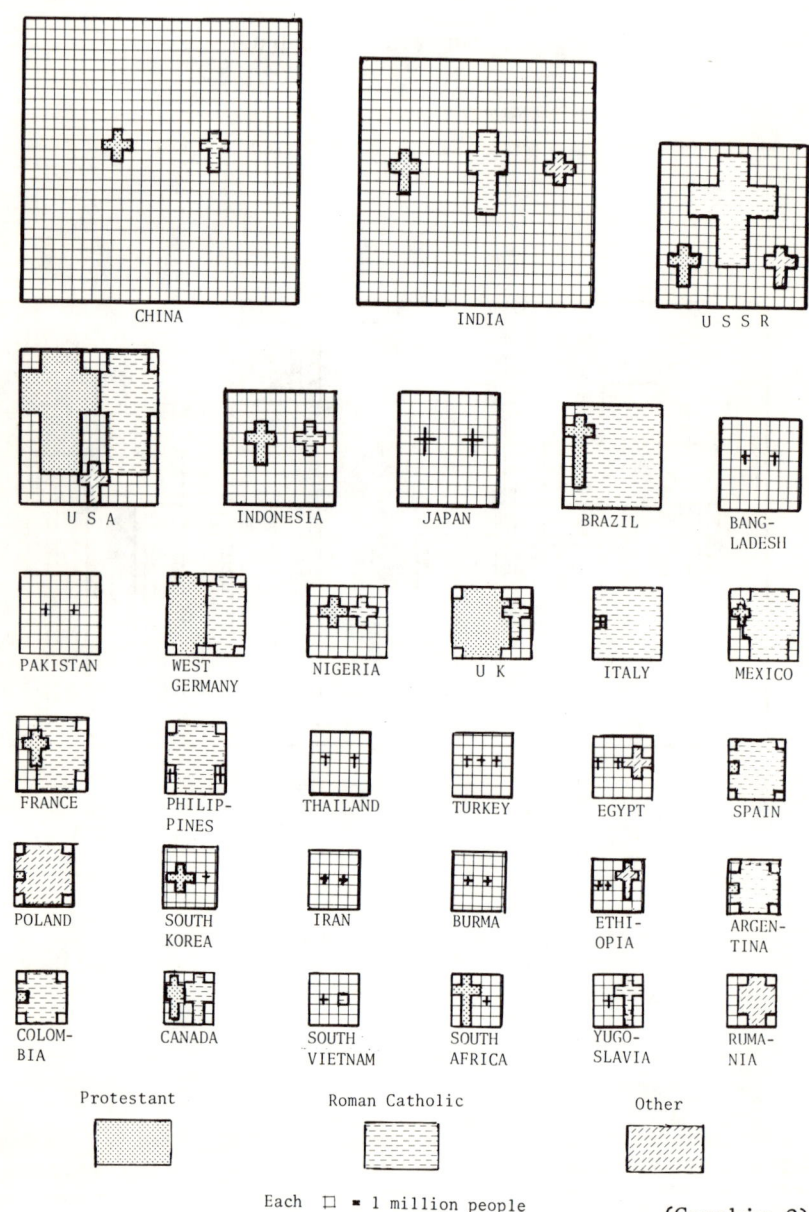

Perhaps the most startling study which has been written on the yet unfinished task is that of Ralph D. Winter, in which he says: "Bluntly, the number of people yet to be won in Africa and Asia has more than doubled since 1900 and will be more than tripled by the end of the century" (1974:3). His graphic presentation (Graphic 3) is reproduced below.

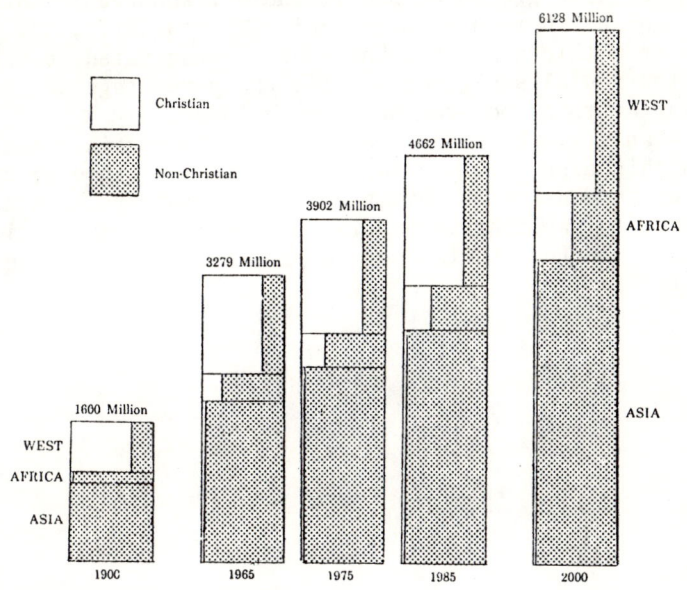

(Graphic 3)

One ray of hope that emerges is the fact that "the number of Christians in Africa and Asia is today *thirteen* times what it was in 1900, and by 2000 will be 34 times as large" (p.2). Nevertheless, in the same reference the fact is brought out that the mission forces are by no means uniformly distributed throughout the world. It is pointed out that 83 percent of the non-Christian world is receiving only 5 percent of the missionary task force.

Whereas Christians in some areas are increasing at a phenomenal rate, and other areas show no Christian percentage, yet on an average the Christian population is increasing yearly.

A second aspect of the scope is the recognition that every generation must itself be evangelized. Each generation has its own responsibility before God and its own opportunity to receive the gospel message. Each must answer for itself.

The Detail

Overall statistics give only a part of the picture. They show general averages which often obliterate the fact that certain specific groups of peoples have responded to Christianity while others are unresponsive. Frequently, the Christians within a given country are concentrated in only a very few social sub-groups, while the percentage of Christians in the total population is much lower.

The ethnic graph of the population of Indonesia demonstrates this aspect very clearly (Graphic 4). Some groups have been responsive to Christianity while others have not. Therefore, to say that Indonesia is 7 to 10 percent Christian hides the fact that some groups are more than 60 percent Christian.

INDONESIA

ESTIMATED CHRISTIAN POPULATION BY ETHNIC GROUPS

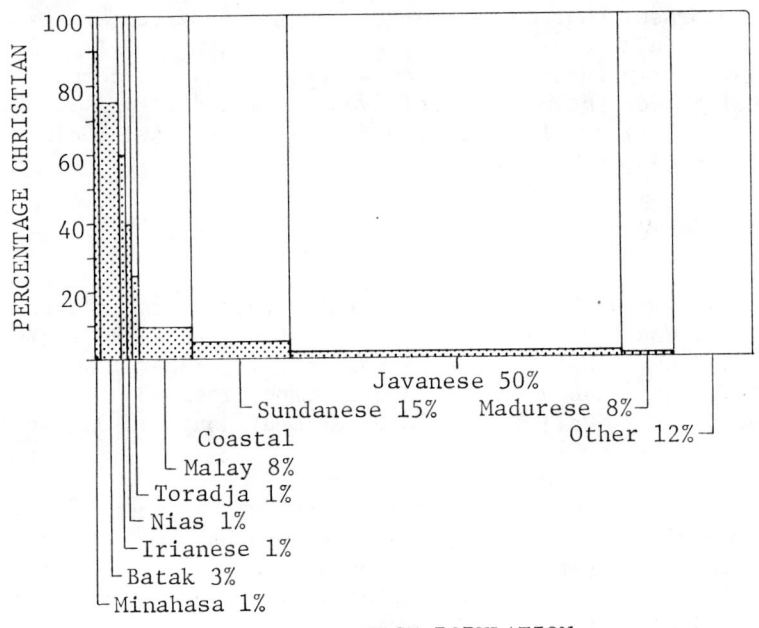

(NOTE: These figures are representative approximations. They should be seen as indications of magnitude, not precise.)

(Graphic 4)

Detailed study of why and how some peoples have responded and others have not would fill volumes. Some case studies are available, and more are being undertaken. Evidence shows that response is measurable and varies within regions. (The reader is directed to the series of <u>Status of Christianity Country Profiles</u>, produced for the International Congress on World Evangelization for examples.)

The indication may be the key to evangelism lies in a consideration of the people of the world in terms of *definable homogeneous units*.

It is well understood that the magnitude of the task is so enormous that one single document, no matter how extensive, could never exhaust the field of study. Also, while many disciplines could be drawn upon to make a complete analysis of the patterns of evangelism and responsiveness, our attention will be confined to Anthropology, Sociology, Communications and Missiology.

THE OCCASION

The immediate occasion for this study is the International Congress on World Evangelization (Lausanne, July 1974), which has assumed as part of its concern the investigation of the unreached and unevangelized peoples of the world. The "Call To The International Congress On World Evangelization" states:

> We are persuaded that God has brought us to one of history's great moments, that the hour has come for Christians everywhere to consider afresh the meaning of "mission," "evangelism," "salvation" and "conversion," and to unite in bold new efforts to proclaim Jesus Christ, to make disciples of all nations, and to welcome them into the fellowship of His Church....
>
> We purpose...to identify those who are as yet unreached or alienated from the Gospel (New Winds of Spiritual Awakening 1973:1).

To this end a research program was established to compile information and produce documents that would present the status of Christianity in representative areas of the world. Part of the program was a study of unreached peoples. The results of these studies are available to the reader in the <u>Status of Christianity Profiles,</u> and in the <u>Directory of Unreached Peoples</u> produced for the Congress.

As Research Coordinator of these projects it was the privilege of the author to have a significant part in the collection and formulation of the information compiled in the documents mentioned. They give a much more detailed treatment of countries and peoples than is possible here and the reader is referred to those portions for detail.

A second motivation for the study is personal concern over the opinion expressed by some that the age of missions has ended. Some are contending that since the Church of Jesus Christ is now present in almost every country, the time for recall, limiting or moratorium of mission personnel and funds has come.

Emilio Castro, Editor of <u>International Review of Missions</u>, summed up the thinking presented at the Salvation Today Conference in Bangkok, January 1973 on the subject of Moratorium, when he wrote:

> It is in the context of this experimental search for new forms of mission that the Bangkok discussion on moratorium ... must be undersood. A moratorium on the sending of funds and personnel may be necessary in a particular situation if it is the best way of rediscovering mission in that place and carrying it out. Moratorium should never be the expression of a desire to break off relationships or to reject the call to mission. Moratorium must be *for* better mission; this is its only justification.
>
> Violent or obligatory moratoria have taken place at various times in the history of the Church, with varying results .... But today we have to examine the idea of moratorium as a means of providing a possibility for the recovery of the freedom of missionary planning for a church in a given situation. The reason for the disengagement of a moratorium is to produce new commitment.
>
> For the sending church, moratorium may mean calling a halt to the routine repetition of their work and the beginning of a consideration of the fullness of mission, starting with that church's own country and moving out towards others .... For the church which requests a moratorium, this can be an opportunity to re-examine its priorities, to rediscover its identity and to develop better communication with its own people. How many churches arising out of missionary work are weighed down by the heritage of missionary institutions, such as hospitals and universities, and thus are prevented from establishing their own priorities? Moratorium is a new weapon in the Christian missionary arsenal (Castro 1973:396).

The real issue comes before us at the level of the third premise. With the first two there would be no debate. However at the third level the concentration is brought to the position of the local congregation. By definition, that "all that the church does within its own local setting is mission" the whole concept of mission is structured to a local witness and service ministry. Castro defined that position when he said:

> It is at the local level that the reality of the church universal must be lived; in today's world, with an ever-growing migration which challenges our communities, all of our churches are called to receive the strangers in our midst as brothers and sisters who manifest the catholicity of the Church and share in its local mission (Castro, 1973:395).

The purpose of moratorium as proposed, and confirmed by such understanding men as Paul Reese, is that by a wise withdrawal at a propitious moment, the local church will be strengthened to perform its own mission. Again, at this point, there would be no problem. Furthermore, if by "moratorium" is meant an end of institutionalized enterprises, then we could also agree.

However, there is great difference of interpretation in several vital areas. The first is that related to the definition of "mission," that defines mission as everything that the church does within its own local setting. The error is that churchmen are defining "mission," and failing to deal adequately with the words of Scripture: "Go, ... and make disciples ... " (Matt. 28:19), and "Pray ye, therefore the Lord of the harvest, that he would send forth laborers into his harvest" (Luke 10:2).

The second is that the ministry of evangelism is a ministry that never can be recalled or limited. It is true that a church which does not evangelize wastes away and dies.

Perhaps the greatest problem with the declaration of a moratorium is the fact that such forgets the yet unreached peoples that reside between the existing churches, or outside of their influence, though within geographical reach. John Dale, General Director of the Mexican Indian Mission, wrote in March 1964:

> Let us begin work in the unreached areas between the various fields where we have churches already established. If one will but consult a map of Mexico, he will see clearly that there are large areas of country between the Tamazunchale and the Tantoyuca fields, between the

Tamazunchale and the Acuatla fields, between the Mecatlan and the Cuautempan fields, and on and on, where no evangelical churches have been established (Dale, 1964:12).

Another lack of facing the problem is that of some who indicate the thought that since the present structure of missions is causing problems, the only solution is to recall the missionaries and thus terminate the cause. The only response to this is "don't throw out the baby with the bath water." One solution to solving the problem is to recall all personnel and finances and close up the ministries. But this is not the only solution. Evangelicals are not willing to accept such a position. Both men in their need, and God in His love, call for action.

Raymond Davis of the Sudan Interior Mission responded to the idea of calling for a "moratorium on missionaries" by saying:

> A great evangelistic offensive has built up momentum around the world. Today, in the last third of the century, the Church of Jesus Christ is pushing back the borders of the kingdom of Satan. He is feeling the heat ...
>
> God helping us, we ... will push ahead. We will not lay down our weapons now! ... We need men and women who will keep going, keep giving, and keep praying, looking not for a cease fire, but for victory! (Davis, 1973:15).

THE HISTORICAL PERSPECTIVE

With the publication of William Carey's now famous: <u>An Enquiry Into The Obligations Of Christians to Use Means For The Conversion Of The Heathens</u>, the Christian world was reawakened to the command of God to the Church. That publication called for evangelization of the heathen and the use of methods to accomplish the task.

With the vision of Carey in 1790 and the subsequent information that was fed back to the Christian Church, interest in the many previously unreached peoples of the world began to penetrate into the minds of the people of the Church with an accompanying sense of responsibility. Latourette writes:

> Before the end of the eighteenth century the rising tide of religious life in England had ceased to be content with fulfilling its sense of duty towards the millions revealed by the rapidly growing British possessions in India through financial support of the Danish-German

mission ... In 1793 ... there landed in Calcutta William Carey, who was to begin a new era in Protestant missions, not only in India, but also in the entire world (Latourette, 1967:Vol. 3; 281).

In this period of awakening of interest the mind of the Church began to be directed toward the "heathen" of the various continents. Interest moved from India to Africa and to China. Africa was described as the "Dark Continent" where uncounted numbers of savages lived in "heathen darkness." China became known as the land of "teeming millions" who needed Christ. People began to be recognized everywhere as great masses of unidentified humanity in deplorable conditions who needed to be reached with the Gospel. Carey wrote:

> The inhabitants of this world ... amount to about seven hundred and thirty-one million; four hundred and twenty millions of whom are still in pagan darkness; an hundred and thirty millions the followers of Mahomet; an hundred millions catholics; forty-four millions protestants; thirty millions of the greek and armenian churches, and perhaps seven millions of jews. It must undoubtedly strike every considerate mind what a vast proportion of the sons of Adam there are, who yet remain in the most deplorable state of heathen darkness, without any means of nature; and utterly destitute of the knowledge of the gospel of Christ, or of any means of obtaining it (Carey, 1962:62).

In 1810 Carey was so concerned about the "unreached peoples" that he called for a World Missions Conference to be held at the Cape of Good Hope. That conference was never convened. It was passed over as being one of Carey's dreams.

A century later, Hudson Taylor was convicted of his personal responsibility to the peoples of inland China. About this he was anything but dramatic, when he expressed simply "The facts were their own argument." His biography identifies two factors behind his concern: "The open Bible and the ever accusing map" (Taylor, 1918:23). He agonized over China's four hundred million inhabitants until he went to work in that land. He could not understand (in 1865) how it was right for Scotland with four millions to have several thousand ministers while the land of China with four hundred million inhabitants had only ninety-one missionaries of all societies, and all of those near the coast.

C. T. Studd was another man who was moved by the recognition of millions of people completely unreached with the

Gospel message. "He heard Dr. Karl Kumm relate his experiences of walking across Africa. Kumm reported that in the middle of the continent there were numbers of tribes who had never heard of Jesus Christ" (Jubilee Edition, "Worldwide," March-April 1964). This prompted Studd's decision to go to Africa. There he formed the beginning of Worldwide Evangelization Crusade (WEC), which in time was to produce studies of the unreached peoples of Africa, Asia, India and Latin America. As a result of those studies, new fields have been opened and new methods of evangelization employed.

In the 1920's the World Dominion Press of London produced a series of books entitled "The Survey Series." These studies were an attempt to describe the Christian situation as it existed in the various countries. Once again statistics were employed to make visible the needs of the world. In the study on India, in The Frontier Peoples of India, A Missionary Survey, Alexander McLeish said:

> These mountainous lands present the distinctive problems of the evangelism of Muslims, Buddhists, Hindus and Animists in their most difficult aspects. Progress is being made in the more accessible regions, but of the total of 22,664 Christians more than half are found in the plains of the North-West Frontier Province and in the Bengal Duaras. The comparatively small force of 189 foreign and 734 Indian workers is distributed among the eighteen million people of these regions.
> It is hoped that this Survey will lead to greatly increased effort on the part of mission boards and of the Indian Church. Careful consideration of the facts revealed show that many of the most difficult religious, racial, economic and geographical problems of the world have still to be faced and conquered within the confines of the Indian Empire (1931:Foreword).

Statistics were being gathered, and their implications being felt. Carey had been moved by the facts that he had. Hudson Taylor responded to the information he received. Studd, likewise was moved by the sheer numbers of people yet to be reached. Each man honestly faced the data that was brought to his attention.

McLeish was aware of the significance of these different peoples, and was able to interpret the results of his research. He wrote:

> Taking the difference in numbers into account, the effort to reach the Hindus is very much greater than the effort to reach the Muslims ... There is one missionary,

although mostly a part-time worker, to every three hundred and ten thousand Muslims, as compared with one to every fifty-seven thousand Hindus. Furthermore, not more than one-tenth of the missionaries in touch with Muslims give their whole time to the work (1931:3,4).

In his evaluation of the work of missions within India, McLeish was able to define the frontiers, and wrote:

> In this long stretch of Frontier, therefore, is to be found the stronghold of Indian Islam on the west, the stronghold of Hinduism in the forests and mountains of Kunaon, and the stronghold of Buddhism in Nepal and Bhutan.
> It requires no great effort of imagination to picture the extreme difficulty of the missionary task. The Christian worker is met at once by linguistic difficulties, accentuated by the geographical problems presented by mighty mountains, swift rivers and wide forests; by racial difficulties, legacies from the history of conquest and reconquest in the past; by religious difficulties, increased by memories of recent struggles for existence among a conservative hill people; by economic difficulties due to the poverty of the soil and the long cold winters (1931:5).

In 1930 C. T. Studd had developed a technique of research for the Worldwide Evangelization Crusade, and wrote:

> Our method is to search and find out what parts of the world remain unevangelized, and then by faith in Christ, by prayer to God, by obedience to the Holy Ghost, by courage, by determination and supreme sacrifice, to accomplish their evangelisation with the utmost despatch (Challenge of India's Millions, n.d.:2).

Norman C. Pateman of the China Inland Mission wrote in 1944 to Mr. Leslie Brierley of WEC demonstrating the concern of his mission:

> Thank you very much for your letter of September 19th. As you say, it is rather difficult to give any geographical indication of the unevangelised portions of China.
> The field, generally speaking, is divided between existing Societies, and in one sense there are few parts of the land which cannot be reached by missionaries or their Chinese fellow-workers. On the other hand, in almost every area there are very many places which are

actually unevangelised. I ought, however, to try to indicate a few of the areas where there are no workers at all.

The outstanding one, of course, is the province of Sinkiang where, as far as I know, there are no missionaries. Former workers were expelled. There is some hope that the door is once again opening.

Inner Mongolia, which is not stricly in China proper, has few workers, although the population is sparse and, to a large extent, nomadic.

As you already know, Tibet, again not strictly within the Republic of China, has no missionary workers, and the border regions to the east of that vast land are very sparsely worked.

There is a corner in south-west Szechwan, just north of the city of Ningyuan (the old name was Sichang); round here are the Independent Nosu people, who are completely unevangelised, and, as far as we know, at present no one is able to speak their language. We have three workers preparing to take the Gospel to them (Personal letter, Sept. 1944).

By 1961 the Worldwide Evangelization Crusade had concentrated its thinking upon the peoples of the world in terms of "unreached peoples," and began to conduct surveys to locate the unevangelized peoples. In The Challenge of India's Millions which was a survey of the unreached peoples of India, is a section entitled, "India's Peoples." It states:

India's millions - 398 millions at the last census and ever increasing - are made up of a medley of tongues, tribes and races, springing from three main stocks - the Aryan, Dravidian and Mongolian.

As we try to picture these peoples, many well-known names come to our minds: the Pathans of the North-West Frontier, warlike and fanatical; the Kashmiris, Dards and Baltis of the mountains and valley of Kashmir; the Baluchis from the deserts and stony wastes of Sind and Baluchistan; the famous Rajputs, who were strong enough to withstand and stem the Moslem invasion; the fighting of Ghurkas from the vastnesses of Nepal. At the other end of the scale are aboriginal tribes whose names have been made familiar to us through missionary literature: the Garos, Boros, Karens and Lushai of Assam and Burma; the Santals of Buhar and Bengal, many of whom have so wonderfully accepted the Gospel; the Mundas and Oraons of Chota Nagpur; the Bhotias and Lepchas of Nepal and Bhutan; the Bhils and Kilis of Sind, Rajputana and the West Indian States, amongst whom CMS and others have gathered such a harvest. Then there are the Lingayats of Bombay and Hyderabad; the Kapus of Madras, and the Telegus, all tribes who loved peace more than war and gave way before the fiercer inhabitants of the north, amongst whom Christ has found many followers.

Most of these races have given their quota to the Kingdom since Carey first led the way to India; nevertheless MANY STILL WAIT the good news and THESE we must locate and reach (WEC, n.d.:3).

THE PRESENT TREND

The present focus is not without its immediate antecedents. In December, 1972, R. Pierce Beaver called for a consultation on "The Gospel and Frontier Peoples," which convened in Chicago. The purpose was to gather missionaries from the different continents together to consider those "frontier situations" that still exist. He was thinking mostly of those untouched and "remote" units of society that have lived in isolation and removed from all Christian influence.

One of the significant participants in the Consultation was David Barrett, of the Research Center in Nairobi, Kenya, who presented what was perhaps the most extensive study made up to that time. His paper was entitled: Frontier Situation For Evangelisation in Africa, 1972, a Survey Report. In this report Barrett presents a comprehensive study of groups from all parts of Africa that are unreached and partially unreached. He deals with the issues of responsiveness and resistance, demonstrates how some peoples are responsive, and gives degrees of responsiveness. His conclusions are based on facts which he collected and analyzed. Some of his data is included in the "Unreached Peoples" section.

Specific mention must be made of the space given in Beaver's report of the Consultation entitled: The Gospel and Frontier Peoples, to the specific case studies. We shall not consider the individual cases, but only call to the attention of the reader the fact that individual groups were identified, and each defined as being "unevangelized" or "evangelized." Every case study is different and illustrates that to be effective, evangelization must consider specific situations and apply the gospel message to each individual people

One of the most recent studies is that which has been produced as Brazil 1980: The Protestant Handbook by William R. Read and Frank A. Ineson. The conclusion of the study rests upon the analysis made of the growth of the Brazilian Protestant Church in the past with projection to its expected growth in the future. The basis for the study was the division of the country into the important micro-regions in which church membership statistics are available. Read says:

> The government of Brazil has recently divided the country into 361 important micro-regions, and the BRAZIL 1980 church growth analysis reconstructs the country by previous years to clearly show the development and progress of the Protestant communicants and community in each separate micro-region.
>
> Church growth past, present, and future has been related to the rapid changes taking place in Brazilian society. It shows the relationship of urbanization, industrialization, internal migration, and population growth to the growth of Protestant churches and what the face of the future might be (Read, 1973:xxvi).

Read asks the questions: Where has the Protestant church grown? Why has it grown? Where will it grow in the coming years? His study includes factors that cause growth, and covers a complete analysis of the ethnic, sociological, and economic factors that are relevant to church growth. His initiation of this type of study for the country of Brazil is certain to produce motivation for an equal type of study in other countries.

Perhaps the broadest study that has been undertaken recently on unreached peoples of the world is that done for the International Congress on World Evangelization. Over 2500 participants from 120 countries of the world are to gather in Lausanne, Switzerland to consider the unreached of this generation. Representatives from seventy-five countries were requested to prepare a study on their country and compile a Status of Christianity Profile that would demonstrate the degree to which the country had been evangelized and determine those peoples who were as yet unreached with the gospel message. These profiles are all to be shared with the participants at the Congress, to serve as a basis of comparison and as a comprehensive statement of the actual status of Christianity in our world today. This pattern will also bring to light many peoples who are unreached with the Gospel. The special characteristic of these country studies is that they are focused on the homogeneous units within the country, and the degree to which there has been a response. Special attention is given to the unit nature, communication pattern, and group receptivity. This approach has tremendous potential as the unevangelized peoples become known to the representatives from so many countries with such potential resources for reaching them. It is anticipated that this time of consultation will prove to be the beginning of action.

Already, the United Presbyterian Center For Mission Studies, located at Fullerton, California, is suggesting to the United Presbyterian Church a plan for extending its influence to reach the unreached peoples who are adjacent geographically to the areas where the United Presbyterian Church is already established. The editor writes:

> Several agencies are already working on general worldwide "unreached peoples" surveys. With only a little more effort the UPCMS can zero in on those peoples, essentially untouched so far, who are within striking range of existing overseas Presbyterian mission operations. This "survey of surveys" could be a vital tool for Presbyterian agencies and Orders in planning future cross-cultural evangelistic strategy (Missions Update Vol.II, No.8; October 1973).

THE ULTIMATE PURPOSE

The end of the survey is the beginning of action. The permanence of this study will not be in the statistics uncovered, but in the patterns of evangelization that might emerge.

No study that deals with people and statistics can be of permanent nature. People change and statistics change. The world is in motion. People are restless and migrate every day. The only permanent thing is change. The recent exodus of Indian peoples from Africa demonstrates changes that are reflected in the people themselves as well as in the countries that receive them. Movements from rural to urban living are creating traumatic changes in almost every country. It is expected that humanity will shift and merge into new groupings.

The value of the present study will be in the application made, and its degree of effectiveness in the evangelization of the unreached peoples. The emphasis therefore is on the general principle enunciated of presenting a methodology for discovering the unreached, identifying their peculiar characteristics, and evangelizing them by units. The evangelist is encouraged to seek out the distinct units of unreached peoples, discover the felt needs of the unit, to determine the best channels of communication to that unit, and to apply the message of the Gospel to the heart of the people in the language they can best understand.

Thus, while it is not imagined that this study will be final, it is hoped that it will stimulate further research and investigation, and that from it will emerge patterns which will not be merely theoretical, but practical and useful for the evangelization of the unreached millions of the world. In spite of deficiencies it is hoped that a system has been developed which, when amplified and perfected, will present a plan for accomplishing the following:

1. Identification of the unreached and unevangelized peoples of the world.
2. Patterns for analysis of the unreached and unevangelized peoples so that they can be better understood in light of their distinguishing characteristics.
3. Plans that will be effective for evangelizing them.

If this can be accomplished, the present study will have served its purpose.

Part One **The Identification of the Unreached**

Chapter 2

The Importance of Seeing the World In Homogeneous Units

To lay a strategy for world evangelization means to consider the world in its beautiful mosaic of intricate design. It means to consider people as God's creation and ask God how each piece of that tremendous pattern can be approached and brought back to Him. The strategy must recognize these distinct units, their particular characteristics and the appropriate media of communication that would be best suited to communicating the Gospel to them.

Donald McGavran has stated that people like to become Christians within their own culture. In the New Testament the Gentiles wanted to become Christians as Gentiles. They wanted to retain their own identity and still be followers of "The Way." The Jews thought they should become Jews, following all the Jewish laws and customs. The first church council dealt with this issue, and made a decisive declaration which said in effect, "The Gentiles can become Christians without becoming Jews." Or in other words, "The Gentiles can retain their own self-identity, and still become Christians."

People like to be themselves. There is an affinity among people for the familiar, and people like to relate to it. Some people hold tightly to family or clan. They recognize themselves by their ethno-linguistic relationships. The Chinese of Lima, Peru, form a distinct ethno-linguistic unit within their adopted country, recognizing themselves by kinship and linguistic ties.

The same pattern is true of many peoples in every major city of the world. When U.S. citizens live abroad, they tend to gravitate together. This is the situation in Mexico City, where the Americans forget the Spanish way of life entirely when closed within their own homes and social circles.

Some people identify themselves by their occupation. Fishermen relate to fishermen. Industrial workers relate to industrial workers. Truck drivers relate to truck drivers. Tokyo is partitioned by industrial workers gathering together in their own distinctive districts.

Countries have been talked about as in need of the Gospel, and country statistics have been given. But when peoples are considered, the country takes on a different character. India is reported as a country having only 3 percent Christians, and therefore a country in need of the Gospel. This is wholly true, but not the whole truth. India is a continent of 600,400,000 people, but that is too many to comprehend. India is divided into 800 different language groups. Some large, some small. The caste system has further divided the country into sociological groupings, where one element has had nothing to do with other elements except insofar as the one group served for the existence or function of the other. When Christianity is considered within India, it is discovered that some groups have responded remarkably to the gospel message, while others have rejected it completely, so that the 3 percent average gives little if any indication at all of the state of Christianity within the country.

The graph following (Graphic 5) gives a little indication of the differences in response that have come to the presentation of the gospel message in India. Only a few of the many "homogeneous units" can be indicated on such a graph, but they are representative of the response by units. Similar variation of response could be shown by geographic areas, or by socio-economic groups.

Donald McGavran has termed these units as "homogeneous units" and stated:

> The *homogeneous unit* is simply a section of society in which all the members have some characteristic in common. Thus a homogeneous unit ... might be a political unit or subunit, the characteristic in common being that all the members live within certin geographical confines ... Sometimes the unit will be a country or city.
>
> The homogeneous unit may be a segment of society whose common characteristic is a culture or a language, as in the case of Puerto Ricans in New York City or Chinese in Thailand (1970:85).

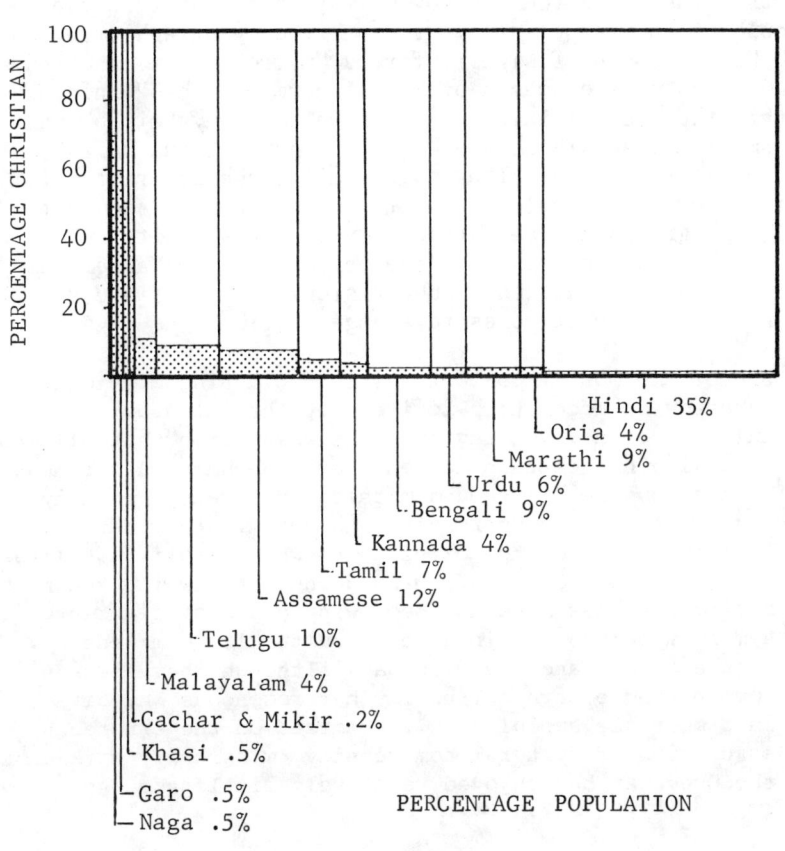

(Graphic 5)

Grady Reed in his thesis on <u>Strategizing Church of Christ Missions In The Light Of Varying Receptivity</u> well states:

> Human societies do not exist as monolithic wholes, but, rather, as 'mosaics' of thousands of smaller social units defined in terms of such differences as race, tribe, caste, class, language, education, occupation, and on and on (1971:107).

The concept of "homogeneous units" may well be considered as the subdivisions of larger entities, into their component parts. There are the "macro" units, which comprise the people of one large entity or country or geographic region. The Hausa people of Nigeria form a "macro" unit. The Indian population of the Amazon of Brazil form a "macro" unit. But within the overall larger unit there are many "micro" units, or small units. These are known as "homogeneous units" or segments of society. They have similar characteristics which are recognizable and unite the members of the unit.

These groups may be further divided in subunits, who act and respond as units within themselves. Peter Wagner has pointed out the fact that subdivisions of groups are very significant when it comes to evangelization. He says:

> One of the most important tasks in planning missionary strategy is accurately to identify the cultures and subcultures of a given region. The assumption that all who live within a certain nation share the same culture has been an obstacle to sound missionary strategy in many cases. Personal observations have indicated that this fallacy is one of the clues as to why in Bolivia Aymaras have been won to Christ in large numbers, while the neighboring Quechuas have not been won to the same extent. Aymara speakers are in general culturally homogeneous. On the other hand the Quechuas, although they speak a common tongue, are culturally heterogeneous and divided into multiple subcultures. Premised on the erroneous assumption of cultural homogeneity, missionary work among the Quechuas has enjoyed relatively little success (Wagner, 1971:89).

Whereas Wagner as an observer from outside the unit could distinguish subcultures within the Bolivian Aymaras, he was unaware of the extent of such subdivisions. Quentin Nordyk, a missionary working with the Aymaras, in his Thesis entitled <u>Animistic Aymaras and Church Growth</u>, distinguished eleven homogeneous units. He says:

The Importance of Seeing the World in Homogeneous Units

In the rural altiplano area of Boliva, we find three main homogeneous groupings . . . .
In the urban center of La Paz, there are four more important homogeneous units . . . .
In the Yungas valleys we find an additional four units . . . . (1972:132,133).

A report of Indonesia given in the booklet, <u>The Isles That Wait</u>, describes Indonesia as follows:

With a population of some 70 millions, divided into 137 tribes, speaking some 60 distinct languages, in an area of about 3/4 million square miles, we have a medley of cultures, religions and languages offering unlimited scope for the Christian message; for this Indonesian archipelago . . . is located at the cross roads of three of the principal currents of human civilisation.
At the present time there are also about 1 1/2 millions of foreign Orientals - Indians, Arabs, and Chinese.
. . . The following figures, whilst showing the unevenness of the distribution of Christians, also reveal some of the greatest conquests of the Christian Church in her world mission:-

Moluccas:	1/4 million	Christians	(25% population)
Celebes:	1/2 million	Christians	(11% population)
Timor group:	160,000	Christians	(10% population)
Sumatra:	1/2 million	Christians	(6% population)
Borneo:	15,000	Christians	(3/4% population)
Java:	100,000	Christians	(1/5% population)

Indeed if we take the total number of the tribe as the basis of calculation, some tribes, such as the Minahassans, are 85 percent Christian! (p. 2,3).

The emergence of studies like these, which were based on research, form some of the basis for recognizing the importance of units in contemplating a strategy for world evangelization.

Mission societies have more and more been turning to the application of the principle of unit evangelization.

The Worldwide Evangelization Crusade has established a strong center for research in London, England. Leslie Brierley has spent years in searching out information on unreached peoples, and the information gathered has been used to guide the decisions of the mission administrators. These findings were published in such documents as: <u>The Challenge Of The Unachieved</u> (1961); <u>World Survey</u> (1961); <u>They Are</u>

Bread For Us (1971).

For many years Wycliffe Bible Translators have concerned themselves with unreached homogeneous units. It all began when Cameron Townsend recognized that the Quatchiquel people of Guatemala with whom he was working were not responding to his preaching in Spanish. He recognized that he was not communicating in the "language of the heart" of the people. To him it became evident that if these people were to be reached they would have to be reached within their own language. Thus a movement began of recruiting missionaries who would be willing to move into new areas and commit themselves to the arduous task of learning the new languages, reducing them to writing, translating the Scriptures into those languages, and then teaching the people to read their own language. Today Wycliffe Bible Translators has a membership of 3,000, and is working among 600 tribes in 24 countries of the world. These are all distinct homogeneous units among whom translators are working. Further, Wycliffe's estimates show 8,000 tribes still in need of the Scriptures in their own language. A fairly recent publication of WBT entitled Two Thousand Tongues To Go is completely out of date because of more recent discoveries of many hitherto unrecognized units (Wallis, 1959).

The work of translation is linguistic in nature, dealing with the most easily recognized single homogeneous units. The work of translation has also been done by many other agencies such as New Tribes Mission, Unevangelized Fields Mission, Christian and Missionary Alliance, Sudan Interior Mission, to say nothing of many missionaries of the traditional denominations as well as Roman Catholic missionaries.

Like Wycliffe, the Bible Societies have for years focused on the peoples of the world with concern to print the Bible in every known language. In pursuit of that goal, the Bible Society publication issued in 1972 entitled The Book Of A Thousand Tongues (Nida, 1972) lists by name and sample of language, 1,399 languages into which at least a portion of the Scriptures has been translated and printed.

The directors of Gospel Recordings have for years recognized the importance of homogeneous units. They have gathered language excerpts and made records of gospel messages that could be distributed to the individual speakers of those dialects. The homogeneous units now identified as being in need of this means of proclamation number into the thousands and records have been produced in 3,000 languages and dialects.

Protestant mission bodies are not the only ones concerned with the study of homogeneous units. Roman Catholic writers are also aware of the strategy of reaching peoples as individual units, and within the culture patterns which observe distinct communication systems. Two outstanding Roman Catholic scholars who are concerned about the recognition of distinct units are Francis Houtart of Belgium and Louis Luzbetak of the U.S.A. Luzbetak writes:

> The concept of subculture has an important bearing on practical apologetics and communication. American Protestantism and American Catholicism are both subcultural forms of Americanism. When explaining Catholic views to our separated brethren, or when attempting to bring about the highly desirable unity among Christians, one should not lose sight of the fact that in such activity one is obliged to cross subcultural boundaries even if one does not leave the American shores. To understand our separated brethren and to be effective in our communication with them, it is of utmost importance to keep in mind that we are separated not only in faith but also culturally; to reach the non-Catholic, the Catholic must cross subcultural boundaries. He must apply essentially the same anthropological principles and techniques here as he would in a strange, far-off land. The Protestant wishing to understand the Catholic must likewise realize that he does not speak the same cultural language (Luzbetak, 1970:120).

We come to the conclusion that today's world is a composite mosaic of many peoples. Many of them are unreached, and unevangelized, but they are all reachable and winnable. The direction of missions during the past few years has turned toward giving attention to distinct units, and recognized the importance of understanding their distinctives. But they are all people whom God loves. There is no people upon whom the Spirit of God cannot move; and God can direct His servants to move in and harvest those who are responsive. The harvest will not come of itself. There must be those who prepare the soil, and those who plant the seed, as well as those who water. We do not forget the entire process as part of God's eternal plan.

DEFINITION OF TERMS

In order to discuss the issue of reaching the unreached, a definition of the term "unreached" should be determined. In reality there is no absolute definition. Various individuals define "unreached" in different ways. To some, a people is "unreached" only when no individuals of the group have become Christian, or heard the gospel message. In this vein, the author has received some letters stating "there are no unreached peoples in this country. All tribes have had some Christian witness." At the opposite extreme, others consider a people unreached if there are still some of its members who have not responded. The response at this end of the spectrum is: "All of the different groups within this area are unreached, for there is no tribe that is totally Christian."

Barrett has discussed this issue quite at length in his paper on "Frontier Situations For Evangelisation in Africa." In his book on <u>Schism and Renewal</u>, Barrett says:

> By the time the number of Protestant or Catholic adherents in the tribe has passed twenty percent . . . a very considerable body of indigenous Christian opinion has come into existence . . . (1968:137).

Based on the agreement of sociologists that a people may have a minority group attitude until that people reaches 15 to 20 percent of the population of the region in which it resides, and for the purposes of this study, we consider that a people is unreached when less than 20 percent of the adults are professing Christians. When this percentage of the population has accepted the gospel message, such a people are then to a point where the members of the unit itself can have sufficient witness to reach those members of the unit who are as yet not reached. This does not mean that all of the group are Christian, but it is accepted as an arbitrary figure, based on sound principle, which serves as basis for our discussion purposes.

This means of course, that the Christian profession will have to be interpreted by the reader in accordance with his understanding of the definition of "Christian." For example, to say that a homogeneous unit is 85 percent professing Roman Catholic, will mean to the Roman Catholic that such a people has been "reached" according to our definition. However, to a Protestant this may mean such a people has not been "reached" or "evangelized." It is not the purpose of this study to make such judgment decisions. They will be left to the interpretation of the individual reader. If the statistics show that a unit is 95 percent Buddhist, then both Roman Catholic and Protestant will make the same judgment that as far as Christianity is concerned the group is unreached. Such a group is by definition "unreached" and "unevangelized."

The Questionnaire used for research of information for

The Importance of Seeing the World in Homogeneous Units   31

the International Congress on World Evangelization has accepted the definition:

> <u>Unreached/unevangelized</u> people: Those homogeneous units which have not received or responded to the Gospel. This unresponsiveness may be due to lack of opportunity, lack of understanding, or because they have not received sufficient information about the gospel message within their own language, cultural frame of reference and communication channels to make Christianity a viable option.
> . . . we consider that a people is unreached/unevangelized when less than 20% are professing Christians. This assumes that a people has a minority group attitude until that people **reaches** 15 to 20% of the population. At that point it may move into a recognition of its own self-identity (Appendix).

SCRIPTURAL VALIDITY

Scripture speaks frequently of the peoples of the world, God showing concern for them though at times displaying His wrath because of their sin. David speaks of the peoples, and of their judgment, (Ps. 9:17-20) but calls for mercy and grace that all peoples may praise the Lord (Ps. 67).

The Scriptural usage of the word translated "nations" is most frequently used in the sense of race, or ethnic group. Strong, in his Concordance, gives the meaning of *ethnos* a *race; i.e. tribe; a foreign (non-Jewish)* one; Gentile, heathen, nation, people.

It is used in Matt. 24:9: "Ye shall be hated of all *'peoples'* for my name's sake." Matt. 24:14: "This gospel of the kingdom shall be preached in all the world for a witness unto all *'peoples;'* and then shall the end come." Matt. 28:19: "Go ye, therefore, and teach (make disciples of) all *'peoples'* . . . ." Mark 13:10: "the gospel must first be proclaimed among all *'peoples.'* Luke 12:30 "do the *'peoples.'* of the world seek after God?" Luke 24:47: "that repentance and remission of sins should be preached in his name among all *'peoples,'* beginning at Jerusalem."

John, in the Revelation, spoke of the *"peoples"* and of the vision of the great multitudes "from all peoples and tongues" that gave honor to the Lamb, and sang in the choir of the redeemed (Rev. 10:11; 11:9; 13:7; 15:4; 17:15).

Luke in writing the book of the Acts of the Apostles recognizes the importance of carrying the message of the Gospel to Jerusalem, Judea, Samaria, and to the uttermost parts of the earth. This was not a geographical concept, but a "people" concept. The message was a message that needed to be applied to the people of Jerusalem, and to the people of Judea. It included the herdsmen of the plains as well as the urban population of the city. It also needed to be carried to the peoples of the whole world.

The question might be asked: Did Paul seek out homogeneous units when he went with the gospel message to Asia? The answer is that he went to the Jewish segment of each city first of all, trying to reach them within their own synagogue. When he was rejected then he turned to the Gentiles, generally a specific group that had gathered around the Jewish synagogue. In any case he adapted his message to each distinct group. This is especially noted at Lystra (Acts 14:8-18), and at Athens (Acts 17:16-34).

Paul was not the only one who recognized the necessity of speaking to people in terms that could be understood. Peter was given a vision in the house of Cornelius by which he learned that the message he had was for the Gentiles as well as the Jews. It was meant for all peoples, and Peter was to give it to all.

THE OBSTACLES OF MAGNITUDE AND COMPLEXITY

The enormous magnitude and complexity of the task of world evangelization demands a division into manageable units. When any business manager has a large task to perform he knows that it will have to be broken into significant segments and done by parts. NASA got men on the moon by coordinating a lot of smaller assignments all of which, when put together, accomplished the objective. The goal set before the Church is the evangelization of the world. The Church cannot expect to accomplish this task of world evangelization by undertaking the enterprise as one majestic endeavour. She will accomplish it by breaking down the task into small units that can be undertaken. Multitudes of laborers must go from every people to every people. Gifted men of God must rise to the occasion to reach out, and reach the unreached. The identification of units makes the job feasible. A homogeneous unit is a tangible element. It can be recognized and its characteristics observed. Its language can be mastered and its channels of communication understood. Its relationship to the Gospel can be studied and its responses known. Prayer can be directed on behalf of the unit and evangelization undertaken with a specific thrust.

In this concept the homogeneous unit becomes as it were, a "living organism." It becomes a vital entity in the life of individual Christians and congregations. Prayers become specific and responses become known.

When the killing of five missionaries by the Aucas in the jungles of Peru became known through the news media, thousands of Christians and non-Christians alike were shocked. As a result hearts and prayers were concentrated on the Auca Indians. The unit, a previously unheard-of lost tribe in the jungle, suddenly took on characteristics of its own. Many prayers were offered on behalf of the killers, and God heard and answered. Today there are Auca believers (Wallis, 1960).

The Nagas of Nagaland, headhunters until 1934, became the object of special concern of the Baptist missionaries of India. Concentrated efforts followed their heartfelt commitment to the tribe and today 60 percent of all Nagas are professing Christians and are the most fully Christian unit of all India (Philip 1972).

The pattern of thinking in terms of units makes possible a focus for prayer, and for the concentration of effort. In turn, this leads to the adjustment of program to fit the specific need. The division of the millions of people into small recognizable homogeneous units makes the task of world evangelization an attainable one.

Likewise, many modern cities are megalopolises of tremendous proportions. Sao Paulo, Brazil, with over 8 million people is an entity which cannot be evangelized as a single unit. The size of the population itself is one reason. The diversity of the people is another. Sociologically, the city can be divided into groups and sub-groups which are more significant than geographical divisions. Sociological affinity causes people to gather into geographical pockets.

When intelligently dealt with, divisions and sub-divisions give realistic means of approach to units which can become manageable segments. No church is too small to do its part when it recognizes that all that God expects is for it to do what it can, and the multiplicity of many small endeavors makes a big accomplishment.

Caracas, Venezuela is one of the fastest growing urban centers in Latin America. It is bulging with high-rise apartment complexes. Many of these are sub-cities within themselves with their own stores, schools, recreational facilities and social centers. Other cities are building in the same pattern. Latin America is exploding with them.

Hong Kong is a city of diverse peoples, 98 percent of whom are of Chinese origin. Within the Chinese ethnic groups are the Mandarin-speaking, and the Cantonese-speaking, as well as various others. The city is also divided by distinct living conditions representing varied economic and social levels. Wayland Wong of Hong Kong says that in Hong

Kong the Baptist Church is growing precisely because "mother churches" are establishing "branch churches" among equal homogeneous segments. The work of evangelization within the city of Hong Kong (with its density of 4,000 people per square mile) can only be accomplished through a multiplicity of varied efforts, by people who can communicate within existing communication channels to peoples they can reach (Status of Christianity Profile, Hong Kong, Section II).

James Wong of Singapore recently wrote of the conditions there. His observation is that within the city of 2.3 million, there are thousands of people living in high-rise apartments who are forming new distinct units. His conclusion is that the only way to reach these units is through Christians who live within the same confines and can relate to the individuals there. His burden is for "house churches" within the communities (Status of Christianity Profile, Singapore, Section II).

In contrast, Paul Rader of the Salvation Army in Korea writes that the homogeneity of the Korean people in language and culture makes a breakdown into small units erroneous and unnecessary (Status of Christianity Profile, Korea, Section II). Others have also noted that Korea is largely one ethnic, linguistic, and cultural unit and that to subdivide the nation is an artificial segmentation.

However, research has shown that there are various significant homogeneous units in Korea. There are Japanese, Chinese and European ethnic groups. The student population is quite different from the rural farm people. The army personnel seem to form into a distinct unit, and reports show that at present the percentage of Christians among the Army personnel is about 30 percent higher than among the rest of the population. Information also shows that there is a segment of society that has banded together because of common social elements. That segment is formed of young people who are about 18 years of age and are the children of U.S. Army fathers and Korean mothers. This unit has formed its own social segment and characteristics and is quite numerous. The bus girls are a peculiar group, with distinctive characteristics within the occupational pattern.

In dealing with the concept of homogeneous units, certain questions should be asked to help identify the distinctives of each group. Such questions should include: What makes it a distinct unit? What are its peculiar characteristics? What is its particular history that distinguishes it from other units? How does the group function? What changes is it looking for? What are its ideals?

The answers to some of these questions should give indications as to how to reach the people, who can best communicate with them, and what they may respond to.

One factor of importance is the recognition that homogeneous units are themselves constantly in the process of change. They are not static, but are on the move constantly. These constant changes mean that the task is a challenging one. The opportunity for evangelism must be taken when it presents itself, for no one can depend on the existing conditions and same unit response to continue indefinitely. Likewise, since change is always occurring, it can also be a sign of hope for the Christian. No group will always remain closed to the Gospel. This implies that the Church of Jesus Christ must always be ready to give the message to every man and people and nation. To be ready for such a moment is the work of many individuals who recognize the magnitude of the total task, and the complexity of its parts.

THE PROMINENCE OF PEOPLE CONSCIOUSNESS

McGavran feels that the most significant aspect of an homogeneous unit is its people-consciousness.

> Castes or tribes with high people-consciousness will resist the Gospel primarily because to them becoming a Christian means "joining another people." They refuse Christ not for religious reasons, not because they love their sins, but precisely because they love their brethren. . . .
> It may be taken as axiomatic that whenever becoming a Christian is considered a racial rather than a religious decision, there the growth of the Church will be exceedingly slow. As the Church faces the evangelization of the world, perhaps her main problem is how to present Christ so that men can truly follow Him without traitorously leaving their kindred (1970:190).

He states that there are two possible solutions to this problem:

> (First) . . . to wait till the society disintegrates, people-consciousness grows low, a melting pot develops, or the military might of a conqueror destroys pride of peoplehood; and (second) . . . to enable men and women to become Christians in groups while still remaining members of their tribe, caste, or people (1970:190).

Homogeneous units vary in their nature, characteristics and structure, but all peoples who have the sense of "people-consciousness" or a sense of "belonging" have a relationship that amalgamates them into a single unit.

Part of this people-consciousness is the result of people asking such questions as: Who am I? Why am I here? Where am I going? The answers they give to these questions are the components of their "world view." Perhaps this searching for answers to such questions is one of the reasons why some animistic peoples seem to be more open to the gospel message than are people who hold to a more integrated and philosophically oriented formalized religion. The established world religions have formulated elaborate responses to such questions. They have taught the answers to their adherents. The animist seems to be living in much more of a state of fear of the unknown, and is thereby more open to something that will give him an answer to his questions.

Christians cannot forget that Christianity is not the only option open to animistic peoples who are as yet unreached. Islam offers another option and is making its approaches to these people. Secular life-systems and ideals as well as religious systems are potential options.

Nigeria is an example of the urgency of the situation in one country. Northern Nigeria is almost entirely Islamic, whereas the southern sector is strongly Christian. In the central belt of Nigeria is the region of the greatest number of still animistic peoples within the country. Islamic forces from the north are vying with the Christian forces of the south for the allegiance of the people who are open and ready to leave animism and accept a new religion that will give answers to their questions. It may be that neither Islam nor Christianity will win these people. In their search they may turn to any one of the many African "Prophet movements" or their own new prophets may emerge. In their search, they may try something new to express their own identity.

A graphic demonstration is presented in the following diagram of Nigeria (Graphic 6). Considering the ethnic groups as compared with the religious profession of each it is readily seen that ethno-linguistic divisions appear which designate the horizontal segments into percentage units, and the vertical segments demonstrate the religious affiliations. Those at the top of the graphic represent the Islamic population. Those in the center represent the animistic peoples. Those at the bottom represent the Christian population. In reality, the majority of the peoples of the north are Moslem, and those at the south are with a much higher percentage of Christians. Those in the central belt of the country are the more highly animistic. In such a situation the peoples in the central belt must look for some alignment, or for

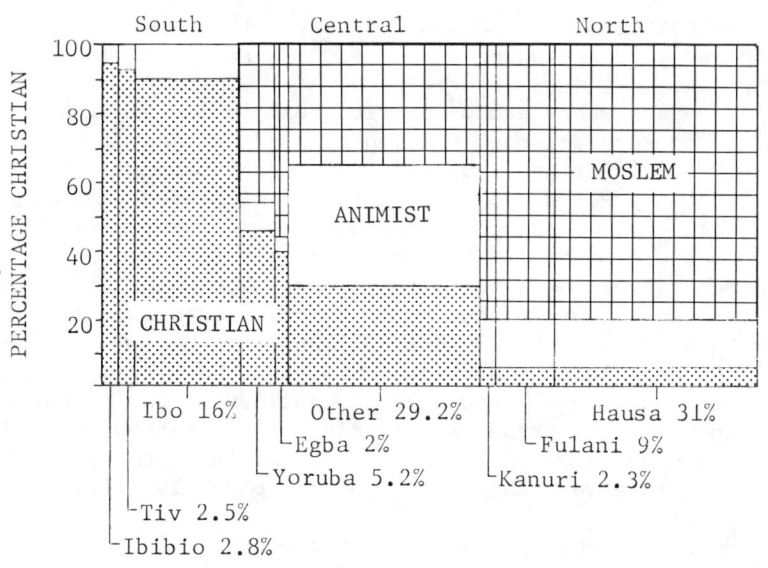

(NOTE: *These figures are representative approximations. They should be seen as indications of magnitude, not precise.*)

some degree of self-expression by which they can retain their own identity.

People seek identity in terms of something that will satisfy a longing for self-recognition, self-identity and people consciousness. Nationalism is one of the manifestations by which satisfaction is derived from the new identity.

Affiliation with some recognized body is another action which offers derived satisfaction. The World Council of Churches offers its status to churches of minority or oppressed groups that will join hands with it. The Roman Catholic Church in its claim of "universality" offers another option.

Luzbetak, a noted Roman Catholic anthropologist discusses the subject of people-consciousness when he writes:

> In areas where group-consciousness is dominant, the Church might very well be referred to as "Christ's Clan" or "Christ's Tribe." Baptism can be described as an adoption into a powerful society, against which even "the gates of hell" cannot prevail. The Head of the Church is the Son of the Almighty. The Head is deeply interested in all the members of the Mystical Body, and each member contributes to the welfare of the other members. Christ comes to the individual in a very special manner in Holy Communion. The relationship between Christ and the Christian is personal and real. Security and solidarity can be further instilled by proper and meaningful instruction regarding Grace and the place of the Holy Spirit in the life of the individual and the whole Mystical Body (1963:174).

When considering a strategy for evangelization the factors of people-consciousness and self-recognition become crucial.

THE DIVERSITY OF EXPRESSION

Emotions are common to all mankind, but expressions of emotion differ from culture to culture. Love and sorrow are expressed more freely in some cultures than in others. We may talk about a people "with very little emotion" or of another people as "very emotional." In reality the difference may not be one of degree, but of display. The Oriental custom of manifestation of friendship and pleasure is very different from the Western. The African is different from the European.

Emotion is a feeling of the heart, as we say in English, but emotional expression is a learned art or pattern. People demonstrate emotion as they are taught. Children learn to display emotion as they observe. In some cultures sorrow is displayed by great wailing and there are professional mourners at funerals. In others there is restraint, for the show of emotion is considered as unacceptable. Religion is a matter that touches the heart of a people, and elicits emotional response. There are innumerable possibilities of expression that may follow. Reactions differ among people, and the display will be conditioned by the emotional patterns that have been acquired.

Probably one factor in the growth of the Pentecostal Church is the fact that it affords a setting for emotional self-expression, and makes the worshipper comfortable in responding to his inner urges. In many cases the doctrinal issues related to the incidence of Pentecostal and many other movements is of relatively little importance to the converts themselves. The sense of freedom of expression is satisfying. Who can doubt that the liberty of freedom from Death and Hell is something to become emotional about!

The evangelist is a bearer of good news. He has a relevant message to deliver. Response to that message has emotional implications. Some will respond with demonstration of joy, others with demonstration of weeping, others with silent worship. The fact that the Friends (Quakers) meet for worship in absolute silence and meditation and the Pentecostals speak out in open response to the preaching of the Word does not in itself make one right and the other wrong. Each has the right of his own form. The fact that a Hindu spends time in silent meditation does not make silent meditation wrong. He is not wrong in his meditation. He is wrong in not worshipping the true God.

It is not the form of worship that is right or wrong. It is the object of worship that makes the difference. Peoples from different cultural backgrounds have developed different habits of worship. They have the right to worship in a pattern and way that is satisfying to the Spirit that is Holy within them. One who does not know the Holy Spirit cannot worship in truth. But when the Holy Spirit enters, then he can worship the true God. The form of worship may not change, but the Object of his worship has changed. New patterns may come into his worship. New patterns can be learned, and may be developed. Old patterns may be abandoned. But it is false to think that an individual becomes a Christian because he worships like a Christian.

One problem an evangelist faces is that of teaching as normative a specific form of worship instead of letting form flow from the expression of the heart. Response follows the acceptance of the message. Otherwise the movement is one of imitation of form without being possessor of the reality.

Among new converts this liberty of expression may take a form very different from the form of the old religion. Many evangelists and missionaries are of the opinion that a new form of worship must be taught, especially if the practices of the old are incongruent with Christian form of expression. If such is the case, then there must be some criteria established for judging what is "right" and what is "wrong;" for determining what is "Christian" and what is not. Very evidently the Bible would have to be the rule book for all situations. Actually in it we find little direct or explicit instructions. The command is given to worship the Lord alone, but as to how to worship is not given. Clearly the Old Testament worship included the offering of sacrifices, but the offering of sacrifices was not the only way. In fact, the Lord rejected sacrifices at times because the hearts of the offerers were not right. In these cases the form did not satisfy. God does not look on the form, or outward expression, but on the intents and purposes of the heart.

Many Christian leaders are concerned about various new movements that are emerging in Third World countries. Two areas of concern are in theology and ritual. Some conclude, as Dr. Harold Turner who wrote of the movement of the Church of the Lord Aladura in Africa, and communicated in personal conversation with the author, that with the Bible as foundational these groups will come to biblical positions through the power of the Word. Others believe that immediate teaching is necessary for groups emerging from one pattern of religious practice and moving into another. They say: "How will they know unless they are taught?" Still others believe that any expression that deviates from a norm is Satanic and to be pronounced as "Apostate."

Each of these positions has weaknesses which must be examined. Turner's positon depends upon a presupposition that the Bible is available and intelligible and accepted as a norm and that people can of themselves discover its light and walk in its direction. This may be difficult for illiterate and confused peoples. It may be too much to assume. Where people are literate and have the Bible certainly the Holy Spirit is able to lead.

The second position presents the danger that an interpretation of practice will be that of the teacher's position without truly being the expression of the heart of the people themselves. This is what happens when a missionary goes to Laos and teaches the Meo people that the way to worship is to start by singing two hymns, offer a prayer, sing another hymn, take up an offering, have a sermon, sing another hymn, have the benediction and go home.

The third position falls into the danger of confusing

The Importance of Seeing the World in Homogeneous Units 41

theological apostacy with ritual. Clear distinction must be drawn at this level. David certainly acted in an unconventional manner when he was so overjoyed at bringing the Ark of the Covenant back to its proper place that he danced before the Lord (2 Samuel 6:14).

Many peoples who have separated themselves from animistic beliefs and practices have sought to express their worship in entirely new forms. Others have fallen into syncretistic practices. To provide a recognized form of worship is urgently needed. Perhaps for this reason many missionaries find success in teaching hymns to new converts. The singing of hymns is one acceptable subsitute and provides expression for the new faith. Singing is often, in fact usually, related to worship. But the missionary cannot forget that the music of hymns must also be a music that gives utterance to the feelings of the individual. What music is worshipful music? It is not necessarily the music of the western hymns. To the westerner the hymn melodies have become traditional, and are accepted. They are related through cultural heritage as being the form of expression of worship. That is why some of the youth groups are finding difficulty with the older generation who cannot accept a different type of music as worshipful. There is a music that is culturally acceptable. But the youth of the west are today living in a different culture from the culture of their parents.

If different modes are apparent in the west, where the culture is so much related, can it be doubted that different cultures will present yet more drastically different forms? Worship is the expression of the heart. Demonstration of worship must be related to the modes of expression that are culturally understood, and the evangelist and missionary must recognize that such individuality will appear, and that is right. To try to dictate form of worship that is not congrous with cultural forms of expression is an anomaly.

Where Christianity is accepted the situation is one where the "advocate" has been a well accepted "witness" to the new faith. But the effectiveness of the new faith depends upon the satisfaction derived from it by the adherents themselves. If satisfaction does not result then the novelty will soon wear off and the people will return to the old pattern. If this should happen it will be far more difficult to initiate any response a second time.

Vital to the evangelist is the recognition that a new form of worship must satisfy the emotional feelings of the worshipper. If a new pattern is introduced, it must be an acceptable substitute for some practice previously performed. As different peoples have different practices, so the demonstration of emotional satisfaction will be different, and any new expression will find outlet in a satisfying manner.

An example of a new expression of a new faith is that of a group of the Otomi Indians of Mexico. When a strong leader of the village of Ixmiquilpan was won to Christ he wanted to demonstrate his new life to the whole community.

> To meet one desperate situation, the church in Ixmiquilpan had itself undertaken, with the help of a government engineer, to build a road into a poverty-stricken valley. The entire congregation would meet Sunday morning at five o'clock to worship, and then the whole day would be given to work on the road, after which the people returned to glorify God. Some members of the congregation, who could spare time during the week from working in the fields or as masons and mechanics, helped on the road, so that actually it was built six months ahead of schedule--perhaps the first time in the history of Mexico that this has happened. Persecution had excommunicated the people from various small towns and villages, but the believers soon banded together, purchased an abandoned hill along the highway, and there built a village of well-constructed homes, which now has electricity and a sewage system. Here the power of the living God has redeemed the work of men's hands, and the whole economic life of the Christian community has been transformed (Nida, 1968:61).

This kind of group-centered manifestation and expression of new-found faith soon led to almost the entire community becoming evangelical.

In conclusion, the evangelist must recognize that the world is a great mosaic of peoples, each different, wanting to be themselves and having the right to be different. People do not need to change to come to Christ, they come to Christ just as they are. The strategy of world evangelism is not to change the world to conform to a pattern, but to recognize how Christ fits every pattern.

The magnitude and complexity of world cultures means the recognition of many and diverse adaptations of Christianity to cultural norms. The importance of recognizing a universal sense of self-consciousness means the strategy for world evangelization allows people to be themselves. The concept of the right of individual self-expression means the right of emotional response in patterns that are soul-satisfying.

The evangelist does not mold the world. He is the clay that fits into the mold.

Chapter 3

Basic Types of Homogeneous Units

In dealing with the question, "Who are the unevanglized?" the Questionnaire used by the Research Committee for the International Congress on World Evangelization defined unevangelized peoples as:

> those homogeneous units which have not received or responded to the Gospel. This unresponsiveness may be due to lack of opportunity, lack of understanding, or because they have not received sufficient information about the Gospel message within their own language, cultural frame of reference and communication channels to make Christianity a viable option (Questionnaire on Unreached Peoples Survey, 1973).

When Beaver convened the Consultation on "The Gospel and Frontier Peoples," he, with the other conveners, planned a consultation to deal exclusively with the tribal peoples who for the most part live in remote places of the world. Yet in spite of such a decision and declared restriction, it soon became evident that

> all sorts of frontiers of mission . . . began to clamor for attention as soon as discussion began . . . . There is the frontier of the encounter with other faiths and that of witness to the seemingly impervious Muslim and Buddhist societies. There is the realm of encounter with the independent, separatist churches in Africa and else-

where. There are peoples of subcultures in every land around the world to whom little witness and ministry are being offered. By-passed peoples, the hordes of displaced political refugees, war victims in many lands, the depersonalized masses of the great cities all demand attention as genuine frontiers where new principles, strategy, and tactics are demanded for effective communication of the faith (Beaver, ed., 1973:4).

Taber in his study of <u>Evangelizing The Unreached Peoples</u> identifies many groups.

What populations are today's unreached? These are not only small, whole, homogeneous populations, such as remote jungle tribes and bands, but definable sub-populations within otherwise well evangelized societies, or groups which were evangelized in a previous century or generation but not in this. This includes a great many churchgoers, e.g. in the prosperous suburbs of Western countries, who for all their churchianity have never come to grips with a clear presentation of the Gospel. For such people, a real obstacle is created by their illusion of knowing what the Gospel is, and by their negative image of those who would present anything different from what they comfortably practice . . . it can well be said that for all practical purposes, these people are just as unreached as the jungle tribes or as the masses of urban ghettos. We must therefore get over thinking in terms of geographical areas, and start thinking in terms of groups of people. A careful survey will not guarantee that a sound strategy will prevail over piecemeal responses to emotional appeals, but lack of it will certainly lead to the opposite. (Beaver, ed., 1973:123).

Our purpose is to discover if possible who those unreached and unevangelized peoples are, in order that somehow the gospel message might be made relevant to them in such a way that they will be persuaded and receive Jesus Christ and His redemption for themselves.

There are units that can be identified and we shall treat some of them, suggesting that recognition of typical groups will aid in the formulation of a strategy of evangelization.

ETHNIC

Perhaps the first significant characteristic of identification of the homogeneous units is the ethnic. All children are the offspring of their parents and carry the ethnic characteristics. One value of this consists in the fact that people of the same ethnic background tend to seek one another out when migrating. The Chinese people of almost every large city have formed themselves into units and developed a "Chinatown." San Francisco is famous for its "Chinatown." Los Angeles has its sector. Philadelphia and New York have theirs. Lima, Peru and Mexico City have theirs. In these areas the close relationships of kin patterns are propogated. Some people term this as being "clannish." Customs are perpetuated because they are taught. All habits and customs are learned, not inherited. Language is a learned habit of speech. Mode of eating is a learned action. Children can learn any language in the world given the same opportunity, just as they can learn to eat in any manner that they are taught.

The importance of the ethnic relationship is found in the fact that by interaction within the ethnic group, certain characteristics are perpetuated that cause the group to remain as a homogeneous unit, even within a foreign society. Some groups, usually small, are assimilated within a generation or two. Others refrain from absorption. Larger groups more easily retain their own identity. The Chicanos of Los Angeles are far from being absorbed. Some of the indigenous Indian peoples of the United States are today demonstrating the fact that they were not completely absorbed after 200 years of co-existence with foreign cultures. The European peoples were never assimilated or absorbed into the indigenous culture of the U.S.

LINGUISTIC

Language is perhaps the most significant characteristic of homogeneity. It unites those of like speech into interrelationships not possible without it. If we were to divide the world into ethnic groups, we would come out with a significant number. However, when we divide the world into linguistic units we find that the number is greatly increased. Wycliffe Bible Translators alone have information on nearly 5,000 distinct languages and dialects.

The division of languages into dialects is demonstrative of the way in which new homogeneous units are formed. Linguistic changes indicate patterns of change. Geographic isolation always produces dialectical changes, which in time become so variant as to be considered different languages. This is the case of the Portuguese peoples, who because of isolation from Spain, developed a language of their own.

Other outside influences also cause dialectic changes, by the adoption of borrowed words and phrases. As linguistic adaptations take place, cultural adaptations also take place.

The coining of new words also is indicative of cultural changes influencing the people. New discoveries mean new words. New words in a language indicate new concepts within the thought pattern.

Expansion of this second characteristic would be most easy to do, but the fact is so well understood that it would seem unnecessary to expand further.

RELIGIOUS

A third characteristic of homogeneity is the religious factor. It has been stated that religion is the cement that binds any people together. Religion is the expression of the beliefs of the heart (mind) manifested in the observances and practices of life as related to the supernatural, the eternal and one's "world-view." Religion is a learned art as far as visible dimensions are concerned, but has inherent within it a sense of invisible and deeper "spiritual" recognition. Man has within himself a sense of "conscience" and fear of the unknown god. This moves him to want to act in such a way as to try to please or appease the god whom he senses. The actions through which he will move are learned expressions.

For example, a Buddhist father will teach his son the art of quiet contemplation on the values that will make him "good." The Hindu learns how to meditate on the philosophies of life that make life worth living. The Islamic instruction teaches one when to pray and how to prostrate himself. The Roman Catholic learns when to go to Mass, how to recite his prayers and when and how to make the sign of the cross. The animist learns how to dance around a fire to scare the evil spirits away.

All of these manifestations are learned practices, by which groups are recognized. But beyond the outward manifestation is the inner communication that only those of like mind and like faith can share. It is communication of understanding and comprehension at the most intimate level. This is a valuable characteristic of each homogeneous unit to recognize.

Within the ethnic and linguistic units there are divisions, one significant division being religion. So that in order to determine the units that exist one must look at the basic groups and then ask: "Into how many religious groups is this unit divided?"

The question can legitimately be asked: "Does it make any

difference into how many sub-groups a unit is divided?" Since evangelization depends on communication it is vital to understand what elements are involved.

Evangelization deals with "conversion," which is repentance of the old and a complete turn toward the new. Evangelization deals with communication as it effects change. Evangelization is the communication of innovation. Therefore it must be understood that if the Gospel is going to be made relevant, it must be understood within the framework of the culture whose center and hub is its religion, and in terms of language that can communicate.

Further, when a new religion moves to enter into any given society, it does so attacking the very strength of the society, and it can be anticipated that there will be sociological as well as religious opposition. The opposition will come on the basis that the new religion is an intrusion which would destroy the very basis on which the unity of the people rests. It is therefore to be anticipated that where Christianity makes its approach against an established religious block, it will meet opposition. Where the people of any group hold a religion that is of lesser degree in affording a base of unity for the society, the religious and social opposition will be less.

An axiom may be stated at this point: THE DEGREE TO WHICH ANY RELIGION HOLDS A SOCIETY TOGETHER DETERMINES THE DEGREE TO WHICH IT WILL OPPOSE THE ENTRANCE OF ANY OTHER RELIGION.

Religion is the strength that unites the Muslim world. There are many factors that would separate sociologically different peoples, but the one factor that unites them together is their common religion.

SOCIO-ECONOMIC

Within a given geographic area there are residents who speak the same language and profess the same religion. Yet there are other differences which separate them. Some are rich and others are poor. These different groups do not have relationships with one another except within well-defined "work" relationships. These relationships define "class" or "caste" systems. In such a situation the factors which distinguish each group are neither ethnic, linguistic nor religious, but socio-economic.

Likewise the distinction may be one of age groupings, or related to education. Dr. Alan R. Tippett describes the age-group differences among the Anuak society in Ethiopia in his book <u>Peoples Of Southwest Ethiopia</u>. He concludes the explanation of the importance of recognizing the age-group differences by saying:

> My pastor-teacher informant, Akwai, saw their Christian need in terms of a strong teaching program in each of the separate age-sets:
> "The beginning of believing began with us when we were still young. The older men rejected the gospel when they became <u>jobura</u>. (Of a certain age that gave distinction). We really need to plan our teaching program to fit each group. When we have a village service the old men and the young men will not sit together. We will have to deal with them one at a time" (Tippett, 1970:62,63).

Many missionaries in Hindu and Islamic areas witness to the fact that the women cannot be reached by a man. They have formed their own patterns which follow well established lines of communication. Only women can establish communication channels with these women. As a result separate operations have been set up to try to reach the women of such groups. Of course it cannot be denied that the husbands of these women have direct communication with their wives, and if won to Christ would be a vital link to reach them. To go directly to the women is, in a sense, by-passing the direct communication channel.

Perhaps one word of caution is in order at this point. Whereas the purpose of the study is to identify homogeneous units, we must not forget the purpose for identifying them. The purpose is to locate those significant units which should be recognized as distinct targets of evangelization, and determine the best means of communicating the gospel message so that people will understand and respond. The purpose is not to simply multiply sub-divisions *ad-infinitum*. Nor does it propose the formation of needless segmentation of the Church into unnecessary sub-divisions. For example, the Anuak society is a society that is divided by age-sets and this division may be respected in instructional settings. Yet it should not mean there is a separate "Church" for each age group. Nor, in the case of the women's evangelism, is there to be a "Church" for the women and a "Church" for the men. If Paul could say the Gospel had broken down the middle wall of partition between the Jew and the Gentile to bring both into one Body, so the "Church" should be that same kind of body, uniting in Christ, not dividing in unnecessary segmentation. We can, however, expect the Church to be sensitive to respected cultural and linguistic differences.

Cultural and linguistic differences do exist and they are real. Where there are linguistic lines and cultural differences, we can expect the Church to fall in line with those characteristics, which are marks of identification and very real. Christians like to be Christians within their own culture.

Subdivisions of sociological groups are occupational and educational as well as economic. Those whose work draws them together, naturally establish close lines of communication. Likewise peoples of educational levels establish a vocabulary of communication of their own. Did you ever try to communicate with a computer technician? His vocabulary is singularly his. So it is with the student world. The mentality is one of doubting, searching and questioning. Here, some individuals are so convinced of the peculiar communication and mental need of this group that they have organized separate "churches" to minister to their individual needs. Their needs are so distinctive as to have given rise to such organizations as the International Fellowship of Evangelical Students (Inter-Varsity Christian Fellowship in the U.S.A. and Canada), Campus Crusade, Youth For Christ, Navigators, etc. to reach them. Certainly the "student" class is a distinct group worthy of being called a separate "homogeneous unit" within the individual countries.

A diagram representing the sociological structure of Brazil serves to display the social class levels, and the ethnic distinctives. Such a diagram identifies nine distinct homogeneous units. (Graphic 7).

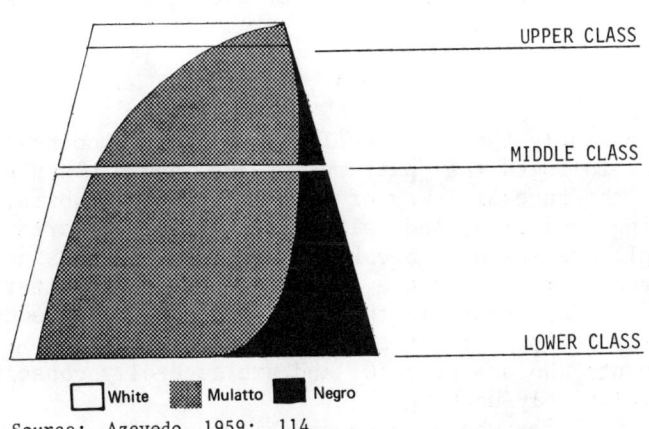

RACE AND CLASS IN BRAZIL

Source: Azevedo, 1959: 114

Source: Interpretive Bulletin I, <u>Continuing Evangelism in Brazil</u>, MARC/MIB, 1971.

(Graphic 7)

URBAN

Within the sociological patterns of the world we discover that the cultural and unifying factors of those who reside in the urban centers are quite different from those who reside in rural areas. Patterns of livelihood are very different. Value systems are distinct. Trade values change, and the economic standard is vastly altered. This is why peoples who change physical location undergo rather strenuous struggles to adjust to their new environment.

Many factors cause urbanization. Some factors such as economic factors may cause rapid changes. Other factors may produce more slowly developing patterns, but all lead to new life styles and the establishment of new values. The people involved, regardless of causes, form homogeneous units, demanding corresponding communication changes to adapt to their changed needs. Here the church might serve as a stabilizing and encouraging force if it is able to communicate with those who may be searching for new foundations and relationships. The evangelization of such mobile groups is a challenging possibility.

Many churches are involved in outreach programs to the newly urbanized groups who often locate in "satellite" areas. In these centers "branch" churches become the pattern. Many individuals do not feel at home in a center-city church where the ways of life are so different. Often the poverty of the recent migrant is a deterrent to his going to a "city" church. The answer is found in separate churches that meet the fellowship needs of the people of the so called *barrios*.

RURAL

Very frequently the rural dwellers are those who have for generations followed the "patterns of the land." This probably means the ancestral way of life in cultural habits, land farming, religion, and value system. In many areas the young people are making a break from the old patterns and going to the cities to seek a new and supposedly "better" way of life. The result is that many areas have a predominance of three distinct age groups:

 1. Parents who are over 50, and are generally conservative and relatively unchangeable.
 2. The families who have young children and remain because it is the only means of livelihood they have, and culture requires that they remain to care for the elderly.
 3. The young children who are of primary and secondary

school age.

Family ties may be very close among such groups, but a growing unrest is felt by the fact that the advanced-age school children are away, seeking for and bringing home reports of a new and more desirable way of life.

Not all find the city way of life satisfying. Bailey and Nasatir wrote concerning a Mexican village:

> By the 1960's many of the young men of the first literate generation had left the poor lands. They went to work on the new highways . . . or on the waterworks project. Several of them migrated to . . . the national capital, where they found occupation in the new industries . . . . Several whole families had moved to Mexico City by 1966, although three of them found no place to live save in crowded shanties in Mexico City's new slum fringes. Their children found no school to attend there, while the children back at home were using fine new free textbooks sent to them (Bailey and Nasatir, 1968:485).

Dr. John Dale, Director of the Mexican Indian Mission, wrote of the Mexican village and the cultural patterns of the people saying:

> There are possible three types of villages or ranches in our area: (1) villages where the Indians have had little influence from mestizo culture, and whose contacts with the outside world are limited to weekly visits to the market in the main market town or county seat; (2) villages where the culture is mainly Indian, but where there are some mestizo families who live as part of the Indian community; and (3) villages where the mestizos form the heart of the life of the community, and the Indians live on the outskirts. You find different degrees of culture in each type, or variations in accord with the national culture. Nevertheless, we can say that where the Indian culture dominates, the life is communal, while where the mestizo is predominant, life is individual (Dale, 1952).

Perhaps the most graphic way of depicting the social structure of rural peoples is one adapted from Whiteford, which shows the village as the outer circle, forming the total community, and inner circles representing the class and sub-class structures, narrowing down to the family. In each area these will be called by different names, but the basic pattern is universal (Whiteford, 1960:33) (Graphic 8).

RURAL COMMUNITY STRUCTURE

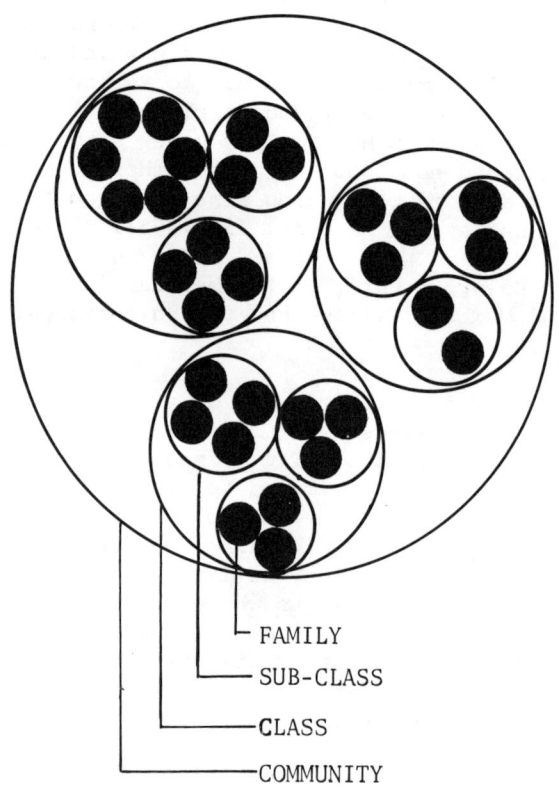

(Whiteford, 1960:33) (Graphic 8)

Basic Types of Homogeneous Units   53

Adapting this same pattern, we present another diagram demonstrating the possible sociological units of a village (Graphic 9). The large circle represents the village, composed of the families (which may be the extended family) represented by the small circles.

The society is represented as divided into two classes, the upper and the lower. Those distinctions will be defined by the village itself, but whatever criteria is accepted will define the relationships of one group to the other. This is represented by the horizontal division, and portrays the fact that families will fall largely into one or the other division.

A second division is possible which may be religion. If the village is a unit with a strong sense of religious unity, religion being the cement that binds it together, then any incumbent religion will be considered as an enemy to the society, and will be rejected. Its entrance will divide the village into separate homogeneous units.

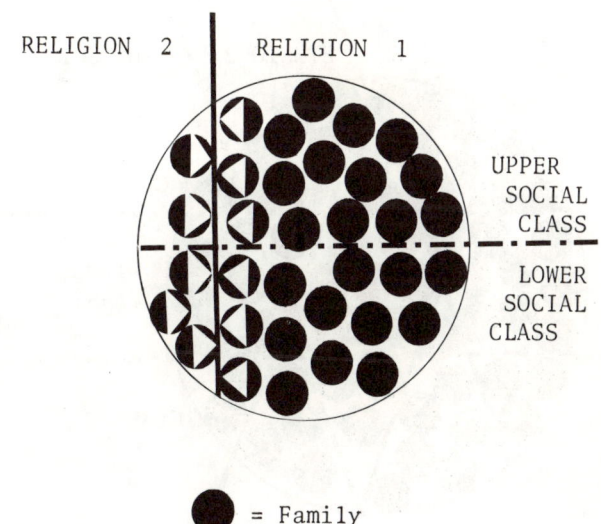

(Graphic 9)

54 REACHING THE UNREACHED

The diagramatic presentation of a city becomes a much more complex design (Graphic 10). Usually there are various sociological classes, defined as, for example, upper, middle, and lower, indicated by the horizontal lines. Secondly there are the ethnic divisions which are indicated by the diagonals from upper right to lower left. Thirdly there are the religious division indicated by the diagonals from upper left to lower right.

The divisions thus indicated multiply the complexity of the urban possibilities, yet clearly demonstrate the fact that urban life is divided into many definable homogeneous units.

It is recognized that very frequently the religious very nearly coincides with the ethnic, as ethnic groups often retain their religion and carefully guard it, even though they may in no sense try to win converts to that religion. In such a case the diagonal lines would be superimposed, and would strengthen the ethno-religious units. If such divisions also become linguistic, then there are three factors that give multiple strength to the unit.

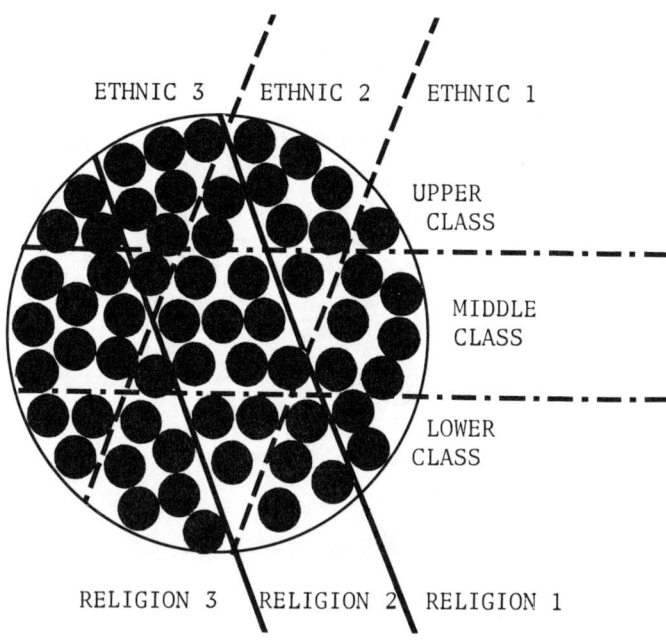

(Graphic 10)

Part Two **The Evangelization of Units**

Chapter 4

Understanding Scriptural Evangelism

One might rightfully ask: "When has a people been evangelized?" Answers differ as perspective and definition of evangelization differ. Barrett says:

> Individuals of another religion, or a family, or a tribe, or a nation, can be said to have been *evangelized* when they have come into contact with Christianity sufficiently for them to have heard the good news about Jesus Christ and to have had an opportunity of responding to it by faith; i.e. people have been evangelized when they have been exposed in one way or another to the gospel (Barrett, 1972:1).

This position understands "evangelization" in terms of "proclamation" only. It accepts "evangelization" as related to the proclamation of the "good news," often called the *kerygma*, and not to the reception of it. Barrett clearly states that "non-Christian peoples can be evangelized without necessarily becoming Christians or professing conversion" (1972:1).

If Barrett's definition of evangelization is accepted, then his conclusion is the only one that can follow. However, in the light of Scripture teaching another definition emerges. Christ said: "Go, and make disciples . . ." (Matt. 28:19). That is evangelization. Anything less than obedience to that comman is unacceptable.

PROCLAMATION

Proclamation of the gospel message is vital. No one related with the Scriptures doubts this aspect. All of the gospel writers except John speak of preaching, and Paul in his epistles gives added teaching with regard to the aspect of preaching. Paul confirms the fact that without it men do not hear (Rom. 10:14). But proclamation is not the end. It is a means.

RESPONSE

The Lord spoke through Isaiah to Israel saying:

My people shall know my name; therefore, *they shall know* in that day that I *am* he who doth speak; behold, *it is* I.
How beautiful upon the mountains are the feet of him that bringeth good tidings, that publisheth peace; that bringeth good tidings of good, that publisheth salvation; that saith unto Zion, Thy God reigneth!
Thy watchmen shall lift up the voice; with the voice together shall they sing; for they shall see eye to eye, when the Lord shall bring again Zion (Isa. 52:6-8).

Jehovah did not intend that there should be a proclamation alone; He intended that Israel should return to Himself.
Paul also speaks very clearly when he says:

Knowing, therefore, the terror of the Lord, we persuade men; . . . God . . . hath given to us the ministry of reconciliation; . . . and hath committed unto us the word of reconciliation (2 Cor. 5:11-19).

He demonstrates his concern for the lost which are ever upon his mind when he says: "For three years I did not cease night or day to admonish every one with tears" (Acts 20:31). "Him we proclaim, warning every man and teaching every man in all wisdom that we may present every man mature in Christ" (Col. 1:28).
Theodore Williams of the Evangelical Fellowship of India writes: "We affirm that in evangelism our primary concern is the transformation of individuals. The individual matters intensely to God" (Ben Wati, 1970:7).
God is concerned about men, and desires a response from men. He gave His Son to bring men back to Himself. God is not satisfied until they come back. Proclamation alone is

Understanding Scriptural Evangelism   59

not sufficient, response is essential. Therefore a people is not evangelized until it has responded to the "good news" of the message. To be evangelized is to be made a follower of the "evangel." To hear is not sufficient.

Too often it is forgotten that evangelism is God-centered. When evangelism is thought of only in terms of man, it results in the concept of preaching a message from God to man. When it is recognized as being God-centered, it results in the concept of bringing men to God. Evangelization is the act of bringing men to God, not only bringing God to men.

Paul told Timothy to "do the work of an evangelist." The context clearly shows what the work of the evangelist is.

> Preach the word; be diligent . . . reprove, rebuke, exhort with all long suffering and doctrine . . .
>   Watch . . . in all things, endure afflictions . . . .
> make full proof of thy ministry (2 Tim. 4:2-5).

If "to do the work of an evangelist" is only one of a list of things that Timothy was to do, then to "Preach the word" is also one of the list and not to be equated. If "to do the work of an evangelist" is the summation of the list, then evangelism includes all that is mentioned; namely to preach, to exhort, to bear a good testimony proving the ministry. Undoubtedly Paul intended all of these and the word "do the work of an evangelist" was the summation.

Certainly Philip, who is the only one called an "evangelist" in Scripture (Acts 21:8), was a preacher (Acts chapter 8). But Philip did not stop with preaching. He "made disciples" as recounted in Acts 8:3. "And the people with one accord gave heed unto those things which Philip spoke, hearing and seeing the miracles which he did." Their belief was demonstrated by being baptized (Acts 8:12). Even Simon the sorcerer was convinced and became a disciple (Acts 8:13). He fell into sin under temptation, but was delivered as a true disciple is delivered (Acts 8:18-24).

Christ's first words after returning from the time of temptation in the wilderness as recorded by Mark are: "The time is fulfilled, and the kingdom of God is at hand; repent, and believe the gospel" (Mark 1:14,15). Christ included response in His message.

MESSAGE

Green writes of the aptness of the term "evangel" as used in the New Testament when he says"

> It was a happy choice of word, for "good news" had, apart from its general appeal, specific overtones both in Jewish and pagan circles, which made it particularly significant.
> The noun . . . is frequently used by Paul and Mark. (It) had little by way of Old Testament background. But it meant much to the Greek world. It was the word used par excellence to announce victory . . . . (Green, 1970: 56).

Thus we find the relationship between the Gospel and its content. The Gospel is "good news," but only to those who receive it and are through it brought into proper relationship with the Author of it. The Gospel is equated with Jesus. It is the "good news" that God has come, suffered on the cross, was dead, buried, and raised again (1 Cor. 15:1-4). To those who reject, it is not "good news" but rather the pronouncement of judgment. Repentance and faith are the essential human responses for reception of it. (See 1 Thess. 1:5-9; Romans 1:16; 2:16; 3:22; 10:16,21).

Paul in Romans 16:25 gives the relationship of the Gospel to the obedience of faith. The proclamation of the message is vital, and essential to its being received. However if the message is not received, the preaching is in vain. The reception of the message is just as important as the preaching of it, and as the message itself, for people to be evangelized.

> My speech and my preaching were not with enticing words of man's wisdom, but in demonstration of the Spirit and of power;
> That your faith should not stand in the wisdom of men, but in the power of God (1 Cor. 2:4,5).

WITNESS

This same verse leads us to the next aspect of the Gospel, which is "witness." Our Lord said "ye shall be witnesses unto me . . ." (Acts 1:8 and Luke 24:48). Witness was to accompany the preaching as an inseparable part of it. Its purpose would be fulfilled not only by word, but by demonstration of power that was convincing.

Scripture relates three aspects of evangelization: MESSAGE, PROCLAMATION, WITNESS, which together produce DISCIPLES.

Theodore Williams of the Evangelical Fellowship of India says:

There are five words associated with Evangelism in the
New Testament. They are preaching or proclaiming (Matt.
3:23, Mark 1:14), teaching (Matt. 4:23), healing (Matt.
9:23), witnessing (Acts 1:8) and discipling (Matt. 28:19).
Healing is mentioned most of the time with preaching.
Thus prominence is given to the verbal cummunication of
the Gospel (Ben Wati, ed. 1970:12).

He further says:

Leighton Ford points out in his book, "The Christian Persuader" that evangelism in the New Testament combines three strands: *koinonia* - the witness of fellowship: *diakonia* - the witness of service: *kerygma* - the witness of proclamation. Jesus followed this pattern. He extended His love and friendship to others (Mark 2:16). He served others (Mark 1:34). Then He proclaimed the Evangel (Mark 1:14). The early Church also did the same. They witnessed through loving fellowship (Acts 2:44) and compassionate service (Acts 3:6) and followed it with faithful proclamation (Acts 5:42). The apostle Paul says, "Though I am free from all men, I have made myself a slave to all, that I might win the more" (1 Cor. 9:19). . . . There is a self-giving in the proclamation of the Gospel which cannot be avoided (Ben Wati, ed., 1970:14).

We must further remember: it takes the work of the Holy
Spirit to win converts. Our Lord said: "No man can come to
me, except the Father, who hath sent me, draw him . . .
(John 6:44). Paul wrote: "For it is God who worketh in you
both to will and to do of *his* good pleasure" (Phil. 2:13),
and "The Spirit himself beareth witness with our spirit,
that we are the children of God" (Rom. 8:16).
In conclusion, I would re-affirm the definition of evangelism, as declared by Billy Graham at the Congress on Evangelism in Berlin, 1966 when he quoted the definition as
given by the Archbishop's Committee on evangelism in 1918:

To evangelize is so to present Christ Jesus in the power of the Holy Spirit, that men shall come to put their trust in God through him, to accept him as their Savior and serve him as their King in the fellowship of his Church (Henry-Mooneyham, 1967:25).

This kind of evangelism produces conversion, disciples
and growth of the Church, which Christ said He would build,
with the promise that the gates of hell should not prevail
against it.

Chapter 5

Effective Communication for Evangelism

If religious conviction is the very hub of man's existence and world-view, then the process whereby a person comes to religious commitment must be the most culturally relevant process in the life of any individual or people. Evangelism, or the activity whereby people are won to religious faith, requires that attention be given to two elements that are vital to the process. First, the message must have cultural relevance. Second, the communication of that message must be comprehensible if the people are to receive it.

COMPREHENSIBLE COMMUNICATION

The deepest concern of the evangelist is the communication of the Gospel in such a way that it is understood and the end result is accomplished. As previously stated, the end result of evangelism is making disciples of the Lord. Yet all who are involved in evangelism are well aware of the practical problems involved in communication of the message, in order to make disciples.
Effective communication is the art of transmitting a message from one individual in such a way that the message is received by another without distortion or dilution. However, to speak of communication without distortion is to speak of an almost impossibility. To consider cross-cultural communication is to multiply the problems of relating without distortion.

Communication is the transmission of "thought patterns." This is why the present trend of Scripture translation is toward what has been called "dynamic equivalent" rather than toward "literal translation." Those who are most deeply involved with Scripture translation, such as personnel of the Bible Societies and those affiliated with Wycliffe Bible Translators, have adopted the term "dynamic equivalency." It recognizes the fact that for each concept there is a different expression in each language, but that usually there is a functionally equivalent expression in each. The burden of the translator is to communicate to the mind of the recipient the dynamic equivalent of the Author's concepts. The burden of the evangelist is to transmit the same image to the mind of the recipient that the Author of salvation had in His mind when He offered salvation. He can accomplish this only when he conveys the image within the cultural context of the hearer. The wonder of the gospel message is its very nature that makes it relevant to every culture.

Here is where we understand the importance of the verbal inspiration of Scripture. God had a message to convey, and the very words the writers chose were the words that best conveyed the thought within the cultural and spiritual context. The words were in the languages of the recipients, and with the Hebrew and Greek context.

Such a position does not weaken the significance of verbal inspiration of Scripture, but rather affirms the fact that even the very words of Scripture were of necessity inspired, in order to communicate exactly what God wanted communicated to the recipients. The words were necessarily culturally framed and culturally understood. In order for people today to understand the Biblical message, most Bible scholars recognize that it is necessary to understand the original context in which the words were written. This means that one must understand the specific biblical culture with all its overtones, whether Patriarchal, Mosaic, or first Century Palestine. This is the reason so many Bible scholars go to such depths in their language study and in their reconstruction of the historical context.

We must remember that cultures change, the meanings of words change, concepts change. There are peoples today who have very different ideas from Old Testament ideas and first century Hebrew and Greek ideas and thus they are confused by many of the Scriptural concepts as they were presented to the Hebrews and Greeks. For people today, even Hebrew and Greek individuals of 1974, different expressions must be used to convey equivalent thoughts. God's Word is so vital to men that it must be continually re-translated into the language of the heart of the recipient, that is, into the thought pattern that will be most completely comprehended. That's one reason why there are so many different and "modern" translations of the Bible in English, Spanish, Chinese, etc. It is not to "change" the Scriptures, but to keep up with the changes of language.

Evangelism is the art of dealing with the most vital message ever given to man. No human message could demand the attention that evangelism demands, because evangelism carrie the message of the love of God manifested toward men. Every man has the right to hear that message and in such a way tha he can comprehend it and respond to it. If the individual i going to get the fullness of the message from God he must hear it in his own understanding pattern. Thus the consideration of homogeneous units is so vital, for it deals with individuals hearing the message in their own thought patterns.

CULTURAL RELEVANCE

Charles Kraft carries the pattern of "dynamic equivalence thinking about language translation one step further when he writes of "Dynamic Equivalence Churches" in Missiology, January 1973:

> A dynamically equivalent church (1) conveys to its members truly Christian meanings, (2) functions within its own society in the name of Christ, meeting the felt needs of that society and producing within it the same Christian impact as the first century Church in its day, and (3) is couched in cultural forms that are as nearly indigenous as possible (Tippett, 1973:49).

His concern is the formation of a church that is functioning within the cultural patterns in the way Christ intended that His Church should function. The ministry of the evangelist is to make the message relevant so that a church will be formed with the culture of the people concerned.

The book of the Acts portrays a God who is committed to the presentation of the gospel message in a culturally relevant manner. From the very moment of the coming of the Holy Spirit it was evident that the message was for every man in his own tongue. Devout Jews were in Jerusalem from all the known nations and the message was given to each in his own language. Jews were always asking for "signs," and the sign of the rushing wind was heard as well as the proclamation by Peter of the fulfillment of prophecy that was well known.

Because the message was both relevant and understandable, many believed and were baptized; the Holy Spirit working through the message.

Peter's continued witness in Jerusalem was that of an advocate, who by his signs and preaching made the message relevant. As a result, Acts 4 records that about 5,000 men believed. Opposition followed from Jewish religious leaders because their traditions were being attacked.

Because the gospel message is completely relevant and applicable in every culture, and because God is no respector of persons, but loves all men equally, the evangelist must recognize that his great problem is to transmit the message without transmitting his culture as part of that message. Jack Shepherd in his article on "Mission--And Syncretism" in The Church's Worldwide Mission (Lindsell, 1966:86ff), calls attention to the danger of cultural accretions accompanying the preaching of the message. He maintains that there is such a thing as a carry-over of cultural additions which inhibit true evangelization, because the potential recipients do not want the weight of the accretions.

God's message is supracultural, and meaningful in every culture. It is above all cultures, and understandable in each. God has given His message for all men, and intended that His message should be meaningful to every individual. John wrote: "These things are written that ye might believe that Jesus is the Christ, the Son of God and that believing ye might have life through his name" (John 20:31). This life is for all men, of every culture, and for every man within his own culture.

The evangelist's concern then, and especially the missionary who is involved with cross-cultural communication, is that of transmitting or communicating the supracultural truth in trans-cultural perception. The truth behind John 1:29, "Behold the Lamb of God, who taketh away the sin of the world," is a supracultural truth. The communication and application of that truth to a people who do not have lambs, nor a concept of sacrifice to cover sin, is a human problem of a trans-cultural nature. It involves both communication problems and cultural relevancy problems.

The evangelist's key to the relevancy problem is to work from the desired goal of producing response to God, back to the pattern of response within the culture, which will produce the desired result--the salvation of the individual.

Cultural relativity is not to be construed as syncretistic adaptation of worship patterns into Christianity. Whereas the gospel message is relevant to all cultures, it is not true that all expressions within cultures are congruent with the Scriptural teaching and message. There are points where cultural practices, especially within religious ritual, are in direct conflict with Scriptural practices and teaching. There is open conflict between the powers of darkness and God Himself. This was portrayed by Elijah as recorded in 1 Kings 18:20ff.

One example of an anti-biblical practice is idolatry. The evangelist's answer is in showing the individual that God would have no image before Him, not in supplying an exchange of images as though putting a different image before the worshipper would make any difference. The only Scriptural response is to bring the worshipper to the One True God away from all images. In this there is no debate. Scripture is clear. God has said: "Thou shalt have no other gods before me" (Exodus 20:2-5).

A clear line must be drawn between a syncretism, on the one hand, which allows basic Scriptural principles to be weakened or subverted by the permissiveness of practices that are anti-biblical, and on the other hand, what we might call *harmonization* which allows a true expression of the *soul* of a people within the cultural pattern but not in conflict with Scripture. Surely the newly formed and growing Body of Christ should harmonize with the culture in which it has been born, with well-defined limits which Scripture indicates. Also Christianity will have a purifying influence on the culture in which it is found. Christianity is really about freedom from sin, within the culture in which it resides. Kraft has expressed it this way:

> A "dynamic equivalence church" then, is the kind of church that produces the same kind of impact on its own society as the early church produced upon the original hearers. In that equivalence the younger church will have need of leadership, organization, education, worship, buildings, behavioral standards, means of expressing Christian love and concern to unconverted people. A dynamically equivalent church will employ familiar, meaningful, indigenous forms, adapting and infilling them with Christian content. At the beginning these may be only minimally adequate but the process of transformation will begin that is exemplified in the history of some of the word forms that the early Church "possessed for Christ" (Kraft, 1972b).
>
> What is desired is a church that will possess indigenous forms for Christ, adapting them to Christian ends by fulfilling indigenous functions and conveying Christian meanings through them to the surrounding society (Missiology, January 1973:49).

There are certain Christian absolutes, stated in the Scriptures, by which Christians in all cultures should live and should be readily recognized by each other. The concept we intend accepts these absolutes. Two such positive elements are the sacraments of baptism and the celebration of the Lord's Supper, both being Scriptural practices and applicable in all cultures. Murder, stealing, adultery, lying, false witness, anger, malice etc. are all under Scriptural condemnation which applies in every culture. Likewise the fruit of the Spirit manifest in love, joy, peace, longsuffering, etc. is relevant to every culture and every language group.

What is the evangelist's relationship to the culture in which he is operating? Perhaps the best course of action is this: "Treat the culture in such a way that discipling results." The end purpose of evangelism is the making of disciples. If true disciples result, following the Lord in the light of His Word, then the relationship between Christ and culture will be a matter decided upon by the believers within the culture. If cultural difficulties inhibit the making of true disciples, then the evangelist has to determine the manner in which the harmonization can be worked out. This involves facing the "power encounter" in the "Power of the Spirit," and the question of dynamic equivalence.

THE RECEPTION OF THE MESSAGE

Another aspect of the communication process is the relationship between the communicator and the recipient. In all phases of life there are inter-relationships that condition communication. People look to people. Political relationships condition receptivity. Religious relationships condition people. Occupational relationships condition people. These may change at any moment. For example, Indonesia was prepared for a great turning to Christ by the political stand taken in recent years of reaction against communism. That condition prepared many people for response to Christianity. Communication channels were established whereby the recipients were conditioned to receptivity.

It is the nature of man to be influenced by many factors, both favorable and unfavorable. Homogeneous units of people react and inter-act according to their own patterns. As the influences which make up life patterns differ, so communication and response patterns differ. Therefore, effective communication which will elicit the desired response must be made in the manner that will communicate what the communicator wants it to communicate, and as a result produce what the communicator wants it to produce.

In this aspect the communicator, or evangelist, becomes an advocate. In order to introduce a new idea that will be acceptable, its expression must meet communication standards in agreement with patterns of receptivity. As people differ, these factors will differ. Thus the need for recognition of homogeneity and individual group response.

Luzbetak shows that "Cultural Anthropology analyzes and compares the way of life of . . . peoples; it interprets their ways in historical perspective; it establishes 'laws' of human behavior" (Luzbetak, 1970:26). He then relates his thought to the missionary by adding: "A failure to grasp the nature of culture would be a failure to grasp much of the nature of missionary work" (Luzbetak, 1970:59).

If the missionary is to understand his task, he must understand how his message relates to people. If he wants to relate to people, he must see people as they actually are, in cohesive units. He recognizes that units are as individualistic as individuals. He recognizes that *Indians* are not all alike. He recognizes that there is no such thing as a typical *African*. He recognizes that there is not even such a thing as a generalized *Eskimo*. He wants to discover very specifically who and where the individuals are that are related to one another as a people and how they relate.

The missionary is interested in the way of life, the total plan of living, the functional system of the group, its learning patterns, and its inter-relationships both internal and external. All of these characteristics differ to a greater or lesser degree between groups. This is what distinguishes groups and identifies each as a *homogeneous unit*.

In dealing with society in this manner, the missionary is dealing with an on-going entity. In fact, two on-going entities. He is dealing with an on-going church, and with an on-going society. He wants the church to continue within the society or unit as a growing entity. He is not interested only in the individual and his salvation, but is likewise concerned in seeing a church established that will continue within the society even after the individual is gone. Individual approach might be fruitful, and meaningful, to the individual; but if the church is to continue, it must penetrate into the unit. It must create a response that will become part of the pattern of life of the unit. Thus we see again the need for recognizing the importance of the homogeneous unit and its response to the message.

At the Chicago Consultation already mentioned, G. Linwood Barney of the Jaffrey School of Missions presented a paper entitled: "The Supracultural And The Cultural: Implications For Frontier Missions." He shows that:

Conversion among the Meo often comes about through a complex series of communicative events concluding in group decisions made by consensus. This can be very disturbing to a missionary who considers individual decision as the only authentic manner of conversion (Beaver, ed., 1973:54).

Barney uses this as an illustration of the importance of recognizing the cultural heritage and adaptation of the message to the individual homogeneous units. He further says:

> Even as Jesus seemed to touch the "key-issues" in the lives of those he encountered, . . . so different cultures may have particular emphases or concerns to which the message of the Gospel speaks most directly and for which Christ is most earnestly embraced as Savior and Liberator. The Meo are as conscious of Christ delivering them from oppressive spiritual powers as from their sins . . . .
>   Despite the movement toward "one world," the popular notion of the world as a "global village" is a gross oversimplification. The demise of overt colonialism and the birth of nationalism are overshadowed by increasing segmentation and tensions related to the self-consciousness of some 3,500 distinct ethnic groups (each with its own language) in the world (Beaver, ed., 1973:54).

Charles R. Taber specifically attacked the problem of evangelizing the unreached peoples when he presented his paper at the same Convocation. In dealing with the matter of the specific nature of evangelism, he wrote:

> Because societies, cultures, and individuals vary so much, the most effective evangelistic approach is the one which is most specifically geared to the particular situation of the hearer. The evangelist, before planning his approach, must discover what assumptions the hearer holds about reality, truth, and value; and more important, must be keenly aware of what problems deeply trouble the hearer, so that he can maximize the fit of the Gospel presentation to the hearer's needs. This is what Jacob A. Loewen has called "scratching where it itches" (Beaver, ed., 1973: 121).

In essence Taber's whole thesis deals with the very basic problems of evangelizing any people within its own cultural context.

THE CHANNEL OF COMMUNICATION OF THE MESSAGE

Channels and methods of communication are also very vital for effective communication. How many children are taught by the "verbal teaching" manner? Most tribes-people teach by the "example" method. A father takes his son out and shows him how to hunt. Or, more often, when he reaches the age of manhood he goes with the tribe and the group teaches him how. The same with planting. He is not given a lesson and then told to "go out and do it" by someone sitting in an arm chair. He goes with the family, clan, or group and learns by observation. How then can Christianity be communicated by someone "telling" all about it?

Well, it may be that the same group that goes out hunting by day might gather around a fire in a circle by night and relate stories of hunting escapades. Personal inter-action takes place and a communication circle is established. The story of "God's hunt for man" might be appropriate.

Here the role of the "story teller" might be very important. In Laos the medium for passing news is precisely by means of a roving news reporter; sort of a "town crier" but he goes from town to town passing the latest events. A natural channel is known within the culture. This is one medium of communication.

Most Americans would have said a few years ago that radio was the most effective medium of communication, and advocate great use of the radio for the proclamation of the gospel message. The reason given was its potential for causing the greatest number to hear. Radio is still a very popular channel for broadcasting the message. It is used as a "seed sowing" method, casting the seed into the wind. Surely some does, and will continue to fall on prepared soil. Yet it may be forgotten that simple hearing may not be the medium that causes people to respond favorably. Radio provides information at an impersonal level and thereby is effective only at that "awareness state." It advertizes, and is effective in making people aware of something. However as the anthropologist Everett M. Rogers states in his <u>Communication of Innovations: A Cross-Cultural Approach</u>:

> If A wishes simply to inform B about the innovation, *mass media channels* are often the most rapid and efficient, especially if the number of B's in the audience is large. On the other hand, if A's objective is to persuade B to form a favorable attitude toward the innovation, an *interpersonal channel* is more effective (Rogers, 1962:24)

Since television has become so popular most Americans would feel that its potential is greater than radio. It is true that television is somewhat more personal than radio, and thereby comes one step closer to the interpersonal level of communication.

When Christianity is evaluated by an individual or group, a "witness" must be received on a personal level before a favorable reaction and choice can occur in the observer. Rogers points out four stages to the innovation-decision process: Knowledge, Persuasion, Decision, Confirmation (1971:100ff).

At the *Knowledge level*, mass communication may be effective. At the *Persuasion level*, the inter-personal relationship comes in, and involves the individual and a "witness" or advocate. The *Decision level* is also personal, where the individual decides what he will do with the innovation; whether he will accept or reject. The *Confirmation level* is that level where others follow or reject his decision. If others follow, he has the confirmation that his decision was right. If he stands alone and others reject, then he is apt to question whether his decision was right. If he finds the confirmation he needs, then he is within a new body of fellowship. If not, he finds himself an "outcast." This is why fellowship within the same cultural group is so vital, for if one turns to another cultural group then he is apt to be ostracized by his own cultural element. If he is rejected by the different cultural group then he will probably turn from the religion which that group professes.

This is where the bringing of a new disciple into the fellowship of a church is so vital to the new convert. As he finds fellowship, he has his decision confirmed. Where he finds no fellowship, he is apt to return to his former patterns and then it will be almost impossible to expect him to change again.

On the other hand, as Tippett points out, there are four possible responses: Rejection, Total Acceptance, Acceptance with Modification, Fission (adaptation of part) (1969:102-104).

The evangelist must be prepared to recognize all of these responses, and with the Holy Spirit moving in His time, the evangelist can expect victory.

The acceptance or rejection of a "witness" or "advocate" is vital to the acceptance of the gospel message. If the "witness" does not approach people through recognized communication channels then the chances are that he will be rejected by the community.

It would seem to the writer that the incident of the Auca Indians' killing the first white men to approach them is an example of rejection of an advocate. When the missionaries decided to contact the Aucas, they did so from the air, making circles in a small plane over the area to attract attention and then dropping down gifts in a basket to the inhabitants of the forest. After several exchanges of gifts, for the Aucas responded by exchanges of gifts to the men in the airplane, the missionaries decided that it was time to make personal contact and flew in and landed on the river bank. Within hours they were all killed.

Later, when the wife of one of the missionaries made her entrance, it was through an entirely different communication channel. She made contact outside of the tribe with a member of the tribe. She became her friend, and began to learn some of the language of the people. Secondly, when she decided that the time had come to enter the tribe she went accompanied by her friend. She, as a woman, posed no threat to the tribe for her presence did not imply danger to the members of the tribe. Also, when she entered, she had a sponsor, a member of the tribe, to introduce her. She was not known as the wife of one of the men that had been killed, so there was no thought that she would be there for revenge. Her presence may have caused curiosity but posed no particular threat. Therefore she was accepted because her presence fit into a pattern that could be more easily understood. As time progressed, she became an acceptable "witness" to the message she carried, and there are believers among the Aucas (Wallis, 1960: The Dayuma Story).

Among the Aztec Indians of the *"Huasteca,"* in Mexico, the proper channel for innovation is through the *"Ancianos"* (Elders) of the village. They are the old men who defend the unity of the village and customs of the people. They are not readily open to change, for the preservation of the race depends upon the preservation of the customs and language. Thus any innovation is usually rejected. Communication that by-passes this channel is usually considered dangerous and thus any who follow a new way that is not accepted by the *Ancianos* are known as *"rebeldes"* or undesirables within the community. If the Gospel by-passes the communication channels, very few turn to Christ for it implies rejection by the unit of which they are a part.

Would not a study of the proper communication channels indicate that the approach should be made directly to the Elders of the village, and that men from another village who were Christians should make the approach? The testimony of the Elders from another respected village would give the inter-personal relationship at the acceptance level, and allow the channels of approval to assert their authority over village-related matters. Unknown outside "advocates" of novelty are generally not well received. There must be a recognized "witness" set before them to arouse confidence. The whole history of the Spanish conquest and the resulting depravation of the Indian speaks against acceptance of outsiders. A deep chasm has been carved. Who can bridge the gap?

It would seem that there are only two approaches:
1. A long term confidence-building period during which an advocate or "witness" would win confidence and a hearing.
2. Elders from another village that would be on the same communication level would make the approach.

The Pentecostal groups are moving within the second approach pattern and finding response previously unknown (Pentecost, 1972:208).

Another communication channel is the kinship channel. One of the churches the author was permitted to see established and grow in Mexico was that which began with one lady who at the time was a retired school teacher of 75 years of age. She was highly esteemed by her family and neighbors. She was personally converted and immediately wanted her family to know what she had received. She took the initiative to invite the author to her home to present the message to her family, where she was the "sponsor" for his presentation. She gave approval as a "witness" to the message, communicating clear approval to the other members of her family. Because of her acceptance, initiative, approval and communication function, the others of her immediate family almost immediately accepted the message. Then they invited other relatives and they responded. Soon the neighbors were brought in and they brought their families. In only a little over a year a congregation of believers with over 85 adults and 100 children was established. The same phenomena can be reported many times over. Where family ties are strong, the communication channels are strongly established.

Japan has a strong family-tie relationship. The father image is very strong. Communication flows naturally from the father to the children in a unilateral direction. When Christianity is offered to the children and bypasses the parental channel and approval, there is a very strong reaction. Parents are turned against the children, and consequently a tension in relationships follows. Communication channels have been defied. The fact that the young people may be apparently the most receptive does not change the communication conflict, and makes the winning of the family unit even more difficult.

It is often supposed that communication channels flow from the upper levels of society to lower levels. Thereby it is often thought that if the elite are won, the lower classes will follow. However, more often than not it is just the opposite. Communication channels often do not flow in that direction. Luzbetak writes:

> The official and wise teaching. . . is to appreciate the special power of communication potential in whatever segment of society it may be found. The fact is that often the elite does constitute the chief "powerhouse" of change and is the chief current of communication; where this is the case, there the policy of the Church is to make good use of its potential in carrying out her divine mission.
> After a careful analysis of the social structure of a people has been made, the missionaries should be able to recognize the corresponding centers of power and the direction and relative force of the various currents of communication. The greatest communication potential is not always from up to down, from the upper class to the lower, from the elite to the ordinary citizen. It is wrong to imagine that once the social and intellectual elite accepts an innovation the rest of society will <u>infallibly</u> follow. We have already seen how, for instance the Guatemalan indigena considers it a sin to imitate the ladinos (1963:299).

Where the elite have been the oppressors it is often the case that opposition to them has been so strongly established that reaction against the Gospel would set in if the elite were to introduce it. Thus the very fact that the elite had accepted Christianity might dictate a counter-action on the part of any subordinate social group. On the other hand, if the elite are a respected group within the total social structure, and their testimony were one of love and concern, then it could easily be that the communication would be clear and accepted.

Two communication possibilities exist, and in each case the actuality must be determined. (Graphic 11)

In the first case "A", there is penetration of communication from the higher to the lower. In the second "B", there is rejection. The first case may be illustrated by considering the elite of Kenya. There is communication from the elite to the lower levels. The lower levels perceive the elite as leaders of a new nation, and are willing to follow in most cases.

The second case is illustrated in Brazil, where the elite have for years been keeping the lower class as peons. Today the economic difference is even greater than a few years ago To such treatment the lower economic class rebel. It is difficult to see the communication of the Gospel flowing from

Effective Communication for Evangelism 75

the elite to the economically depraved. Rather, the communication is on the level of equal to equal, with very little penetration from the upper level to the lower. This is indicated in diagram "C".

COMMUNICATION BARRIERS

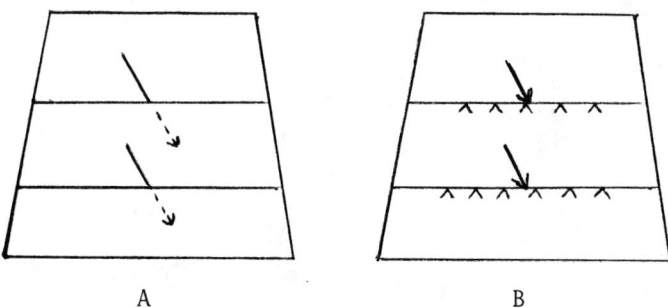

A   B

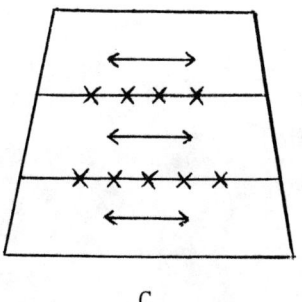

C

(Graphic 11)

Part Three **The Evidence of Responsiveness**

Chapter 6

Use of Indicators to Determine Readiness to Respond

The use of "indicators" to determine a people's readiness to accept Christianity is a relatively new consideration. The concept of indicators for use in the study of social sciences has been developing and has been used to provide information on national economies and such social problems as population trends, government activities, mass transit systems, etc. City planners look at "indicators" with deep interest and lay plans according to the conclusions indicated.

In the present context an indicator is a phenomenon that can be determined and measured and which demonstrates direction and degree of change of human communities, with respect to values and goals so as to enable us to evaluate and determine the outcome and impact of this change. The importance of discovering the indicators is the help they give us in the process of planning to meet those changes and to be prepared to act accordingly.

Bruce Russett, et al, published a book entitled: The World Handbook Of Social And Political Indicators in 1964. He contends that the use of indicators can provide valid information for the study of national economies and can be applied to different nations. The principle presented is: *the activity of a complex set of relationships can be generally determined by observing the activity of a few key variables.*

In 1968, the "Information Service" bulletin of the Department of Research of the National Council of the Churches of Christ in the United States of America, published an article

entitled: "Indicators for Planning in Bibliographical Perspective." The purpose of the article is to: "help Churchmen and others to discover the availability, quality, and usefulness of social and economic indicators for purposes of planning and related fields."
It states:

There has been a mushrooming interest in social and economic indicators by varied groups in the United States and Europe during the past few years. This interest has spread also to the field of religious indicators . . . . One reason for these developments has been the importance of indicators for both the planning process and for related speculation on the future states of a society leading up to the year 2000 (Sat., Oct. 5).

In the spring of 1973 a "Center For Coordination of Research on Social Indicators" was opened with its headquarters in Washington.

The Center's focus is on future research on social indicators. Its role will be to stimulate, facilitate, and guide research, by providing a locus and source of information on research under way, and by encouraging communication among researchers and between researchers and the broad constituency that has need for what they produce.
Published and unpublished documents describing past research and present projects, including materials on religious indicators, will be assembled and catalogued . . . (ADRIS NEWSLETTER, Spring 1973:29).

In adopting the concept of indicators to our study it will be helpful first to consider their validity, their limitations, and some examples of their usage.

VALIDITY OF INDICATORS

Students in the social sciences are attempting to look at social change to try to determine those factors by which any peoples' actions or movements can be predicted. Such students want to know how to plan for the future. They want to know how to be ready for mass migration, what causes mass migration, and how to put to use the results of their findings in order to predict what may happen in the future to know how to be prepared to meet that social change.
George Samuel, in his study of church growth in Bombay, entitled: Growth Potential of Urban Churches made a study

of sociological factors which influenced church growth. He observed

> . . . that churches in the city grow largely out of migrant Christians from different parts of India, and that there are 9 language groups among the 90 fully organized congregations which comprise 41,778 communicant members. The linguistic, denominational, ethnic and economic background influenced worshippers (Christians) to form or join congregations which suited their background (1973: iii).

Some of the important sociological factors with which Samuel dealt are indicated as he states:

> The social change stemming from urbanization is accelerated by the open-mindedness of the city dweller in responding to new ideas. The movement of people from rural to urban society results in far more than a geographical dislocation. It involves a change in the way of life and particularly a change of work, values, and relationships. Functional relationship in societies increases and, because of the necessity of accommodating people of different backgrounds, social tolerance also correspondingly increases. Exposure to the influence of the new techniques of mass communication, journals, magazines, movies and the like, is multiplied. As the exposure becomes longer, the older ties and influences becomes more and more remote. The city dwellers tend to retain the inner attitude of their upbringing. But their external life conforms to an entirely new pattern (1973:156).

As an individual concerned about social change, and peoples' movements, the evangelist is one who is definitely concerned about changes, direction and degree of changes, causes of changes, and the results that changes will produce on individuals. He is vitally concerned about the prospects of a movement among people that could predict a readiness to move God's way.

Is such a prediction possible? What would the results of such a foreknowledge be?

To begin with, foreknowledge of peoples' movements would give the evangelist and missionary societies direction by which they would know where to move and where to send missionaries, what approaches to take, and what kind of missionaries would be the most effective. The wrong approach could easily turn off a potential people movement to Christ. Likewise a proper approach to a people ready to respond to the presentation of the Gospel could mean a rich harvest for the glory of the Lord. If the missionary's desire and purpose is to see disciples made who would follow Jesus Christ, an indicator of readiness to respond to the gospel message would certainly encourage him to move into the field that is prepared.

The use of indicators would also allow missionaries and evangelists to know just what part their ministry should play. Some would know that their ministry was as sowers of the seed. Others would know that their ministry was that of plowing and preparing the field. Others would know that their ministry would be a teaching ministry.

The use of indicators would also lead to the discovery of the movement of the Holy Spirit of God over a people, preparing that people for a movement of God. Consider the people of Israel in Egypt: When God was ready to move His people out of Egypt He raised up a national leader. That leader had to prove himself to the nation Israel, which is recounted in the first chapters of Exodus. The record shows how a spirit of unrest and tension grew between the slaves and the slave masters. An explosion of the slave population also added pressure. This spirit of tension and unrest is an indicator of dissatisfaction on the one hand, and fear on the other. Pharaoh felt fear at Israel's request to go out to the desert because he recognized the seriousness of the situation and the implications for Egypt (Ch. 5).

The officers of Israel felt the unrest, but were unprepared to offer a decision. As a nation, Israel needed a strong leader. The leader would have to emerge from among the people and be strong enough to control the movement. One factor that was present was anguish of spirit over cruel bondage (Ch. 6).

The plagues added strength to the position of the leader, and confidence on the part of Israel toward Moses, unifying the nation. When Moses reached his necessary stature as a leader, the time had come for a people movement; the slaves of Egypt were now to exert their strength and move out (Ch. 11,12).

God was at work, and displaying His power and there were indicators of the direction and magnitude of God's working. Perhaps these signs were not understandable to the Israelites at the time, but looking back we can see the signs and so now when the same signs begin to appear we can anticipate new movements. History can be put to work for our advantage if we learn to read the signs of history. God's plan was to lead His people out of slavery to freedom. He planned a change for them. He led them out to freedom.

There are times in the history of nations, and peoples,

when God moves through His Spirit to prepare people to respond to His call. It is these signs of God's working that the evangelist desires to perceive. He wants to know where to move. He wants to be able to read the indicators of a people ready to respond to the message he has to offer. A missionary can move wisely and meaningfully if he can interpret indicators that will help him know which people are ready to respond. It would be a sad mistake for a missionary to go to the people at his left if they were not yet prepared by the Spirit of God to receive the message that he had, and let the people at his right go unreached who might be the ones ready to respond to his message.

To understand the indicators of a people-readiness would be to understand the movement of the Holy Spirit of God; to know where He is preparing a people to respond to His call.

Luke 10 records the account of our Lord's sending out His disciples "into every city and place, where he himself would come." The Lord planned to move into certain selected areas. He sent His messengers to go before Him because He had determined to go to those villages. In the same way the purpose of the missionary is to determine the mind of the Lord to know where He would enter, in order to go and to prepare the way for Him.

LIMITATIONS IN THE USE OF INDICATORS

It is to be understood that the study of indicators will be complex and that there must be very definite limitations placed upon them. One limitation of indicators is the fact that conditions change. It may be that by the time indicators can be interpreted, the conditions will have changed and therefore the indicators are no longer valid. In order to be meaningful any indicator must be relevant at the time it is being read. The study of conditions in history may give insight into the use and application of indicators at the time that such indicators are valid. The length of time that an indicator may be valid will vary according to different phenomenon.

A second limitation is the fact that there may be signs which would appear to be indicators but which might be false. Any given indicator may only be proven true by submitting it to the test. It could also be that an indicator is misread, or it could be that other factors counterbalanced the sign of a given indicator. No one indicator could be considered valid by itself.

Also, the validity of indicators must be considered in the light of the reliability of the indicator. It must meet certain criteria, such as: What is this an indicator of? Is it quantifiable? Is it readily related to the system to which it is being applied? Is data available that will test the indicator? Is the same indicator readable or understandable to others?

Albert D. Biderman ennumerates certain limitations of indicators as follows: (1) invalidity; (2) inaccuracy; (3) conflicting indicators; (4) lack of data; (5) incompatible models; (6) value concensus (<u>Information Service</u>, Sat. Oct. 5, 1968).

Indicators will ultimately be broken down into two classifications: (1) "hard data" which consists of hard statistics on past, present and future, and (2) "soft" or non-quantitative data.

Accumulation of "hard data" may be relatively easy. The problem will be with the interpretation of such data and the validity of the indicator. Conflicting data will have to be evaluated. Compatability of data to the model may be questionable. Judgment decisions may be influenced by desire rather than fact. All of these areas provide for questionable results.

Non-quantitative data may be even more prone to subjective interpretation. The fact that it is of such a nature that it cannot be statistically evaluated means that it will be more suspect and thus doubted. However, recognizing that indicators do have their limitations does not mean that the whole process should be discarded. To recognize limitations is to be prepared to evaluate and prove, and to operate accordingly.

The fact that the first airplane made by the Wright brothers did not fly very far does not prove that the laws of aerodynamics were false. The fact that it flew at all is the verifying fact that the laws of aerodynamics did work and were worth developing.

EXAMPLES OF THE USE OF INDICATORS

There are several examples of the use of indicators which deserve recognition. They may not have been designed for the purpose of discovering peoples that would be ready for acceptance of the gospel message, but serve as illustrations of the usage of indicators.

David Barrett in his book <u>Schism And Renewal In Africa</u> dealt with a problem. He looked at the multiplicity of independent movements in Africa and determined that there must be a recognizable cause for so many movements emerging:

The enquiry should determine what it was that the two

hundred and ninety tribes [of Africa] with independent church movements had in common, in order to arrive at some overall explanation of the whole vast complex (1968:4).

The author sees the independency and movements "as movements of renewal attempting to create a genuinely indigenous Christianity on African soil" (1968:7).

His studies of indigenous movements lead to the correlation of information in such a way as to determine significant factors in the formation and pattern of the movements. These factors then provide what we have called *indicators*, against which any known group can be measured to determine its readiness to follow an independent line of action. Thus the work of Barrett has laid a foundation for one pattern of indicator analysis:

By means of a representative sample of tribes and the use of standard statistical tests, we have arrived at eighteen basic factors correlated with the presence or absence of independency in all parts of the continent (Barrett, 1968:108).

His listing of the 18 factors is as follows:

A. IN TRADITIONAL CULTURE
 1. Is this a Bantu tribe?
 2. Is it over 115,000 in population
 3. Is ploygyny general or common, and not limited?
B. IN TRADITIONAL RELIGION
 4. Is the ancestor-cult important?
 5. Is there an earth goddess?
C. IN THE COLONIAL PERIOD
 6. Did colonial rule arrive more than 100 years ago?
 7. Have white settlers occupied tribal land?
 8. Is the national *per capita* income over 25 pounds (US$70) per year?
D. IN THE MISSIONARY PERIOD
 9. Did the missions arrive more than 60 years ago?
 10. Have scripture portions in the vernacular been published?
 11. Has the New Testament been published?
 12. Has the Bible been published?
 13. Was the New Testament published more than 60 years ago?
 14. Is Protestant missionary density in the nation more than 22 ordained missionaries per million

population?
- E. IN THE CURRENT PERIOD
  15. Are Muslims in the nation less than 50 per cent?
  16. Are Protestants in the tribe 20 per cent or over?
  17. Are Catholics in the tribe 20 per cent or over?
  18. Is there independency in any physical adjoining tribe?

Barrett gives the following conclusion:

> It could be termed an index of propensity to independency. It appears to be a measure of the socio-religious pressure to separatism in a tribe. It seems to be assessing the atmosphere in a tribe and its ripeness for schism. Composed as it is of social and religious factors, it will later be shown to be a measure of the *Zeitgeist*, [spirit of the times] by which we mean here the socio-religious climate of opinion favouring independency, protest or renewal in a given tribe at a given time (109,110).

We should call the attention of the reader to two matters: First, Barrett's system is worked out on the basis of obtainable "hard data." Definite answers can be given to the questions asked. Second, the pattern is a display of the fact that "yes" and "no" responses are relatively accurate indicators. Barrett's table of the Incidence of Independency should be carefully considered. It is reproduced on page 87.

TABLE IX

Tribal Zeitgeist and the Incidence of Independency
Using a Sample of 336 Tribal Units

	ZEITGEIST (Scale of Religious Tension)	Tribal units in Sample	INDEPENDENCY	
			Present	Absent
A. DORMANCY (low on scale)	0	0	0	0
	1	7	0	7
	2	15	0	15
	3	18	0	18
	4	23	0	23
	5	21	0	21
	sub-totals:	84	0	84
B. MARGINAL SEPARATISM (medium low)	6	46	11	35
	7	43	13	30
		89	24	65
C. PRESSURE (medium high)	8	40	15	25
	9	28	12	16
	10	19	11	8
	11	20	10	10
	12	24	18	6
		131	66	65
D. INEVITABLE INDEPENDENCY (high on scale)	13	14	14	0
	14	7	7	0
	15	6	6	0
	16	4	4	0
	17	1	1	0
	18	0	0	0
		32	32	0
TOTALS:		336	122	214

Notes:
1. The sample of 336 tribal units used here is an expanded version of the sample of 164 tribal units representative of sub-Saharan Africa (see Appendix E, paragraph 5) with the addition of a number of tribes for which information on the zeitgeist was available including those listed in Appendix B. It is not itself a properly representative sample.
2. For a diagrammatic presentation of these four levels of the zeitgeist see Figure VIII, p. 209.

Bertram M. Gross in his book <u>Social Systems Accounting</u> presented what he terms a *P O I S E* profile (p. 211). This is a system of a *high-low* indicator analysis which takes into consideration several pertinent variables as a sociologist sees them. He set up the pattern to determine the degree to which any group would act in a free style as over against restraint. His P O I S E profile is given below:

```
Political Democracy        (Free participation)         H
                                                         \
Organizational Democracy   (Self-rights)             H    L
                                                      \
Individual Democracy       (Juridical rights)        H    L
                                                      \
Social Democracy           (Race-religious freedom)  H    L
                                                      \
Economic Democracy         (Individual freedom)      H    L
                                                      \
                                                          L
```

(1966)

In his pattern Gross deals with a scale analysis in each case, to predict the probability of social action. He has ascertained certain factors which vary, and by placing those in measurable format, is able to differentiate between the two extremes quite readily. He then adds the total. If all add up low, the percentage of predictable response is high. If all add up to a high, then likewise the percentage of predictable response is high. Those that fall in the mid-range are less certain in their prediction.

Abler, Adams, Gould in <u>Spatial Organization</u> present a third pattern of social indicators, known as the "Venn diagram." It consists of separating any society into groups that are divided by responses to "yes-no" questions. When correctly questioned and then responses analyzed, surprising information becomes known.

Use of Indicators to Determine Readiness to Respond   89

The most spectacular application of this type of study was to the famous Watts riot in Los Angeles in 1965. A consideration of the study is valid.

Venn diagrams are a way of representing a division of a population in a concise and often highly useful way. Consider the census tracts of Los Angeles in terms of conditions thought to underlie the pathologies that contributed to the Watts riot of 1965. Five conditions or attributes define five sets: (1) median family income in the tract less than $5,000; (2) blacks were 75 percent or more of the population; (3) the tract contained the highest population densities in the city; (4) school drop-out rates were at a maximum; and (5) crime rates were the highest in the city. The five attributes define five sets which intersect one another. Where all five sets intersect we would expect living conditions to be the worst (Fig. 6-4). Turning to census tract data and other social area indices we discover that only in the Watts area of Los Angeles did all five conditions prevail at the same time (Fig. 6-5) (Abler, et al, 1973:153,154).

VENN DIAGRAM

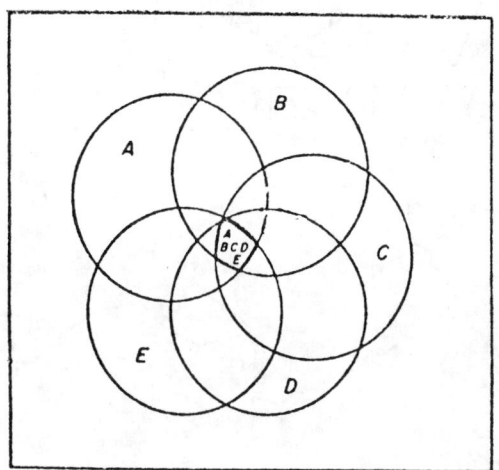

FIGURE 6-4
Five intersecting sets identify locations with maximum potential for violent civil disorder.

(Graphic 12)

WATTS RIOT

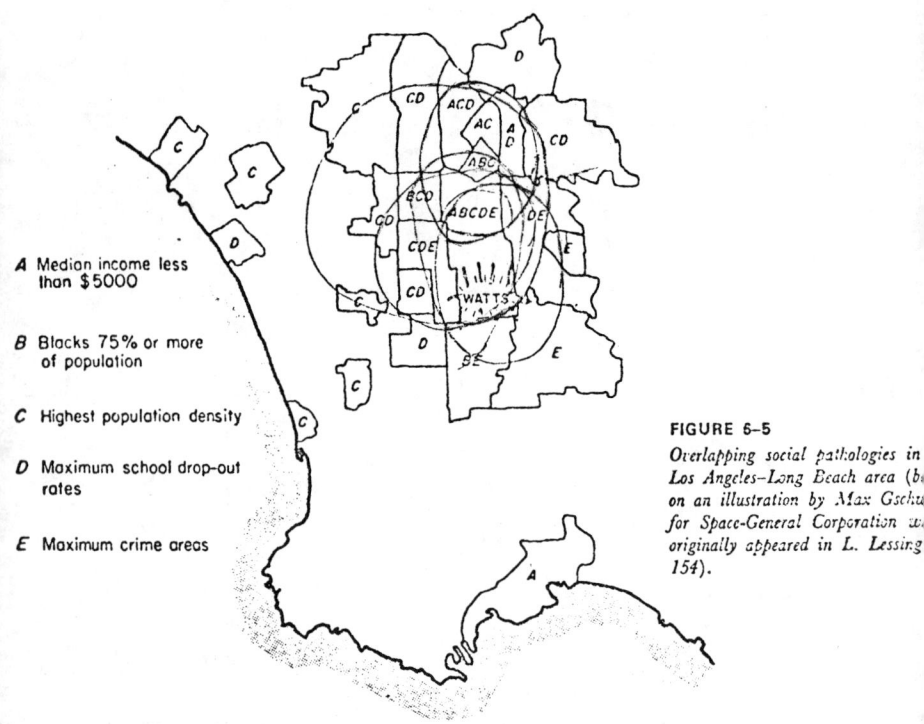

A Median income less than $5000

B Blacks 75% or more of population

C Highest population density

D Maximum school drop-out rates

E Maximum crime areas

FIGURE 6-5

Overlapping social pathologies in Los Angeles–Long Beach area (based on an illustration by Max Gschu... for Space-General Corporation ... originally appeared in L. Lessing 154).

(Abler et al, 1973:Chapt. 5)

(Graphic 13)

Chapter 7

Proposed Indicators

Now we turn to the question: Are there indicators that might be discovered in the discipline of missiology that would provide indications of a people-readiness for response to Christianity? It is without doubt that if readiness could be determined it would be wise for mission executives to have the right kind of missionaries at that point when the time was right.

DISSATISFACTION

A well-known anthropologist, Anthony Wallace, in <u>Revitalization Movements</u>, introduces the first aspect of our search for indicators as he presents his 5-step program of movement from steady-state to steady-state. He show that all cultures move from one period of relatively fixed state to another period of relatively fixed state, but that the new state is arrived at by passing through three levels of progress. The first is decline from the old, to a rapid recovery usually produced by some crisis, which gives rise to a new position. Then a more gradual rise to tapering off in the new steady-state.
That movement might be demonstrated as follows:

WALLACE DIAGRAM

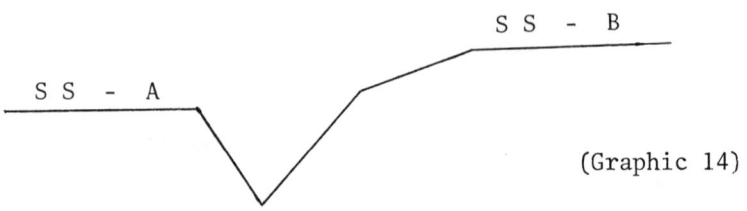

(Graphic 14)

Wallace indicates that just after finding a steady-state, it is most difficult to persuade any group to seek further change. However, within every society, there comes a time when dissatisfaction level increases, and change is indicated. If a slight change corrects the dissatisfaction, then cultural alterations are slight. But the more serious the cause of dissatisfaction, the more serious will be the change necessary. As dissatisfaction grows, change becomes more and more desirable, until finally existence without change is intolerable. Usually the dissatisfaction level is recognizable at a given point of time, demonstrated by a set of observable circumstances.

Dissatisfaction is the basic observable key. Dissatisfaction will produce a desire for change, ever increasing to the point of demanding change as it approaches intolerability. When this occurs the change adopted must be in agreement with the felt need.

The diagram shows the first decline as increasing dissatisfaction, which sooner or later demands a change which will give satisfaction and a new and supposedly higher level of steady-state, that will prevail until a new dissatisfaction arises. The dissatisfaction or unrest is usually related to some change in the value system. It may be produced by any of a number of factors such as economic, political, or physical unrest, and will produce dissatisfaction according to the degree of severity.

One of the first recognizable signs of unrest will be the reaction against the old value system, which has somehow ceased to serve its function. Where there is harmony with the existing value system and satisfaction derived from it, there is little felt need for change. Unrest is not present. To the degree to which the value system does not give satisfaction, there is disagreement with the existing system. Unrest becomes prevalent.

The missiologist is interested in these signs of unrest. They form the key to understanding a "people-readiness" for

Proposed Indicators 93

change, and the direction of change.

CULTURE CHANGE

Cultural manifestations are among the first signs of people readiness for change, since they are an indication of movement already in progrss. These manifestations may be seen within the institutional pattern, reflected by marriage, family, environment, etc., but all reflect change in the value system. These changes reflect displeasure with the existing institution. The youth of America have gone through a serious period of drastic change within the last few years. Dissatisfaction with the existing institutional system has been clearly manifest. Broken homes have betrayed a value-system where the home was previously idealized as the center of the American system. A government that could not keep us out of an undeclared and non-understood war gave reason to question the basic institution upon which the country was built. The value-system of the youth was shattered. Dissatisfaction arose and call for a new value-system became evident. The insitutional church was found to be lacking in supplying a value-system that satisfied. This is why so many young people turned to one of two answers: either to the "hippie" movement with an attitude of "return to nature," or to the "Jesus People." One was a reaction against the affluent society that provided all but happiness, and the other was a reaction against the formal church that provided all but love and satisfaction.

Within the existing social system, including family, marriage, religion, community, etc., certain patterns of relationships are discernible. When these patterns begin to change, the indication is that there is a change in the value system, and displeasure and dissatisfaction with the existing institution is in progress. As dissatisfaction rises, the demand for change rises correspondingly.

Not all people within a given culture feel the same lack or need. Often the elite who are recipients of those things which are considered to be "values" will be very satisfied with the existing insitution and patterns. They are in agreement with the value system, and they receive their satisfaction from the existing pattern. This would explain why so often the felt need for change comes from those who are at the "bottom" of the "value-system." They are the ones who first feel the dissatisfaction, and are thus ready for change. But until there is recognition of felt need there will not be readiness for change.

The recognition of felt need may be conscious or

unconscious. Often unrest will begin to move the subconscious of an individual, or a group. Until the discontent and unrest has reached a certain level, it may not be recognized. When unrest becomes felt, then the demand for change becomes urgent. Society may demand a functional substitute for that which is causing the unrest, as a political figure, or it may demand a complete change of the institution attributed to be the cause of the unrest.

The noted Anthropologist, Bronislaw Malinowski, points out in The Dynamics of Culture Change:

> One kind of institution can be replaced by another which fulfills a similar function. But such change is difficult, and it always has to move toward something which is better in the cultural sense, that is, better endowed, giving greater scope and opportunities to the people who live in that institution.
>
> A comprehensive institution endures because it is organically connected and satisfies an essential need of society (Malinowski, 1949:53).

This truth suggests to the missiologist the fact that change will be extremely difficult where the existing institutional pattern is intact and where those who are living within the institution are satisfied with the pattern.

There would seem to be no doubt but that peoples within the large historic religious blocks of the non-Christian world fall into this category. Apparently there is solidarity, and functional satisfaction derived from the various religious practices, or existing systems. Perhaps it is because man's conscience is quieted and he feels satisfied with the cultural pattern, which gives a derived sense of satisfaction and provides security for the individual and for the society.

In such a situation if one were to seek change and satisfaction through another religion, he would encounter the group dissatisfaction and be denounced by his own society. This would tempt one to return to the position of security found within the existing pattern. Thus a break with group practice would be a costly experience, and could only be done when the new satisfaction were recognized to be greater than the satisfaction of conformity. In such a case it would hardly be expected that there could be more than individual turning to Christ, and among those converts would be the dissatisfied persons, who would be recognized as outcasts from their own society.

Barnett points out that within any society there are three groups: the *indifferent*, the *disaffected* and the *dissenters*.

The *indifferent* will not cause any upheaval, for they are satisfied with their indifference. The *disaffected* will not cause any change, for they are not concerned because they feel no need for change. The third group, the *dissenters*, may be dissenters for any one or a combination of reasons. Christianity would not always be happy with having its name attached to the dissenters group. Consequently, a church formed of any of these three groups is destined to slow, almost "individual" growth.

Christopher Dawson, speaking of the Pueblo Indians in his book, Religion and Culture, states:

> Material and spiritual factors interpenetrate one another so completely that they form an inseparable unity, so that religion and life have become one. Every moment of life, every social occasion, every gesture and form of expression is consecrated by religious tradition and invested with religious significance . . . the whole society obeys the same laws, moves with the same rhythm, breathes the same spirit (Dawson, 1948:197).

Thus with the Pueblo Indians it would seem that as long as such a situation as that described continues, there will be very little expectation of change, and very little individual response. Only the dissenters would welcome change.

Turning to consider other society patterns, where the society structure may not be so tightly knit, imbalance within the society might be a growing factor that would indicate dissatisfaction of one or more segments, developing dissent. In other words, *imbalance* may cause *dissatisfaction*, and dissatisfaction cause *dissent*. All three may be viewed as indicators of readiness for change. But by their very nature, these may be indicators of a negative nature as well, and could be signs of danger.

When any group begins to look for a substitute, there is the indication that satisfaction with the existing pattern is not complete. At times the seeking may be on the part of the few, and at times the seeking may be on the part of the whole. If there is social detachment on the part of a segment of the society, the detached elements may respond to novelty. Segmented detachment may not indicate readiness for the whole ethnic group to accept the change. But it may be a strong indication that the particular group is ready.

We may conclude: *where stability and coherence of the heterogeneous elements are unmoved, there will be little receptivity to change.* When factors enter into a culture so as to change markedly the stability and coherence of the heterogeneous elements there will be more readiness for change. The more closely the instability approaches the religious core of the people, the more will the people be ready for religious change.

Barnett speaks of "satisfaction of wants" as he speaks of readiness for change:

> An individual will not accept a novelty unless in his opinion it satisfies a want better than some existing means at his disposal.
>
> A novelty has less appeal for those who are enjoying the benefits of its functional alternative than for those who are not (Barnett, 1953:328).

Christianity is the novelty that is offered to the unsatisfied want, to the dissatisfaction, to the imbalance, and to the dissent. But Christianity must be offered in a way that is *compatible* with both the felt need and the culture of the ethnic group to whom it is offered as an alternative. Barnett continues:

> Novelty acceptability is often discussed with reference to the concept of compatibility . . . . It is imperative to bear in mind that compatibility or its opposite entails a specific referent. An idea or a behavior, new or old, is adaptable or harmonious with something known, believed, or done by a potential acceptor, not with abstractions like statistical averages, censensuses, trends, common denominators, or cultural patterns. These abstractions summarize or describe compatibilities. They do not determine them . . . .
>
> Basically, compatibility from an acceptor's standpoint is a question of the possibility of a substitute in a particular situation. As far as intrinsic characteristics are concerned, this means that the acceptor admits an equation between something new and something old. Either he identifies the novelty with something familiar to him, so that it can be substituted in the context of the familiar entity; or he identifies the correlate of the novelty with something familiar, so that the latter is an appropriate substitute for the former; or he identifies both the novelty and its correlate with a familiar form and its correlate, so that there can be a double substitute. Unless one or another of these possibilities presents itself either spontaneously or through explanation and persuasion on the part of its advocate, the introduced idea must remain alien and unacceptable as far as the particular acceptor in question is concerned (Barnett, 1953:329).

Kinship Structures

Within the cultural framework is the kinship relationship. This touches a very emotional area with some peoples whose kinship relationships are very strong. For example, the extended family relationships of many peoples of Africa are very well defined and functional. When outside influences begin to encroach upon the privacy of the intimate family pattern a serious change is pending. An element causing movement and unrest in the U.S., and therefore presenting an unsteady state, is the educational pattern that is encroaching upon much of the extended family relationships. Individuality is replacing group solidarity. Young people leave the family and go to school. The kinship relationship is being destroyed. In this instance while one aspect of culture is rising, the other is on the decline. A society is being affected. Kinship structures are deteriorating. Old people are left without anyone to care for them, and the young children are deprived of their older brothers and sisters. In such a situation the society is forced to look for new value-systems to satisfy the changing demands. One option is Christianity. If it is seen as the enemy and destroyer of culture, it will be rejected. Such may be the concept of the elderly who see the decay of the old system. They may view Christianity as the cause of the decay. The young may see education as the bright horizon of the future. If it is related with Christianity in the minds of the young then they may be ready to embrace Christianity. This of course may be selective, and only that part which appeals may be accepted.

History has shown that where there has been evangelization that took the family and kinship pattern into consideration, peoples have responded to the Gospel. The Karen and Kachin movements in Burma are examples. The Batak movement of Sumatra is another. Whole family units responded as units. The Lutherans ministering in New Guinea followed patterns of approaching the whole unit, working with kinship units. Kinship ties were not broken, but respected. People movements in tribal response followed. Today as much as 80 percent of many of the formerly animistic tribes of Papua New Guinea are professing Christians.

Perhaps part of the reason there are so few Christians among the Aztec Indians of Mexico is the fact that the very self-preservation of the tribe depends on the strength of the kinship relationships so it unitedly rejects anything that might challenge its very existence. Here is a group that is not ready for social change. It is an indicator of very negative level.

One difference between the peoples response of Paupa New Guinea and the Aztecs of Mexico is the fact that the approach of Christianity in the first case took into account the preservation of the kinship structure and built on it, while in the second case Christianity was viewed as an enemy that would destroy culture and kinship ties. The real difference was in the view the two groups had.

Communication Channels

Social indicators cannot be considered without giving due attention to the established lines of communication. This has already been done earlier, but the reader is reminded of this fact in his contemplation of the potential indicators of people-readiness for change, and possibly turning to Christianity.

Readiness for change is enhanced by a novelty offer coming from those who are most highly esteemed and recognized within the culture pattern. Where kinship ties are strong, kinship communication is effective. Christianity, as any other religion, spreads most easily along lines of kinship and other established intimate relationships. These lines of communication "prevent system disintegration, and influence group performance" (Gross, 1966:183).

POLITICAL CHANGE

It has long been recognized that political tensions indicate people readiness for change. Barrett says: "(Political) movements . . . arise primarily from the need for a political outlet of some sort" (1968:93). Frontier situations often present points of tension, where political ties (or tribal ties) are being broken, but new relationships are not yet established.

Barrett says of the Tiv people of Nigeria: "Islam has made scarcely any converts and has been opposed for political reasons." But people are accepting Christianity, and by 1967 the "Protestants had grown to twenty per cent of the entire tribe" (1968:248).

Perhaps the most significant illustration of political influence causing change is the response to Christianity in recent years in Indonesia. The analysis of that situation is complex and beyond the scope of this study.

Russett points out the fact that political instability is closely related with economic development and social inequality. If Christianity is presented as the answer to the felt needs of economic, social and political unrest and dissatisfaction, then it may receive a hearing at that level.

It is clear that many aspects of economic development - growth of income, literacy, education, health facilities, urbanization, industrialization - bear some fairly close relationship to political development . . . . when other influences such as per capita G.N.P. and the percentage of the labor force engaged in agriculture are taken into account (Russett, 1967:9).

Political indicators then cannot be considered as standing alone. They rest upon many variables themselves, and their inter-relationship with other factors cannot be overlooked. Probably discontent in political matters is itself caused by failfure to satisfy the felt needs of those under its control, and inability to meet the felt needs turns the group under its administration to turn against the system, or institution.

The many political changes of such countries as Zaire affect response to Christianity with tremendous implications. Favorable response is seen in Papua New Guinea. In December 1973 the new independent nation came into being, with a politically favorable encouragement to Christianity. (See Profile, Section II). The felt need of the people seems to be satisfied, and there has been very little even reported in the communication media of radio and newspaper because the transaction has gone so smoothly. There is nothing of note to report.

National political unity may be significant, but it is suggested that for the missiologist, the recognition of the local political scene is equally important. By this is meant the pattern of government of the local area, whether geographic or tribal, multi-tribal or mono-tribal, with external influences or internal factors. For example, in the country of Mexico among many of the rural peoples there exists a very strong political and governmental force. It is adapted to the Mexican form of government in a recognized way, in that the town authorities are legally under the governmental district officers. However, in practice, the local town people name their own representatives, and those names are submitted to the government. The government finds it very convenient to "appoint" to office those whom the townpeople have themselves chosen in their own way. If the government were to send any other representative into the town to govern the town he would be removed from the town very quickly. Both the local way of choosing the officials and the officials chosen are very much "indigenous" (Pentecost, 1972:36).

ECONOMIC CHANGE

Many peoples are caught up in changing economic conditions over which they have no control. These economic changes however exert their influence over the unit. At the present time the few remaining untouched tribal peoples are largely caught in this struggle. For example, the Indians of the forest regions of Paraguay are being forced to change their pattern of life to an agricultural form from a hunting form simply because the economy of the country is demanding that the forest be used for raw material for the rest of the population's needs (Unreached Peoples Survey Questionnaire). By virtue of their forced change, a whole new life style is imminent. In this change of economy a sense of uncertainty and unrest is forced upon the people. Some will adapt; others will probably rebel; but all will be influenced. Which of the two attitudes would present the most receptive environment? Undoubtedly the group that rejects the encroaching cultural end economic pattern will be the group of greater resistance to the Gospel. Probably the group that is open to the new life pattern will be the more likely to listen to the Gospel.

The Indian population of the Amazon basin is about to be introduced to a traumatic experience in the next five to ten years as the new roadway is cut through the jungles. Economic changes will be forced upon the people. What will the result be? The only prediction that can be made with certainty is that it will result in change (Read, <u>Brazil 1980</u>).

There may or may not be a likeness in Argentina. When the interior of Argentina was opened up by the railroad bed being laid into the interior, many people were brought to salvation through the witness of the English Christian engineers in the survey teams. The Plymouth Brethren found responsiveness in many centers and planted many assemblies as they moved with the teams. However the remoteness and history of the tribes of the Amazon is very different from the Argentinian frontiers of the 1880's.

Other areas of economic change are those related with rural to urban migration and agricultural to industrial occupations. Economic adjustments are either the cause of or related to such changes. In either case, the relationship exists.

When fluctuating uncertainty in economic insecurity is prevalent, people begin to feel frustration and despair. Desire and hope when unfulfilled, are often accompanied by an opposite and contrasting fear and frustration, and people find themselves in a fluctuating uncertainty. This may be the opportune moment when people are ready for that which will give satisfaction to their souls.

Russett points out that a study made of 84 countries revealed the fact that "the highest levels of instability are associated with <u>middle</u> levels of economic development" (Russett, 1967:9). This is probably due to the fact that the lower level income group is the most indifferent; the higher level income bracket is less likely to profit from change. However, when the lower level becomes awakened to the new potential of a better income and economic standard, there may be great mass and political force set loose, demanding change.

In considering the movement of the Pentecostal forces in Chile, Peru, and Brazil, it is noted that the greatest movement is among the lower class, and the movement is accompanied by many economic changes in living style.

Norbert Johnson, a missionary to Chile, writes:

It cannot be forgotten that Pentecostalism [in Chile] has grown during an era of great social upheaval. Masses of people . . . unable to make a living in the country, started crowding into the city slums. Uprooted, leaderless, frightened. These people found within Pentecostalism an opportunity to express themselves and release intolerable tension (1970:39).

In referring to the Pentecostal movement in Chile, Wagner says:

Sociologists such as Emilio Willems and Christian Lalive who have studied Pentecostalism from their professional perspective, invariably comment on the proletarian nature of the Pentecostal churches. Without using the term, such writers provide accurate pointers toward identifying Latin America's fertile soils. In particular, peoples found in the areas of new urbanization and industrialization are receptive to the gospel. In the rural areas Willems found some receptive and some resistant . . . . But those who had been uprooted and relocated in new agricultural areas were found to be highly receptive (Wagner, 1973:68).

Unemployment is a factor related to economic and social stability. For the sociologist this is a vital factor in indexing social stability.

Unemployment percentages are of great interest to the economist as indices of activity. A high unemployment rate clearly indicates important unused resources and an economy operating at a lower level of production than that of which it is capable. Unemployment rates are of obvious relevance to theories of social stability. High unemployment may have magnified effects on certain subgroups within a population (e.g., Negroes in the United States). High unemployment may make it virtually impossible successfully to integrate such subgroups more fully into the society. Even moderate-appearing overall unemployment rates may, in underdeveloped countries, conceal a high rate of urban unemployment, and consequent social tension (Russett, 1967:188).

Taking this seriously, the missiologist would be concerned about subgroups, or ethnic groups, that would fall into the category of high rate of unemployment. The proportional unrest felt by the group would be directly proportional to the unemployment factor.

No doubt each culture would have its own definition of what constituted "unemployment" which would have to be ascertained. But the factor is one which seems to be a universal factor.

MIGRATION

Unemployment, industrialization, educational patterns, political maneuvers, all affect migratory patterns just as much as natural disasters, etc. Europe is one whirlpool of migratory groups seeking employment in different areas. All modern industrial centers have their "barrios" or "satelite" centers of immigrant peoples either working or seeking employment in the new industries. Some are moving away from the old out of felt need. Others may be attracted to the new as a star on the horizon. Some will find satisfaction. Others will find only frustration. (See Status of Christianity Profiles - Portugal, France, Section II).

Among immigrant peoples there is unrest. People are seeking. Hopes are aroused and dashed. Yet few will return to their place of origin. May it be that the unrest and delusion will have prepared these peoples to be open to the Spirit of God?

Much of the turning to Christianity in Mexico is among the migrant peoples who are moving to the cities, leaving the rural farms. They are dissatisfied with the old, and seek satisfaction in something new.

Proposed Indicators   103

The question can be asked, do migratory peoples display a readiness to accept Christianity? Barnett says:

> Land alienation and its equivalent, migration, forces some cultural readjustments if the disposed group is to survive. Migrants and dispossessed populations are characteristically receptive to new ideas, whether those ideas are developed by their own members or suggested by outsiders (Barnett, 1953:87).

This aspect of the importance of migration groups and patterns is a necessary consideration for every missiologist. Numerous examples come to the attention of the student of missions when considering people-readiness for change and people-readiness to accept Christianity. Read has written:

> The Gospel has great capability of reaching people who are in the midst of transition, people who are encountering new experiences, leaving behind old ways and finding new needs. When homes are uprooted and people migrate to new areas, they leave behind them many of their traditions (Read, 1973:27).

Migrant peoples often display unrest, dissatisfaction, and felt need. The reason for the migration of course is a major factor in determining the degree of pleasure or unrest. It may be only segments of society that are migrating, or it may be a complete unit of society. The Meo people that migrated into Northern Laos were a segment of society that left their homeland. They have responded to Christianity more than all of the rest of the population of Laos

The following graphic of Laos displays this pattern (Graphic 15).

Many factors produce migrations, but regardless of the causes, the very fact of the migration brings new cultural conflicts, new needs, new desires, and upsets the old established patterns. Wars cause rapid migration with many refugees. Famines cause migrations. Plagues cause migrations. Discovery of gold causes migrations. But the one thing in common is the fact of change, which in turn produces both readiness and desirability for immediate change. Change produces change.

It is therefore undisputed that every refugee area is a center of a people in process of change, where Christianity has its opportunity of being the newly adopted religion and pattern of the new culture.

The question can be asked very sincerely: Do migratory peoples display a readiness to accept Christianity? History

LAOS

ESTIMATED CHRISTIAN POPULATION BY ETHNIC GROUPS

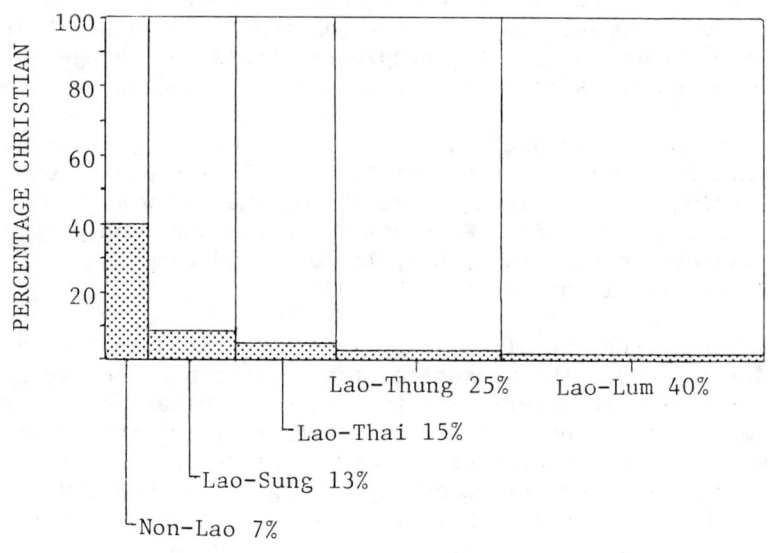

(NOTE: These figures are representative approximations. They should be seen as indications of magnitude, not precise.)

(Graphic 15)

seems to indicate that people who migrate out of attraction to the new are quite open to accept the patterns of the new that appeal, and retain the old that was satisfying. People who are forced to move adopt new forms less readily.

If people migrate in groups they are more apt to retain their own self-identity, characteristics and religion. Reports from Australia and New Zealand show that the peoples who migrated to those countries have adopted some of the economic patterns, but have tenaciously held to their own religions and very few have turned to a different form of religion. (See Status of Christianity Profiles, Section II). Very few individuals have united with the Christian churches of those countries, while most prefer to hold to their old form of worship in their own language. It may be that the group-solidarity feeling is fostered in the worship practices of each, and satisfaction is derived from it. We cannot forget that every Christian home would try to instruct its children that wherever they might move to live, they should in no way forget the religion they were taught. Religion is a very deep emotional factor in the life of every individual, the very cement that holds a society together. Therefore it cannot be forgotten that even in migration, peoples are often reluctant to turn from their old religion and adopt a new one. We would conclude that migration patterns display change, but not necessarily openness to religious change. The student should not be misled into thinking that receiving Christianity is easy for a migrant people.

However history tells of many peoples who in the course of their migrations came into contact with Christianity and were won by it. That is, they were ready for a change of religion, realizing that the old did not satisfy, and found in Christianity that which satisfied. There have been great movements of response to Christianity in cases like these. Such was the case of the Lisu people who migrated out of China into Burma.

LINGUISTIC CHANGE

Another factor to which attention can be given is the linguistic factor. Little linguistic change may be an indicator of homogeneous unity, and thereby an indicator of group solidarity. In such a case, one may be prepared to find that group action is an important element of the culture. If this is so, group action of turning to Christ is a potential, based upon the group solidarity element. In such a case the missiologist would do well to consider carefully the patterns by which that society changes, and discover which persons within the group would be the best innovator to introduce change.

On the other hand, significant change of linguistic patterns, and especially the readiness to adopt new forms of speech, may be indicators of both contact with sources introducing the changes, and esteem for those groups whose language is being adopted.

Linguistic changes within a segment of the society may be indicative of segmentation of society, and perhaps be an indicator of people readiness for change on the part of one or the other element of that society. Most probably the segment open to adoption of the new language is the segment which would be more ready to receive the Gospel. The one retaining the old language patterns is probably in the midst of tightening its institutional control and proclaiming its tradition, as a response of fear and reaction against a certain amount of change being felt.

Many groups such as Wycliffe Bible Translators, Unevangelized Fields Mission, New Tribes Mission, have long been concerned with linguistic analysis. They recognize the power of the linguistic influence within a given culture.

One of the most significant linguistic changes is that related to the reduction of a language to writing and the publication of Scriptures in the language. All languages are in a state of flux but there is no particular significance in the normal change, except to note the place from which the linguistic influence comes. However when drastic changes are brought about by the reduction of a language to writing and the subsequent appearance of the Scripture in that language, then response to Scripture can occur. The Bible Societies and the Wycliffe Bible Translators have on record dramatic changes which occurred among many linguistic groups after the New Testament was introduced.

It is hard for members of a group to accept something that has not been adequately communicated to them. The written Word gives a substance and permanence to the message. It is indisputable that the Holy Spirit uses the Word of God to prepare peoples to receive the gospel message.

The enormous power of literature to generate religious movements has long been known (Barrett, 1968:134).

RELIGIOUS CHANGE

When people are ready for religious change there are often clear signs. Attendance at religious functions drops. Participation becomes formalistic or non-existent. Disaffection becomes apparent, or a spirit of indifference and lethargy appears.

Self-satisfaction and occupation with pleasure may mean also that religion is losing its significance. This is not to be confused with a state of dissatisfaction with the old. Many people in the United States find themselves quite satisfied with religion that allows them to spend Sunday playing golf, boating, or at the football stadium. They would never say they are ready for religious change. In contrast, many of the youth of the United States recently have demonstrated readiness for religious change. They stopped attending services that were "institutionalized" and "formalized." When a new "Jesus People" option was offered that allowed freedom and gave satisfaction, many young people turned to that. The present charismatic movement is seen by many to be a reaction against formalism and ritualism in institutionalized religion.

Donald Fabun, a "Futurist" sociologist in The Dynamics of Change gives reason for the tightening grip of an old religion when change begins to become evident when he says: "To protect themselves against further change, institutions harden their resistance by formalizing rituals, customs and 'traditions'" (Fabun, 1968:9).

We may conceptualize these examples of dissatisfaction with old religious patterns by stating that restlessness appears before a new satisfaction is sought. The missiologist must look for those signs of restlessness and dissatisfaction with the existing religious status quo, and measure the intensity of those signals.

PROTOTYPE

Barnett has maintained that:

The fundamental processes of identification and substitution are dependent upon the existence of a prototype configuration which reacts with a stimulus configuration to form a new idea (1953:242).

His concept of a "prototype" is "a standard of reference" (1953:243), an image, or model that is present in the mind of a potential receptor. To accept Christianity means to accept a form that is conceived in the mind. There must be an image in the mind of the receptor before he can accept it, and that image must be not only recognizable, but also attractive. "[A Prototype] is dependent upon a complex of conditions involving the attitude of the individual, his purposes, his retention of past experiences, and the frame of reference upon which he draws at the moment" (Barnett, 1953: 207). The prototype must hold new ideas which are desirable, corresponding to a felt need. It is therefore in order to ask: What image does the ethnic group or the individual have of Christianity? What is the prototype that he knows or idealizes?

Readiness for change and readiness to accept Christianity are correlated with the image of the prototype recognized as offering the desired novelty, and seen as the answer to the existing tension or dissatisfaction as the desirable change in the existing value system or institution.

Prototypes may not be accepted in their entirety. As previously expressed, people may accept the whole, or part, or accommodate a part. People may look at the prototype and select the desirable and discard the undesirable. Barnett calls this process "selective imitation:"

> History reveals that the members of one ethnic or subethnic group frequently become paragons for another. Almost always a certain amount of eclecticism standardizes the imitative pattern that results. Thus, for many years, and to some extent even at the present time, Americans admired and copied French fashions and French artists; but scientists, especially the applied scientists, looked to the Germans for leadership in chemistry and physics . . . . During one period of their history the Japanese imitated the humanistic accomplishments of the Chinese; at a later time they turned to copy the industrialism of the United States (1953:51).

It is worthy of note that no people will be ready to accept the religion of another whose culture they do not esteem highly. If culture and religion are vitally united, as they are, then the reception of one usually indicates reception of the other. Thus, while Western culture was viewed as being superior to many others, it was natural that missionaries from the Western culture block should receive good acceptance. But when the culture image lessened, the desirability of Western missionaries lessened. As a result, a sign of readiness for reception of Christianity is the indication that any given people is beginning to adopt the culture of a people that could be representative of Christianity. And yet, we cannot be so naive as to think that many peoples want everything that pertains to another culture without selection. Nor do peoples necessarily want "Christianity" without being selective concerning the elements they would adopt.

Nevil P. Andersen, Principal of the Melbourne Bible

Institute of Australia, writes:

> In discussing the matter of the large numbers of tribal people who have become Christian, motive and cause have been very much to the fore in such discussion. Verrier Elwyn puts the emphasis on the motive of the social progress among the tribals "Christianity has made an appeal to the tribals, of Assam, because it has been associated in their minds with the idea of progress. Christianity in the past has meant hospitals, education in the English language, a larger, richer material life, a Gospel of universal brotherhood. Its flexibility with regard to food rules has more than compensated for its rigidity about such matters as rice beer and polygamy" . . .
>
> The spiritual freedom, giving relief from a bondage that was very real and evil, was deeply appreciated. A whole new world of faith and courage opened up - Christ, the Bible and their Church became a living force. External pressures from other cultures, Government, education and commerce were helping bring about a disintegration of tribal culture. Christianity brought a new code and helped evolve a new culture. In many cases it meant having standards by which to know what could be retained from the old and how to mold on the new ways so that a stable culture could be developed (Personal communication, March 1974).

DEGREE OF CHRISTIAN INFLUENCE

People move toward that which in their concept offers the greatest degree of satisfaction, and thus are ready to try a system that fills most completely their image of a desirable prototype. Alternatives will be considered when there is choice and the one that most exactly fulfills the ideal situation they have in mind is the one that will be chosen.

Here is where the Holy Spirit is seen, molding together the change factors and the witness factors in His omniscience, to bring about the desired results of a people turning to Christ. The work and the results are not of the missionary, but of God.

One of the vital factors in determining the direction of choice is the degree of influence of each alternative. This influence may include time of exposure as well as the nature of the attraction. If Christianity is going to attract peoples, it must be through an influence which presents desirability, and it must be presented over a period of time sufficient to make its influence felt.

In North Africa the influence of Christianity is known and has caused antagonism. Christianity and Islam always causes antagonism, as Isaac and Ishmael. Each has its creed, and each has its scriptures. Each has its life-pattern. Christianity presents a life-pattern that is free and apparently very unrestricted. Islam has a total life-pattern that is governed. Christians are accused of not praying, because their pattern and time of prayer are not controlled, and probably Christians do not pray as frequently as Moslems. As a result, each judges the other, and a spirit of antagonism results. This is why it is so difficult for missionaries working in Moslem countries. The two religions are not unknown to each other; they have faced each other for 1,500 years. Somehow, Christianity has not presented a desirable image.

In contrast, in Central Africa, where the traditional tribal religions have been followed by the great majority of the peoples, there has been a much different response to Christianity. It was not so at the beginning. However as missionaries persisted, demonstrating Christian love in the face of bitter opposition, the witness and influence of Christianity penetrated more and more, and peoples responded to that influence, finding the image desirable. Today, many peoples in Central and Southern Africa have accepted the gospel message. Many homogeneous units have turned to Christ, and in many groups more than 50 percent of the people are professing Christians. (See Status of Christianity Profiles, Section II).

In many countries today the growth rate of the Christian church is greater than the growth rate of the total population. Christianity is becoming more and more acceptable, and its degree of influence is on the rise. However, a word of warning must be interjected at this point. Distinction must be made between the form and the message. To accept a form of Christianity is not necessarily congruent with accepting the message of Christianity. It is all too true that it is possible for a people to accept the form of religion, because the image of the religion is related to cultural image that is highly esteemed. The evangelist must be aware of the dangers of the dilema into which he is placed.

The church must have its influence, and increase that influence. Such is the purpose of a clear "witness," that people will see and believe. Yet on the other hand the witness must be to the gospel message and to the results of that message. The evangelist does not desire people to respond to his culture image, he wants people to respond to the Gospel. Recognizing the need for witness, and the need to extend its influence, how can the Church consider any retrenchment? God's orders are marching orders: "Go, and make disciples."

Chapter 8

Pragmatics

Now we turn to the pragmatics of the thesis presented. Having established certain factors as possible indicators of people-readiness for change, and recognizing these indicators as being possible indicators of people-readiness to accept Christ and His way if properly presented to them, we present the following as a list of possible indicators:

1. Culture change
2. Political change
3. Economic change
4. Religious change
5. Status of Scripture translation
6. Migratory patterns
7. Prototype image
8. Degree of influence of Christianity

HIGH-LOW SCALE PATTERN

Once the indicators are decided upon, they are to be arranged in order. A "high" / "low" scale is determined for judgment of each factor. Then each factor is considered in order and a point determined, as nearly as possible, giving a placement on the "high" / "low" scale for evaluation.

	Cult. Chng.	Polit. Chng.	Econ. Chng.	Relig. Chng.	Status Script.	Migra. Chng.	Proto. Image	Degree Infl.	Change Index
High									
Low									

If the culture is changing rapidly, the culture change column is marked with an "x" at the "high" side. If there is no change evident, it is marked at the "low" side. If political change is evident, an "x" is placed at the respective position. The same procedure is followed for each factor. When the details are determined and marked, an "index" of change becomes evident. If the indicated positions reveal a majority of "high" coordinates, then the observer can expect to see change, and prepare accordingly.

Looking at the University students of Mexico, (among whom the author worked) we find something like the following:

	Cult. Chng.	Polit. Chng.	Econ. Chng.	Relig. Chng.	Status Script.	Migra. Chng.	Proto. Image	Degree Infl.	Change Index
High							x		
		x	x		x				x
	x					x		x	
Low			x						

The change index is approximately in the low middle range.

The same procedure can be carried through with the designation of a value for each position, assigning a figure of 1 to 5. High would be marked with 5, and low with 1. In this way a value can be assigned to each position. The degree of potential change is indicated by the sum of the individual values divided by the number of indicators. An index of 5 would indicate a people with an extremely high propensity to change. A people with an index of 1 would not be demonstrating readiness for immediate change.

Considering the country of Chile, and taking the homogeneous unit of migrants that are moving into the city of Santiago, based on general information such as supplied by Wagner and Johnson, we assign values as follows:

1. Culture change is taking place as families are moving from rural to urban centers. Value is relatively high - 5.
2. Political change is at the present time very high, with overthrow of government - 5.
3. Economic change is high for the group, with new income and a new value system - 5.
4. Religious change is taking place as old ties and patterns are broken - 3.
5. Status of Scripture is relatively unchanged since the majority are moving within the same language structure and translation is unaffected. However Scriptures are more readily available - 3.
6. Migratory change is very high, since we are dealing with a migrating unit - 5.
7. Prototype image has not been high as regards Protestant Christianity, but as a new witness is received the prototype image rises in many cases - 3 to 4.
8. Degree of influence is somewhat low in many cases, yet with the witness of an active church within the area the degree of testimony and influence is continually on the rise - 3 to 4.

Our pattern would give the following:

	Cult. Chng.	Polit. Chng.	Econ. Chng.	Relig. Chng.	Status Script.	Migra. Chng.	Proto. Image	Degree Infl.				Change Index
Rating	5	5	5	3	3	5	3	3	=	$\frac{32}{8}$	=	4.0

(These figures were arrived at only on the basis of information at hand, and are completely subjective. They are suggested only as illustrative, and it is hoped that the interested party will be able to assess his own group situation more accurately.)

Here the index of change is 4.0 which is high. When we consider the observable factors we find that the prototype of Chilean Pentecostalism is very acceptable and the degree of influence is increasing constantly. The response to the Gospel among this group bears out the change index. Many of the migrating unit are responding to Christ and bringing others also to Him. That same response to Christ is adding daily to the influence of Christianity so that the degree of influence is constantly augmenting.

In giving due consideration to such a change index plan, it is understood that we are talking about directive for determination of action, based upon indicators available. We use the index as an index, recognizing that it has its limitations. It will never replace other directives of the Holy Spirit of God. We also recognize that certain questions should accompany the study of the index, such as: What image of Christianity do the people have? How long have they known Christianity and how deeply is its influence felt? What near neighbors are Christians, and what is their relationship to this unit? What clear witnesses do the people have?

Looking at the refugee people of Bangladesh, we find quite a different pattern from the pattern of the industrial workers of Chile. General information concerning the Moslem refugees indicates a pattern something like the following:

	Cult. Chng.	Polit. Chng.	Econ. Chng.	Relig. Chng.	Status Script.	Migra. Chng.	Proto. Image	Degree Infl.		Change Index
Rating	1	2	2	1	2	5	2	2	= $\frac{17}{8}$ =	2.01

Here the index of change is 2.01, which is very low. Also, only one factor is above 2. In addition, the prototype image has been very low, and the degree of Christian influence has been very low. They have not had Christian near neighbors, and Christian witness has been very little. However, with the programs of assistance that are being offered, this people is being made aware of a Christian witness, and the image of the prototype is being changed. With continued influence and witness, it is forseeable that in God's time these factors will begin to penetrate and have their effect upon the refugees, who may be the first people in Bangladesh to respond to the message of love and receive Christ. If they are going to do so, they must have the opportunity presented to them. This door of love may well be the door through which the gospel message will enter and begin to influence the people.

Apart from a very special working of the Holy Spirit of God, it would not seem that the time is propitious to expect any great people movement to Christ in Bangladesh. The change index indicates a very low possibility at the present. This should not discourage God's people. It should help them to understand reality, and understand the type of ministry that is needed. Here is a field to be plowed and the seed sown before a harvest comes.

The missionary who goes to Bangladesh should understand that his ministry at present is one of plowing and preparing the soil, and planting the seed. He should recognize that his ministry is one of "witness" and demonstration of the power of the love of Christ and of the gospel message. He should also be assured that God is able to use His servant to change existing factors, as He is also able to use many other means to bring a people to that point of being ready for change, and to accept the message being offered. The harvest may delay. That is not the missionary's responsibility. He must not judge himself as a failure if he does not see the "harvest" he had anticipated. Understanding the facts can alleviate a lot of wrong suffering and self-inflicted chastisement on the part of dedicated and commited missionaries.

With this understanding the missionary is not discouraged when he does not see the "abundant fruit" that he would like to see in a short term of ministry. Understanding the situation should never discourage anyone. It might indicate what kind of person it is going to take to "stick with it" even when he may know that the time is not propitious for the harvest just yet.

VENN DIAGRAM PATTERN

A second pattern of study is the "Venn Diagram" approach. The outline is to determine the given geographic areas where the "high" factors are noticed, and draw circles around these areas or possible areas of concentration. If the circles

Pragmatics 117

converge in a given center, then a geographic center for operations is disclosed. A people ready for response to the Gospel may have been located. If, as the circles are drawn, the pattern indicated below emerges, one will be directed to a "Ready response" area; one in which it would be well to concentrate missionary personnel.

READY RESPONSE AREA

A = CULTURE CHANGE
B = POLITICAL CHANGE
C = ECONOMIC CHANGE
D = RELIGIOUS CHANGE
E = MIGRATION CHANGE

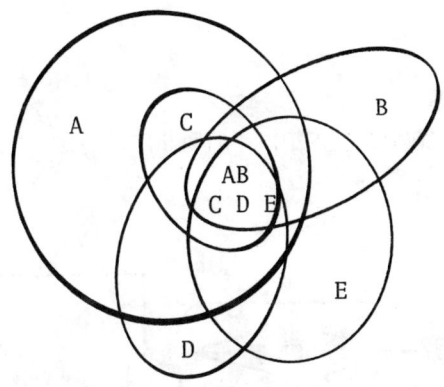

(Graphic 16)

This pattern can only be studied with a map of the population spread out before one. Information about the distinct groups must be secured, and then the lines drawn around those groups as information reveals people who are affected. Are there any peoples who are in the midst of culture change? If so, draw circles around those groups. Are there any who are influenced by political change? Draw a circle around those peoples. Are there any groups that are in economic change? Draw a circle. If not, don't include within a circle. When the circles are all drawn, a geographic center may appear which would indicate the center of highest propensity for change. One word of warning is necessary: let the facts speak for themselves. Don't try to force a circle, for you are then only misleading yourself.

COMMUNICATION PATTERN

A third pattern of approach to the discovery of any group that is ready for change, and possibly turning to Christ, is the consideration of the communication pattern. All communicators know the pattern:

COMMUNICATION PATTERN

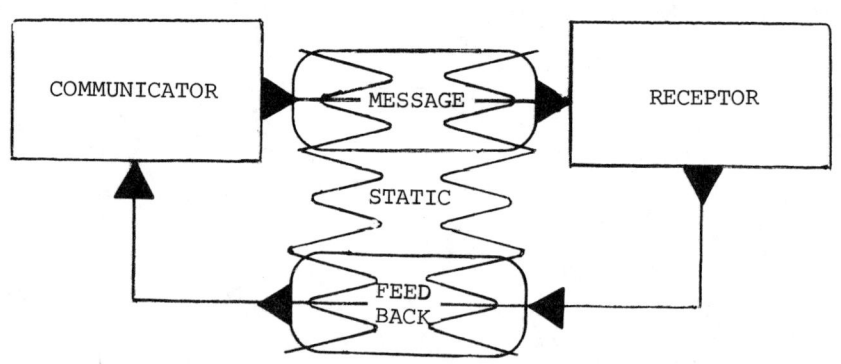

(Graphic 17)

Since the communicator is an advocate, and since his acceptance is so vital, he must be evaluated on a "high" / "low" scale. He may have a high degree of acceptability to the receptor, or he may have a low. The mission administrator must ask the question: Who will be acceptable to the target group, and why?

Next the message must be considered. It cannot be considered in the light of its absolute nature or meaning alone, but also in its relevance to the receptor as the receptor perceives it. The discovery of the application which will be relevant is vital, for this is the point of contact and of individual relationship with the receiver. The missionary seeks for a "high" in application of message.

The noise level or "static" is the area of outside influence and opposition. Where the noise level is high, the message may not get through.

Other influences are too great. This is where non-Christian religious influences are at their highest. Islam offers an extremely high noise level that hinders the passage of the gospel message. All monolithic religions offer very high noise level to Christianity. Family and kinship patterns may also offer a "high" noise level, unless the whole family and kin are also involved in the communication process.

At the receptor's position again there are variables to be determined. They have to do with the actual state of the receptor himself. Is the time appropriate? Is the message relevant to him? Is the application functional? Only the feedback will tell. But the feedback will itself pass through a distortion or static level.

Assuming that a value can be applied to each factor, we can assume that an index is possible. Assigning a "5" to a "high" level and "1" to a "low," we can easily discover a pattern which would register degree of possibility. A "low" communicator, with a message of "low" applicability passing through a "high" static would hardly be heard even if the receptor were ready. Also a "high" communicator with a "high" applicability of the message, passing through "low" noise, would hardly be effective if the receptor were approached at an inopportune time or if he did not perceive the message as being able to satisfy his needs.

Perhaps the communication pattern is the more subjective pattern, but it should be considered as relevant to the evangelization of any given group. The communicator, (advocate, missionary or evangelist - whichever he may be called), will do well to consider the aspects and application of the pattern to know where and how he fits into the scene of carrying God's redemptive message. Of course, if the evangelist is only there to "proclaim" the message, then he need not concern himself too seriously. But if he is looking for "disciples" then he will be greatly concerned.

    The evangelist, pastor, missionary, servant of the Lord, is interested in knowing and understanding people so he can communicate the message of God's love in a way that will be received, and disciples follow. He will do well to know the potential of the people among whom he is working, and be advised of those among whom the Spirit of God is working, and prepared to face the reality of the conditions before him.

Part Four **The Potential Ambassadors**

Chapter 9

People from All the World

The sun never sets on the world. It only goes down on one portion as it rises on another. One half of the world is always in the light of day. In our scientific age we know that the sun does not go around the earth, but that the earth rotates and any point constantly passes through the phases of sunrise, morning, high noon, afternoon, evening, sunset. We also know that according to God's clock of history there are periods of the rise of nations, the successful operations of nations, the decline of powers. Would it seem strange that the same God who has ordered the universe, and who also said: "I will build my Church and the gates of Hell shall not prevail against it," might have a similar plan for carrying out this work? Would it seem strange that a missionary movement begun in England, and to a great degree passed to the West would follow on in the Pacific Countries, and in the Land of the Rising Sun? Would it seem strange that the Continent that was known as the "Dark Continent" should burst into light and give light to all the world? Would it seem strange that God would in the last days pour out His Spirit upon all flesh and allow men of all nations the joy of being co-laborers together with Him?

MISSIONS NOT A WESTERN MONOPOLY

Christianity did not come from the West. It came from Palestine, the land of the Jews. It was not born in Western culture, and many of the cultural settings of biblical lands are lost to Western thinking. Western cultural patterns have been added to the image of Christianity so that in some cases the real core can hardly be discovered. God has been given some of the characteristics of a Western God. Christianity has often been equated with the West.

Christians in the Western world have tried to interpret Scripture within its own cultural context, and have succeeded quite well within the framework of Western thought patterns. But are these patterns always transferable to other cultures? African Christians say "no." The "time" concept of the West is not congruent with the "already" and "not yet" concept of Africa. The absolute "yes" and "no" concept of the West is not comprehensible to the oriental mind that operates within a "ying" - "yang" context.

One Asian evangelist expressed his feelings when he wrote:

Missionary who came to Sarawak during this time also from Western countries. Of course the Western influence is still very strong. They had tried their best to present the Spiritual knowledge of gospel. But according to their ways or Western ways of thinking and culture. You know that to transfer the seeds from cold climate to the hot and humid climate is no very easy thing. Suppose I bring seeds of rubber to Korea to be planted, its sure does not grow because the climate is not suitable for the rubber.

Asian Christian <u>MUST</u> evangelise Asian to fulfill the command of our Lord which as given "all authority in heaven and on earth. Go, then, to all peoples everywhere (Asian) and make them my disciples: (says the Lord) baptize them in the name of the Father and the Son and of the Holy Spirit, and teach them to obey everything I have commanded you. And remember (Lord's say) I will be with you always, to the end of the age" (TEV Mat. 28:18-20).

Two ways traffic Missionary must be organized-by means sending and receiving churches. And the Spirit of SHARING TOGETHER must be posses in the heart of Asian community. Not in terms of money only, but any ways they be able "SHARE" with Asian community. We must encourage our Asian people strong to keep the image of <u>Asian</u> <u>Church</u> <u>Identity</u>. For instance, I am a Christian, but I love God, but I want to express that love in my own way. Christianity has to be rediscovered in the life and struggle of Asian people, in whatever we face in joy or strife. We have to express our faith in Asian ways. How do we Asian evangelise Asia in Asian ways? How do Asian praise God as an Asian?

Asian churches of sending churches should be very clear that is to develop the national church in Asian style rather than Mission Station (All-Asia Mission Consultation, Seoul, Korea; 1973).

God, being a God who loves all mankind, is concerned that "all peoples" shall hear and understand the truth of His redemption. God is not limited to working through Western missionaries, but is working through His own from among all races and nations. God is moving in new ways, and the whole Body of Christ is more and more involved in that movement.

A recent publication entitled Missions From The Third World (Wong, Larson, Pentecost) has brought to the attention of many of those interested in missions the fact that a new day has dawned and we are in a new era of missions. The Third World churches are sending out their missionaries, and new societies are being formed in every continent to complete the work of the Great Commission. More than 3,000 missionaries have gone from Third World churches, and more than 200 agencies are responsible for sending them.

EFFECTIVE COMMUNICATION

As we consider effective communication of the Gospel, the point of issue is not one related to the truth of Scripture. We believe there is an absolute truth and message, and that the message is applicable to all peoples. The issue is one of communication. Scripture was given within a cultural context. The message was clear to those who received it. When that message is translated into another language and context there are inevitable changes of concept that take place. Such is the case when Scripture is translated into English, and a Western culture. Then again, when that English and Western concept is re-translated into Afrikaan more is lost. When the English is re-translated into Korean, or Tagalog, other aspects are lost and concepts changed.

Theological issues become real issues. Questions are raised. Answers are sought. God is not confounded by the problems, but men are. God is still in control of the situation, and capable of raising up new individuals to meet the new demands. God is able to move new communicators to add to the task of communicating His eternal message.

God is raising up leaders in the churches of every continent. He has his leaders in key places. They are men prepared and called of God to take their place in the Church of Jesus Christ.

Pastors have been leading congregations for years. Now, theologians are emerging in the Third World, and their voices are going to be heard. Not all will speak with clarity. Some will sound a voice of confusion. Not all will be biblical. Some will be syncretistic. Standards must be established as criteria for the judgment of Scriptural theology, lest an "African" theology and an "Asian" theology and a "Latin American" theology emerge in place of a biblical theology, and cause confusion. God is not the author of confusion, nor of falsehood. Theology belongs to the whole world of God's people. The truths of God are for all, and not for private interpretation by any. The day of theological inter-change is going to be an exciting day as emerging theologians begin to express in new terminology their understanding of the eternal message within changing cultural context. How will the unchanging message be communicated in a fast-changing world? Fear, excitement, reticence, all emotions are displayed at the thought. But new expressions are sure to come.

Many of those who attempt to write in the field of theology will be individuals who have been trained outside of their own countries. Two things will characterize their writings. First, there will be those who hold strongly to those forms that they have been taught, and their writings will appear very much like their teacher's. The other group will be the reactionaries, who will try to break away from the patterns, and invent new patterns and styles that they will attempt to show are more understandable within their culture. The reaction will be to twist the truth in order to try to conform to an "image" which they would like to present as being "African" or "Latin" or "Asian." In this there is great fear, for this will be the image that is presented, and the message that will be communicated.

All of these varied positions are going to be presented, and they are going to be faced by all the Body of Christ, for no longer is isolationism a possibility, except for those who hide their head in the sand and let the world pass by.

ACCEPTABLE PROTOTYPE

The image of Christianity must be separated from Western culture. People accept that which is acceptable to them; that which offers what they are looking for. People have a concept in their minds of what Christianity is. As long as that image is Western, more and more people will reject it. There are many reasons for that: nationalism, loss of Western prestige, failure of "Christian" testimony through human weakness, Christian "professionalism," "imitation," etc. Some of these are legitimate and inevitable, some are Satanic, but they are all "real" in the mind of the potential "receptor." Here is where God will not be left without a witness, but will raise up new witnesses to Himself. He is raising up those who will make the prototype a new image. Not that it is new, but that it is new in the minds of the receptors, and that is what is happening. Missionaries are emerging from the Church in the Third World, carrying a new "image" of the Christ of the Gospels. This is not a new "statue." It is a new living testimony to the power of the gospel message.

The new prototype is supracultural and multi-cultural. It speaks Chinese, and Japanese, and Indonesian, and Tagalog, and Telegu, and Korean, and Ibo, and Hausa. The faces are tan, and brown, and black, and white, and olive, and yellow. The witnesses speak, and a new prototype, formed from the great mosaic of languages, and tribes, and peoples, and nations, is coming into being. The day of universal testimony is on the horizon! God is at work. He is not going to say to any people: "I have no need of you." He is going to move men from all nations to go to all nations. A new day of missions is emerging! And as the Church in each country sends out its own emissaries, it is going to find a new spring of life bubbling up within. New life will fill the Church, as the Spirit of God manifests His power and fills with His joy.

GIFTED OF THE SPIRIT

God has always chosen His own, throughout all history, to be His servants. His plan is to endow with a special gift those individuals that they might fulfill His purpose. In the Old Testament He chose His Moses, and Joshua, and Elijah, and David, and Christ. In the New Testament He has chosen His Apostles, and prophets, and evangelists, and pastor-teachers, "for the perfecting of the saints for the work of the ministry for the edifying of the body of Christ" (Eph. 4:11,12). Those whom He chooses, He endows with the gifts, graces, love, and whatever necessary to accomplish His purpose. God is not limited to working through any one nation or people, but is moving through gifted men today in many parts of the world. Today there are gifted Indian evangelists, gifted Japanese, gifted Indonesian, gifted Nigerian, gifted Filipino evangelists. They are all ministering with the gift of the Spirit in what has become known as E-1 evangelism. Others have become active in what is known as E-2 and E-3 evangelism.

> E-1 is defined as that sphere where we can reach people of our own language and culture and . . . expect to bring them into our own churches.
>
> E-2 includes all those people with whom we have some common ground culturally . . . but who are far enough away so as not to be candidates for membership in our own local church.
>
> E-3 includes all those people beyond any significant common ground of language and culture, that is, people totally strange to us (Winter, <u>Christianity Today</u>, Jan. 19, 1973:11).

Africa's outreach has for the most part been E-2 evangelism, where peoples of adjacent areas are reached. It has been like the early Church, first in Jerusalem, then in Judea, and to Samaria. Few have been involved in E-3 evangelism so far, though there are some working in Newark, New Jersey and in New York City among the Blacks of the U.S. This is culturally a new world for those missionaries, though still largely confined to working with the black population. But the fact of being black does not change the fact of cultural differences. (See <u>Missions From The Third World</u>, Wong, Larson, Pentecost, 1973).

Chinese have become increasingly concerned with reaching Chinese in many centers of the world, and there are hundreds of thousands of them. Almost every major city of the world has its Chinese center. Japanese are also leaving Japan to minister to Japanese in other countries. There are many Japanese in Brazil who are being ministered to by Japanese pastors from Japan. These are pastors who were raised in the churches and trained in Japan who have accepted the call to serve these congregations. This is E-1 evangelism.

Others have gone from Japan supported by Japanese congregations to minister in other countries as E-3 evangelists. That is to say, not all Japanese serving in overseas ministries are ministering to Japanese. Countries in which Japanese are serving are: Afghanistan, Bolivia, Cambodia, Canada Ethiopia, India, Jamaica, Kenya, Laos, Malaysia, Peru, Singapore, Thailand, Taiwan, Indonesia, Nepal, Brazil, Ecuador, and the Philippines. Ministries are divided among evangelism teaching, medicine, and linguistics with 103 Japanese serving under 29 mission groups at present (Japan Report to the First All-Asia Mission Consultation, August 1973). These are forerunners of others to follow.

The challenge of missions is expressed today by many leaders from different countries. Grace Church of Manila is excited about its missionary program, sending missionaries from the Philippines to India, and Taiwan, as well as to Indonesia. Korea is rejoicing in its outreach, and growing in its intentions.

The first All-Asia Mission Consultation, held in Seoul, Korea, August 27 to September 1, 1973, determined to place: "At least two hundred new Asian missionaries by the end of 1974." This means from fourteen Asian countries alone.

As new leaders are emerging in the Third World, they are constantly taking more and more responsibility and leadership in the evangelization of the world. With such a rise of competent men of God, the image of Christianity is being re-discovered. The communication channels are being enlarged, and the potential receptivity is increased.

INCREASING INFLUENCE

Not only is the concept and image of Christianity changing, but the degree of influence is rapidly changing also. The multiplicity of voices is emerging like a great choir in the distance, coming closer. Voices are becoming louder and clearer. Recent studies have shown that Third World agencies are now on the move, sending out missionaries to reach beyond their own boundaries. This action is not completely new, but recognition of it is.

Asia is now sending at least 110 missionaries, with a goal of sending an additional 200 during this year, 1974. Latin America is sending at least 62. Africa is reported as having 33 (Wong, Larson, Pentecost, 1973:107). But this is only the initiation. What movements will the next few years see?

It must be remembered however that non-Western missionaries and evangelists are not going to find an easy road. The fact that they are ministering in cross-cultural and cross-lingual situations means they face the same problems of cross-cultural communication that Western missionaries face. They will have language barriers to overcome, cultural obstacles, and communication problems. They will not all be well received. Much consideration will have to be given to the question of understanding who can best reach whom, and who will be most openly received. Not all Asians are acceptable in all Asia. Not all Africans are well received in all Africa.

All missionaries are together facing the same problems, issues, and decisions. All are facing the temptations of the world, the flesh, and the devil. All are attacking the same strongholds of Satan. All are approaching people held in the grasp of false religion, false gods, idolatry, secularism, nominalism, indifference, fear, hate, disillusion and believing a lie.

The fact that new forces are coming on the scene in no way implies that the present forces can or in any way should diminish. The Christian message is a message that requires all attention and all potential forces working together.

If the percentage of the Christian population is going to keep pace with the rising world population, then the church in every country must grow as the population grows. If the church is going to grow in the world to fulfill the purpose of its existence, which is to be a light unto the world and draw men into it and expand its influence, then a yet brighter and stronger testimony is needed. Personnel from every country and every potential source is needed. An expanded witness is vital. If the church just keeps pace with the percentage rise of the population, that means that in actual numbers there are just that many more thousands without a Christian witness.

Today's rising world population of 2.2 percent per year means an increase of 2.2 percent per year in missionary personnel, just to keep up with the same ratio. Much of that personnel may come from one of two sources: either the local church adding personnel to expand the ministry, whether by laymen or full time servants, or from personnel outside its own circle. Considering the North American missionary force as 35,000, that means 770 missionaries must be added this year of 1974 just to keep the same ratio. They may come from the United States, or they may come from other countries, but the number must be increased to maintain the same percentage force. Next year 777 others must be added. In 1976 there must be another 793 added. This means a total of 37,350 missionaries by 1976, either from the U. S. or other sources just to keep the same ratio.

Further, with an approximate 3,000 Third World missionaries in service at the present time, the Third World is going to have to produce 66 more this present year, 67 next year, and another 69 in 1976 just to keep the same proportional strength it now has. That means 202 new missionaries by 1976 apart from the normal replacement of missionaries necessary to maintain the actual numbers, in order to maintain the same strategic strength that it now exerts. But the purpose of the members of the Church is to work together with God to increase the influence and testimony of the Church in the world. "We then, as workers together *with him*, beseech *you* also that ye receive not the grace of God in vain" (2 Cor. 6:1).

God did not intend that the Church should remain static in the world. He intended that the Apostles would go and make disciples, and the disciples would make more disciples. God intended a duplication plan that would reach out to make disciples of all nations, with the message of Christ spreading faster than the population increase. In order to fulfill this purpose of God, the Church is going to have to increase its witness and outreach faster than the world is multiplying. Anything less than that means an actual loss. With such a purpose and program set by God, how can any consider doing less than God would have? With almost two and one half billion people who have not responded to the gospel message, who can say that there is not need for servants of the Lord to still go from every country to every country and for every local church to lift up its eyes, and look on the fields "white unto harvest?" It is granted that the patterns of ministry and outreach may change, but the fact of ministry and outreach in evangelism must never diminish.

Movements are under way to consider how the existing evangelistic forces can be best deployed to reach the yet unevangelized of our world. No one plan is going to be satisfying for all, nor is such necessary. Many programs and relationships will have to be coordinated. But the most important is the overall leading of the Holy Spirit of God upon all concerned. We are moving into a period of internationalization of missions. Not necessarily in organic internationalization, but in inter-relationships. That means fellowship, purpose, action, training. It may mean church oriented programs, and para-church operations. It may mean national mission societies, and it may mean international societies. It means training, and mobilizing the laity as well as the specialist. It means all becoming involved.

One thing is certin: the challenge of reaching the yet unevangelized is so great and diverse and so humanly overwhelming, that all those who truly love Christ and are called according to His purpose are going to have to go "all out" for the program of God to reach the unreached.

Who can best reach the unreached? You and I. No one can take our place. Nor can we turn our responsibility over to anyone else. When we begin to do our part, and communicate the message we have, and make our disciples, and others begin to make theirs, then the Christian influence will begin to increase and spread as God would have it. This "you" and "I" also corresponds to local churches, and it expands to local churches in Asia, Africa, Europe, Latin America, Oceania, everywhere. It is the Body of Christ in all the world, in action, witnessing by all means to all peoples everywhere, according to the Gifts of the Spirit on all men who are of the Body of Christ.

Bibliography

ABLER, Ronald; John S. ADAMS & Peter GOULD
   1973   *Spatial Organization, The Geographer's View of the World.* Englewood Cliffs, Prentice-Hall.

BAILEY, Helen Miller & Abraham P. NASATIR
   1968   *Latin America: The Development of its Civilization.* Englewood Cliffs, Prentice-Hall.

BARNETT, H. G.
   1953   *Innovation: The Basis of Culture Change.* New York, McGraw-Hill Book Co.

BARNEY, G. Linwood
   1973   "The Supracultural and the Cultural" in *The Gospel and Frontier Peoples* R. Pierce Beaver, ed. South Pasadena, William Carey Library.

BARRETT, David B.
   1968   *African Initiatives in Religion.* Nairobi, East African Publishing House.

   1968b *Schism and Renewal in Africa.* Nairobi, Oxford University Press.

BARRETT, David B. et al (ed.)
   1973   *Kenya Churches Handbook: The Development of Kenya. Christianity 1498 - 1973* Kenya, Evangelical Press.

BAUER, Raymond A. (ed.)
   1966   *Social Indicators.* Cambridge, MIT Press.

BEAVER, R. Pierce (ed.)
1973 *The Gospel and Frontier Peoples.*
      South Pasadena, William Carey Library.

BEGUIN, Olivier (ed.)
1970 *Directory of Bible Societies.*
      London, United Bible Societies.

BEN WATI, I
1970 *Into the Seventies with Christ.*
      Bangalore, India, Evangelical Literature Service Press.

BIEDERWOLF, William E.
1921 *Evangelism: Its Justification, Its Operation and Its Value.* New York, Fleming H. Revell Co.

BRIERLEY, Leslie
1961 *World Survey 1961.*
      London, Worldwide Evangelization Crusade.

1971 *They Are Bread For Us: Continental Surveys of the World Mission Situation.*
      London, Worldwide Evangelization Crusade.

BRIERLEY, Leslie (ed.)
1961 *The Challenge of the Unachieved.*
      London, Worldwide Evangelization Crusade.

1962 *Atlas of W.E.C. Mission Fields.*
      London, Worldwide Evangelization Crusade.

CAREY, William
1962 *An Enquiry into the Obligations of Christians to Use Means for the Conversion of the Heathens.*
      New facsimile ed. London, Carey Kingsgate Press.

CASTRO, Emilio
1973 "Bangkok, the New Opportunity" *International Review of Missions.* Vol. LXII, No. 246.

DAWSON, Christopher
1948 *Religion and Culture.*
      London, Wheed and Ward.

DAYTON, Edward R. (ed.)
1973 *Mission Handbook: North American Protestant Ministries Overseas.* Monrovia, MARC.

EVANS, Robert P.
1963   *Let Europe Hear*.   Chicago, Moody Press.

FABUN, Donald
1968   *The Dynamics of Change*.
       Englewood Cliffs, Prentice-Hall.

1971   *Dimensions of Change*.   Beverly Hills, Glencoe Press.

GREEN, Michael
1970   *Evangelism in the Early Church*
       Grand Rapids, Wm. B. Eerdmans Pub. Co.

GROSS, Bertram M.
1966   *Social Systems Accounting*.   Tavistock, B. & M.

HENRY, Carl F. H. & W. Stanley MOONEYHAM
1967   *One Race, One Gospel, One Task*.   Vol. I & II.
       Minneapolis, World Wide Publications.

HERENDEEN, Dale
1972   "Conversion Receptivity and Church Growth Among
       the Ethnic Vietnamese."
       Unpublished thesis, Fuller Theological Seminary.

JOHNSON, Norbert E.
1970   "The History, Dynamic, and Problems of the
       Pentecostal Movement in Chile.
       Unpublished thesis, Fuller Theological Seminary.

KELIHER, Alice V.
1931   *A Critical Study of Homogeneous Grouping with a
       Critique of Measurement as the Basis for Classi-
       fication*.
       New York, A.M.S. Press, Inc.   Reprint.

KENNEDY, D. James
1970   *Evangelism Explosion*.
       Wheaton, Tyndale House Publishers.

KIETZMAN, Dale Walter
1972   "Indian Survival in Brazil."
       Unpublished Ph.D. dissertation University of
       Southern California Graduate School.

KRAFT, Charles H.
1973   "Dynamic Equivalence Churches." *Missiology*,
       (A. R. Tippett, ed.)

KUIPER, R. B.
  1961   *God-Centered Evangelism*.
           Grand Rapids, Baker Book House.

LARSON, Peter
  1972   "Receptivity among the Migrants in Northern Argentina." Unpublished Thesis, Fuller Theological Seminary.

LATOURETTE, Kenneth Scott
  1936   *Missions Tomorrow*. New York, Harper & Bros.

LEAVELL, Roland Q.
  1951   *Evangelism: Christ's Imperative Commission*.
           Nashville, Broadman Press.

LEBAR, Frank M., Gerald C. HICKEY, & John K. MUSGRAVE
  1964   *Ethnic Groups of Mainland Southeast Asia*.
           New Haven, Human Relations Area Files Press.

LINDSELL, Harold (ed.)
  1966   *The Church's Worldwide Mission*.
           Waco, Word Books.

LUZBETAK, Louis J.
  1963   *The Church and Cultures*.
           Techny, Divine Word Publications.

MALINOWSKI, Bronislaw
  1949   *The Dynamics of Culture Change*.
           New Haven, Yale University Press.

MC GAVRAN, Donald A.
  1970   *Understanding Church Growth*.
           Grand Rapids, William B. Eerdmans Pub. Co.

MC GOWAN, Patrick J. & Patricia BOLLAND
  1971   *The Plitical and Social Elite of Tanzania: An Analysis of Social Background Factors*.
           Syracuse, Maxwell School of Citizenship & Public Affairs.

MC LEISH, Alexander
  1931   *The Frontier Peoples of India, A Missionary Survey*.
           London, World Dominion Press.

MURDOCK, George Peter
  1965   *Culture and Society*. University of Pittsburgh Press.

NEEDHAM, William L., Edward C. PENTECOST & Ellen GILBERT
1973   *Unreached Peoples: A Preliminary Compilation.*
        Monrovia, MARC.

NIDA, Eugene A.
1960   *Message and Mission.* New York, Harper & Bros.

1968   *Religion Across Cultures.* New York, Harper & Row.

NIDA, Eugene A. (ed.)
1972   *The Book of a Thousand Tongues.*
        New York, United Bible Societies.

NORDYKE, Quentin H.
1972   "Animistic Aymaras and Church Growth."
        Unpublished thesis, Fuller Theological Seminary.

PENTECOST, Edward C.
1972   "A Church Growth Study."
        Unpublished thesis, Fuller Theological Seminary.

PETERS, George
1972   *A Theology of Missions.* Chicago, Moody Press.

PHILIP, Puthurail Thomas
1972   "The Growth of the Baptist Churches of Tribal
        Nagaland.
        Unpublished thesis, Fuller Theological Seminary.

READ, William R. & Frank A. INESON
1973   *Brazil 1980: The Protestant Handbook.*
        Monrovia, MARC.

READ, William R.
1973   "New Patterns of Church Growth in Brazil."
        Unpublished thesis, Fuller Theological Seminary.

REED, Grady W.
1971   "Strategizing Church of Christ Missions in the
        Light of Varying Receptivity."
        Unpublished thesis, Fuller Theological Seminary.

ROGERS, Everett M.
1962   *Diffusion of Innovations.* New York, The Free Press.

ROGERS, Everett M. & F. Floyd SHOEMAKER
1971   *Communication of Innovations, A Cross-Cultural
        Approach.* 2nd ed. New York, The Free Press.

RUSSETT, Bruce et al.
  1962 *World Handbook of Political and Social Indicators.*
        New Haven, Yale University Press.

SAMUEL, George
  1973 "Growth Potential of Urban Churches: A Study in Bombay. Unpublished thesis, Fuller Theological Seminary.

TABER, Charles
  1973 "Evangelizing The Unreached Peoples: What To Do And How To Do It," in *The Gospel and Frontier Peoples.* R. Pierce Beaver (ed.) South Pasadena, William Carey Library.

TAYLOR, Howard, Dr. & Mrs.
  1918 *Hudson Taylor and the China Inland Mission.*
        London, Morgan & Scott.

TIPPETT, Alan R.
  1969 *Verdict Theology in Missionary Theory.*
        Lincoln, Lincoln Christian College Press.

  1970 *Peoples of Southwest Ethiopia.*
        South Pasadena, William Carey Library.

TURNER, Harold
  1967 *History of an African Independent Church.*
        Oxford, Clarendon Press.

WAGNER, C. Peter
  1971 *Frontiers in Missionary Strategy.*
        Chicago, Moody Press.

  1973 *Look Out! The Pentecostals Are Coming.*
        Carol Stream, Creation House.

WALLACE, Anthony F. C.
  1958 "Revitalization Movements" in *American Anthropologist* 264-281.

  1964 *Culture and Personality.* New York, Random House.

WALLIS, Ethel E. & Mary A. BENNETT
  1959 *Two Thousand Tongues To Go.* New York, Harper & Bros

WALLIS, Ethel Emilia
  1960 *The Dayuma Story; Life under Auca Spears.* New York Harper

WHITEFORD, Andrew Hunter
  1960   *Two Cities of Latin America: A Comparative Description of Social Classes.* Beloit, The Logan Museum of Anthropology.

WILLEMS, Emilio
  1967   *Followers of the New Faith: Culture Change and the Rise of Protestantism in Brazil and Chile.* Vanderbilt University Press.

WINTER, Ralph D.
  1973   "Existing Churches: Ends or Means?" in Jan. 19 *Christianity Today,* Harold Lindsell (ed.)

  1974   "Seeing the Task Graphically" in *Evangelical Missions Quarterly*, Vol. 10, No. 1, Jan. 1974 Wheaton, EMIS.

WINTER, Ralph D. (ed.)
  1973   *The Evangelical Response To Bangkok.* South Pasadena, William Carey Library.

WONG, James, Peter LARSON, & Edward PENTECOST
  1973   *Missions From The Third World.* Singapore, Church Growth Study Center.

DOCUMENTS

BRIERLEY, Leslie
  1968 "Missionary Opportunity Today."
      Port Washington, Worldwide Evangelization Crusade.

DALE, John
  1952 "Report of Indian Villages."
      Tamazunchale, Mexico, Mexican Indian Mission.

  1964 "Five Year Plan of Work."
      Tamazunchale, Mexico, Mexican Indian Mission.

ELLIS, Ted
  1974 "Status of Christianity Country Profile - Taiwan."
      Monrovia, MARC.

JACQUET, Constant H., Jr.
  1968 "Indicators For Planning In Bibliographic Perspective" in *Information Service*, Sat. Oct. 5, 1968. New York, NCCCUSA.

MELLIS, Charles
  1973 "Missions Update." Newsletter of the United Presbyterian Center For Mission Studies, Vol. II, Nos. 7-9, 1973. Fullerton, UPCFMS.

PATEMAN, Norman
  1944 Personal letter to Leslie Brierley, Sept. 1944. Personal file.

WILSON, C. Elwood
  1974 "World Report of Christian National Evangelism Commission." Vol. 32, No. 1, Feb. 1974. San Jose, CNEC.

1973 "All-Asia Mission Consultation Seoul, Korea" Aug. 27 - Sept. 1, '73. Mimeographed document No author indicated.

1972 "Asia Pulse" Vol. III, No. 3, April, 1972. Wheaton, EMIS.

n.d.   "The Challenge of India's Millions."
       London, Worldwide Evangelization Crusade.

1971   "Continuing Evangelism in Brazil" in *Interpretive Bulletin I*.
       Monrovia, MARC.

1973   "The Evangelization of the Modern World."
       Washington D.C., United States Catholic Conference.

n.d.   "The Isles That Wait."
       London, Worldwide Evangelization Crusade.

1974   "Japan Report to the 1st All-Asia Mission Consultation, Aug. 1973."
       Personal correspondence.

1973   "New Winds of Spiritual Awakening 1973."
       Lausanne, Switzerland, ICOWE.

1964   "Worldwide" Jubilee Edition, March-April 1964.
       Port Washington, Worldwide Evangelization Crusade.

Index

Advocate - 41,65,68,70,71, 72,119

Africa - 5,12,16,18,30,40, 43,85,124,129,130,132

Andersen - 108

Animism - 36,41

Animistic - 36,41

Anthropolygy - 8

Asia - 5,32,124,125,129,130, 132

Barnett - 94,96,103,108

Barney - 68,69

Barrett - 16,30,57,84,86,98, 106

Beaver - 1,16,69

Bolivia - 26,128

Brazil - 26,33,49,74,101,128

Brierley - 14

Burma - 97,105

Carey - 11,12,16

Castro - 9,10

Chile - 101,114,115

China - 12,14,105

Christian - 9,11,13,14,16, 27,30,35,38,39,40,48,66,67, 105,109,110,116,130,131

Christianity - 24,31,36,42, 47,66,70,73,79,91,95,96,97, 98,99,102,103,105,108,109, 110,114,115,119,124,126,127, 129

Christians - 2,5,6,11,13,23, 24,29,32,33,34,36,49,81

Church - 9,10,11,13,17,18, 23,32,35,39,48,61,64,66,68, 71,95,110,123,127,128,130, 131

Churches - 9,34,73,81,105, 125

Communication - 8,17,18,29, 31,34,43,44,46,47,48,49,50, 61,62,63,65,67,70,71,72,73, 74,80,98,99,118,119,125,129

Conversion - 8,11,47,69

Cross-cultural - 62,65,70, 129

Cultural - 31,34,39,41,42, 46,48,63,64,65,66,69,71,93, 124,125

Culture - 24,26,27,29,39, 41,42,45,47,49,51,63,65,67, 68,69,93,97,98,108,109,110, 112,113,114,117,118,124

Dale - 10,51

Davis - 11

Dawson - 95

Disciples - 1,10,57,60,62, 67,71,82,111,120,124,131

Dissatisfaction - 91,92,93, 95,96,99,103,107,108

Dynamic-equivalence - 63,64, 66,67

Eclecticism - 108

Economic - 17,50,74,80,81, 98,99,100,101,105,112,114, 117,118

Engstrom - 1

Ethiopia - 47,128

Ethnic - 6,17,31,33,34,36, 44,45,46,47,54,69,81,102, 104

Ethno-linguistic - 23,36

Ethno-religious - 54

Evangelism - 1,8,10,13,35, 42,58,59,60,61,64,67,69,128

Evangelist - 18,39,40,41,42, 59,62,64,65,66,67,68,69,71, 80,82,110,119,120,124,129

Evangelistic - 11,69

Evangelization - 2,11,13,14, 16,18,19,23,26,27,30,32,33, 34,38,42,44,47,48,50,57,59, 65,129

Evangelize - 10,61

Evangelized - 2,6,16,17,33, 44,57,59,60

Fabun - 107

Frontier - 1,13,14,15,16, 30,43,44,68

Gospel - 1,6,13,15,16,17,19, 23,24,28,30,31,32,35,36,43, 44,47,48,57,59,60,61,63,65, 70,72,74,82,84,97,100,103, 106,110,115,116,124,125,127

Gross - 88

Harmonization - 66,67

Homogeneous units - 17,23, 24,26,27,28,29,30,31,32,33, 34,35,43,44,45,46,48,49,50, 53,54,64,67,68,110,114

Hong Kong - 33,34

Houtart - 29

India - 11,12,13,14,15,16, 24,25,33,60,128,129

Indicator - 79,80,82,83,84, 85,91,95,97,98,106,112

Indonesia - 6,7,27,67,98, 128,129

Ineson - 16

Innovation - 47,70,71

Innovator - 106

Johnson - 101,114

Kenya - 16,74,128

Korea - 34,124,125,129

Kraft - 64,66

Kumm - 13

Laos - 70,103,104,128

Larson - 125,128,129

Latin America - 129,132

Linguistic - 34,46,47,48,54,
81,105,106,129

Luzbetak - 29,38,68,74

Malinowski - 94

McLeish - 13,14

Mexico - 10,24,42,45,51,72,
73,97,98,99,102,113

Migrate - 45

Migration - 80,102,103

Missiologist - 92,94,99,102,
103

Missiology - 8

Mission - 8,9,10,12,13,27,
28,43,65,74,125,131

Missionaries - 11,12,14,15,
16,28,40,48,72,74,91,108,
125,127,129,130

Missionary - 5,9,13,15,26,
68,69,82,83,85,109,116,117,
119,120,124,130

Missions - 9,11,12,14,29,
129,131

Moratorium - 9,10,11

Multi-cultural - 127

Nida - 42

Nigeria - 26,36,98

Papua New Guinea - 97,98,99

Paragon - 108

Pateman - 14

Pentecost - 99,125,128,129

Pentecostal - 39,73,101

People - 11,13,15,18,29,30,
31,32,33,34,35,36,42,57,69,
83,100,116,117,118,126

People-consciousness - 35,
36,38

People-readiness - 91,92,
93,98,103,112

Peoples - 1,2,6,8,9,11,13,
16,17,18,24,27,29,31,35,43,
44,82,100,110,118,124,127

Peru - 23,33,45,101,128

Political - 98,99,101,112,
113,114,117

Proclamation - 57,58,60,61,
64,70

Protestant - 2,3,12,17,28,
29,30,86,114

Prototype - 107,108,109,112,
114,115,116,126,127

Reached - 13

Read - 16,100,103

Reed - 26

Religious - 11,13,14,46,47, 66,94,95,96,105,106,107,112, 114,117

Resistance - 16

Responsiveness - 8,16

Roman Catholic - 2,3,28,29, 30,38,46

Rural - 50,52

Russett - 79,98,101

Samuel - 80,81

Self-consciousness - 42,69

Self-expression - 42

Self-identity - 23,38,105

Self-recognition - 38

Shepherd - 65

Singapore - 34,128

Socio-economic - 24,47

Socio-religious - 86

Sociological - 17,24,33,47, 49,50,53,81

Sociology - 8

Strategy - 2,18,23,26,27,29, 38,42,44

Studd - 12,13,14

Supracultural - 65,127

Syncretism - 65,66

Syncretistic - 41,126

Syncretistic - 41,126

Taber - 69

Taiwan - 128,129

Taylor - 12,13

Thailand - 24,124

Theology - 40,126

Third World - 40,125,126, 127,129,130

Tippett - 47,64,71

Townsend - 28

Transcultural - 65

Tribe - 15,27,28,31,33,35, 38,72,85,98,99,106

Turner - 40

Unevangelized - 1,2,8,14,15, 16,18,19,29,30,31,43,44,131

Unreached - 2,8,10,11,12,13, 15,16,17,18,19,29,30,31,32, 44,69,83,100,131

Unresponsive - 6,31

Urban - 50,54

Urbanization - 50

Value-system - 92,93

Venn Diagram - 89,116

Verbal inspiration - 63

Wagner - 26,101,114

Wallace - 91

Whiteford - 51

Winter - 5,128

Witness - 41,60,61,71,72,73,
110,116,130

Wong - 125,128,129

World-view - 46

Appendix

PART I

Following is a set of GRAPHICS which demonstrate the estimated CHRISTIAN POPULATION BY ETHNIC GROUPS. In each case, as stated, the graphic is presented to demonstrate the ratio of the ethnic group to the total population, and the proportion of that group which has responded to the Christian message. The graphics are demonstrative of degree, and drawn to the best proportions according to information available, which is itself often an estimate. The author therefore presents these graphics to encourage a way of thinking, rather than to portray accurate and reliable information.

Certainly many will react, and some will respond with more accurate information. This is encouraged. It is hoped that by introducing these as an initial investigation, much more research will follow. Such will allow further and more detailed development of the pattern of study. It will also provide more accurate statistics that will portray more precisely the actual status of Christianity among groups, and within countries.

As a key, the following is presented:

Protestant:

Roman Catholic:

Other:
(Orthodox, Syrian, Coptic, etc.)

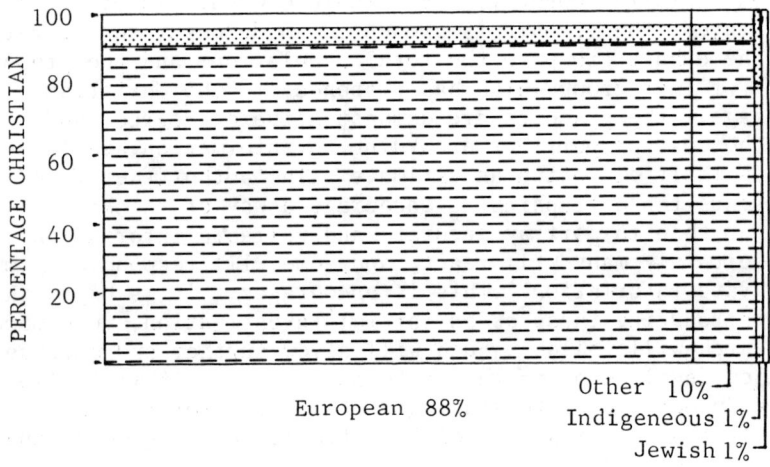

(Note: These figures are representative approximations. They should be seen as indications of magnitude, not precise.)

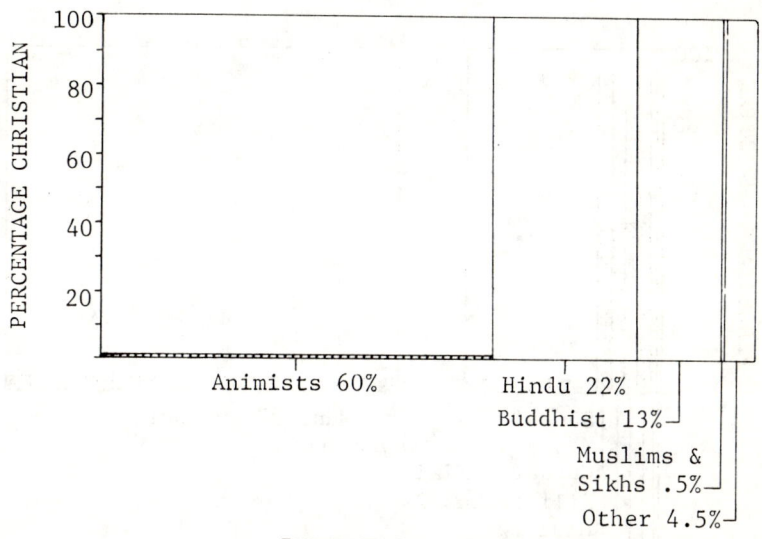

(NOTE: These figures are representative approximations. They should be seen as indications of magnitude, not precise.)

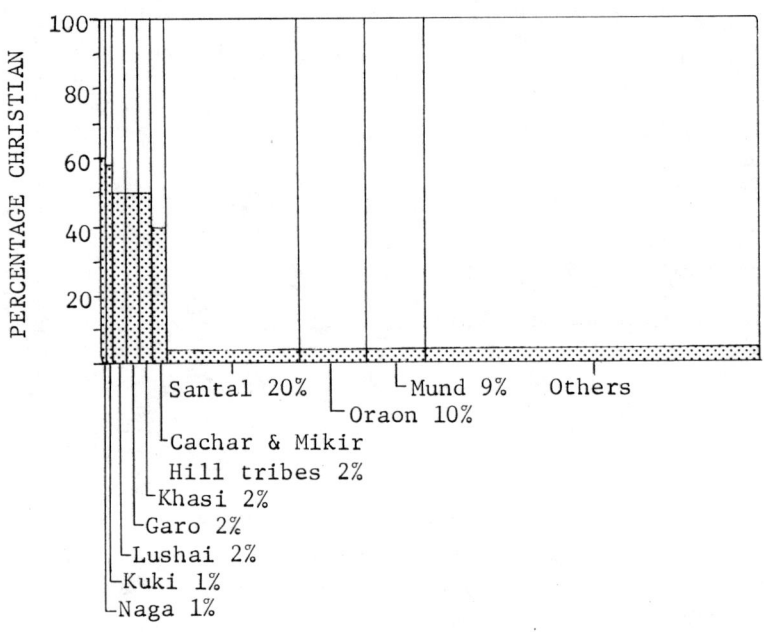

(NOTE: *These figures are representative approximations. They should be seen as indications of magnitude, not precise.*)

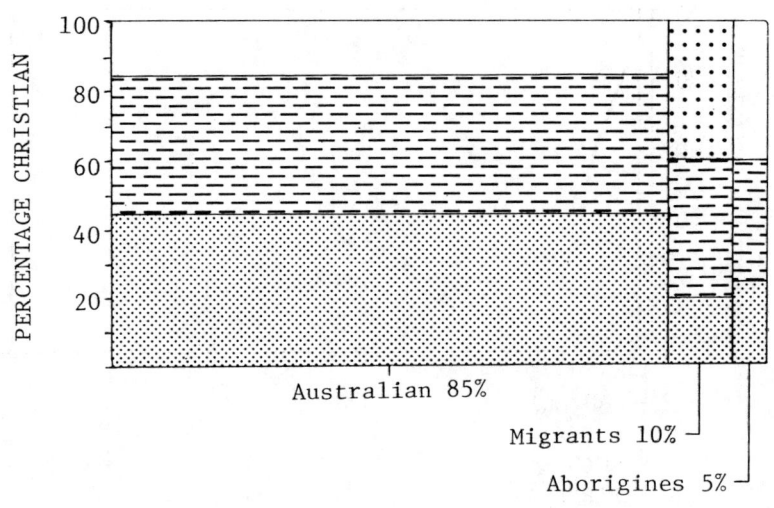

(NOTE: These figures are representative approximations. They should be seen as indications of magnitude, not precise.)

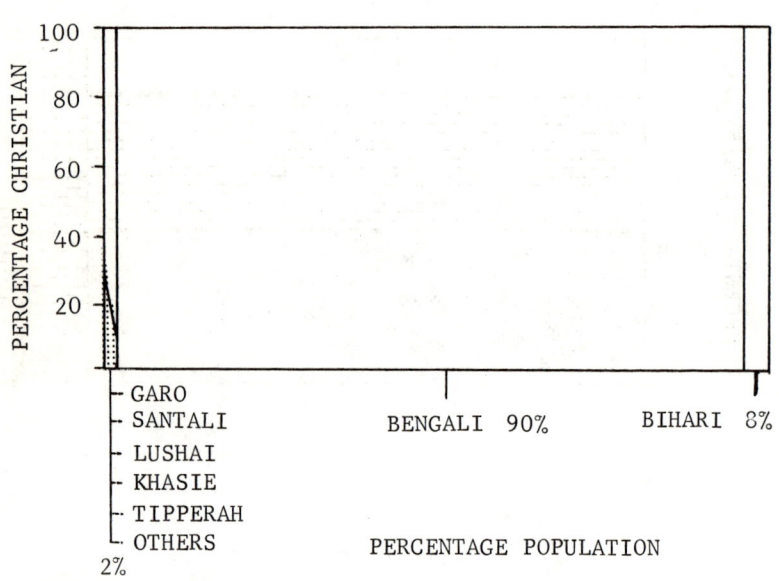

(Note: These figures are representative approximations. They should be seen as indications of magnitude, not precise.)

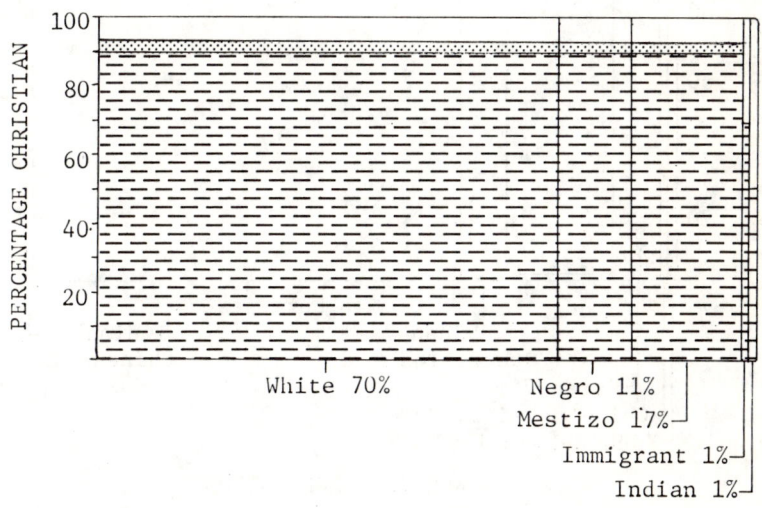

(NOTE: These figures are representative approximations. They should be seen as indications of magnitude, not precise.)

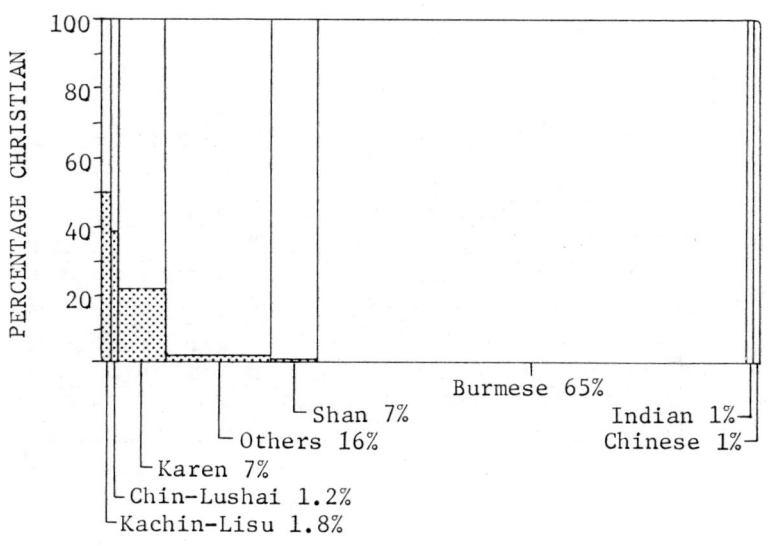

(NOTE: These figures are representative approximations. They should be seen as indications of magnitude, not precise.)

CAMBODIA

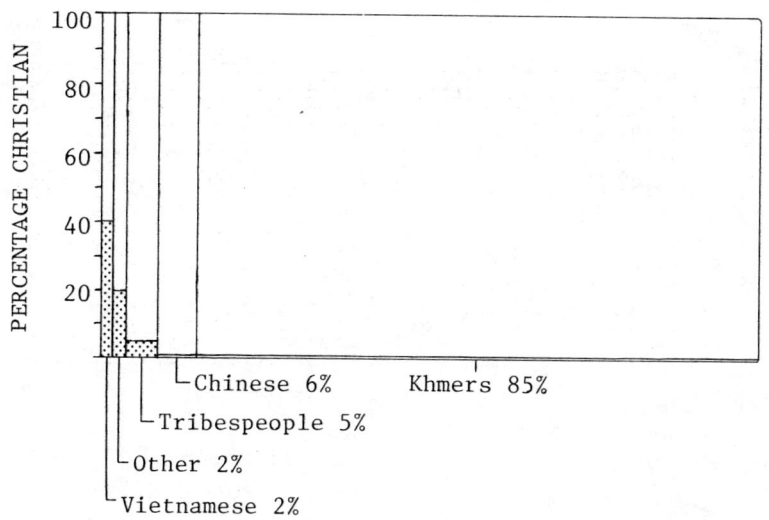

(NOTE: These figures are representative approximations. They should be seen as indications of magnitude, not precise.)

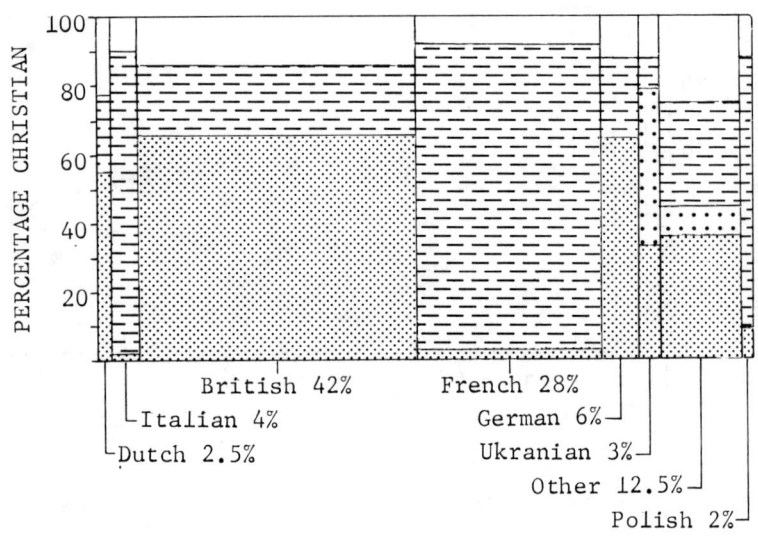

(NOTE: *These figures are representative approximations. They should be seen as indications of magnitudes, not precise.*)

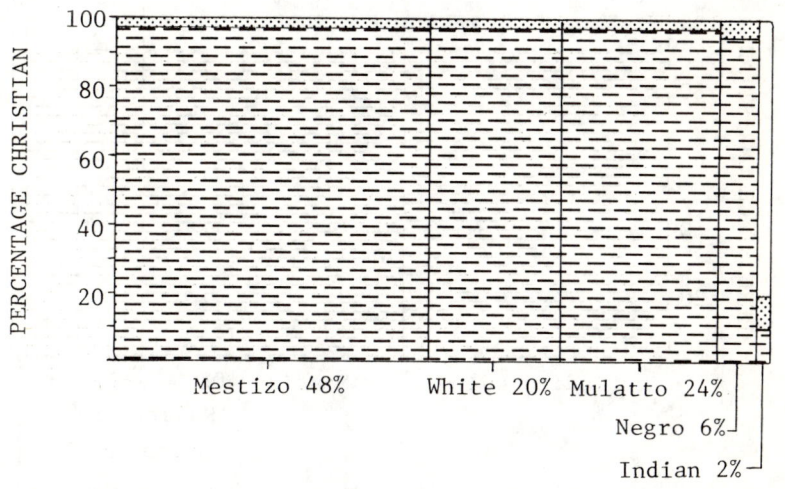

(NOTE: These figures are representative approximations. They should be seen as indications of magnitude, not precise.)

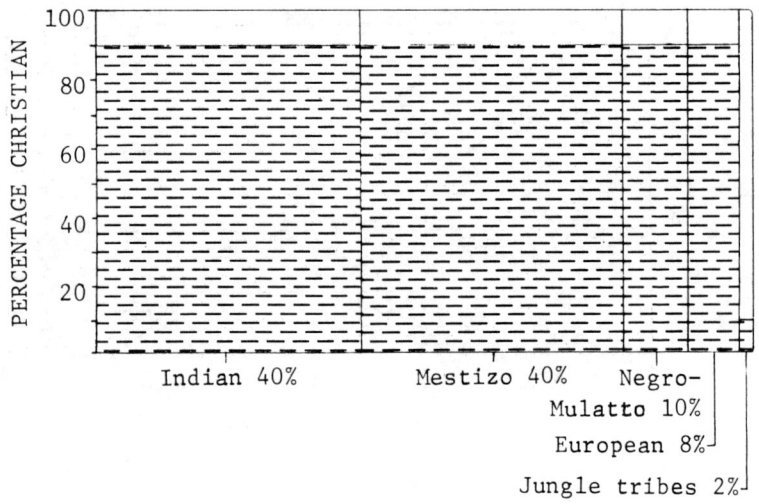

(NOTE: These figures are representative approximations. They should be seen as indications of magnitudes, not precise.)

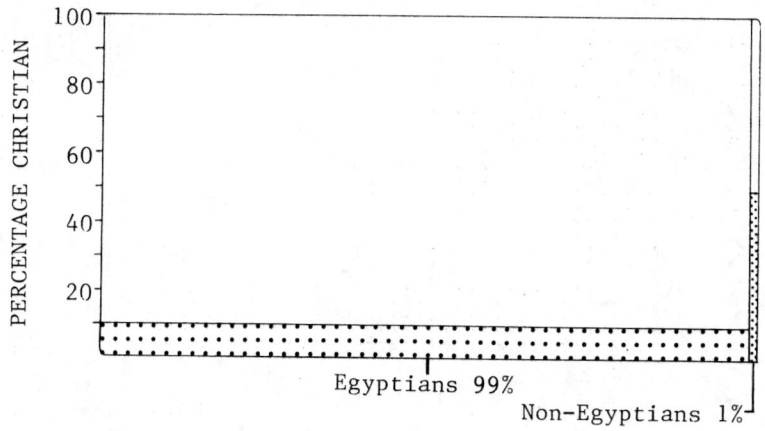

(NOTE: These figures are representative approximations. They should be seen as indications of magnitude, not precise.)

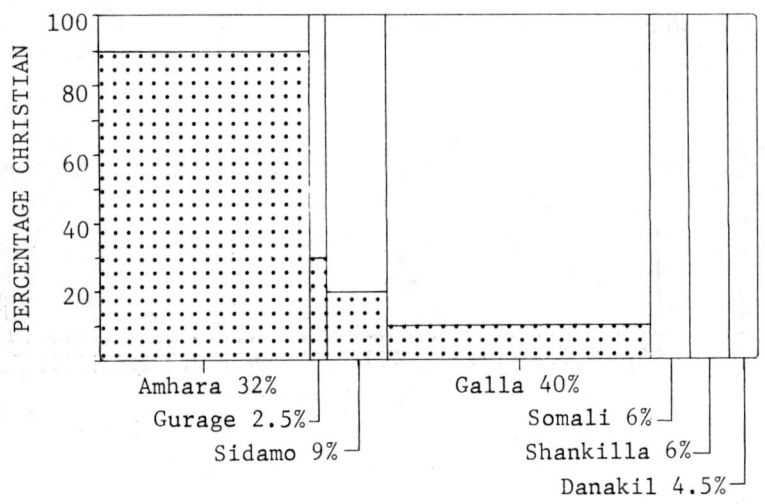

ETHIOPIA

PERCENTAGE POPULATION

(NOTE: These figures are representative approximations. They should be seen as indications of magnitude, not precise.)

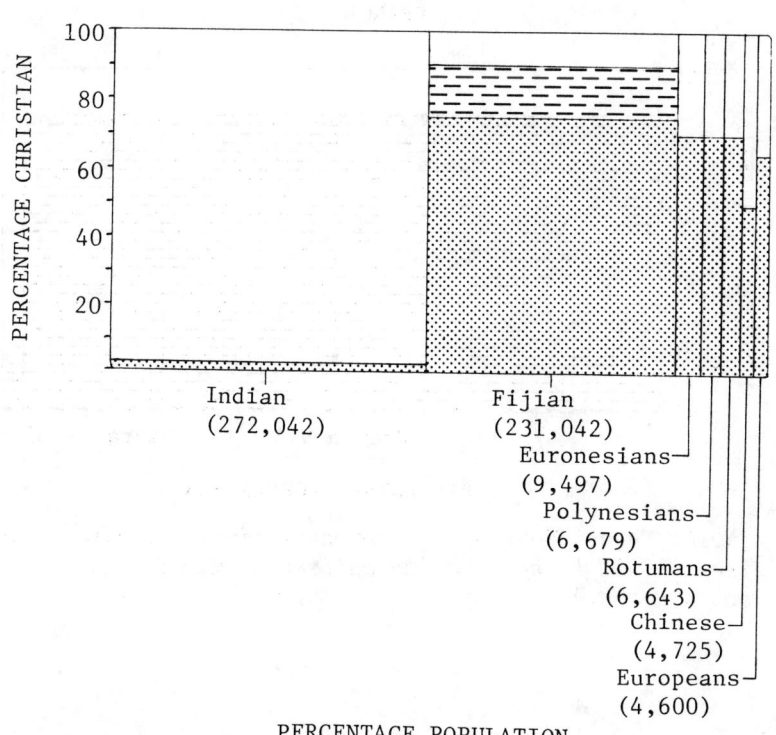

(NOTE: These figures are representative approximations. They should be seen as indications of magnitude, not precise.)

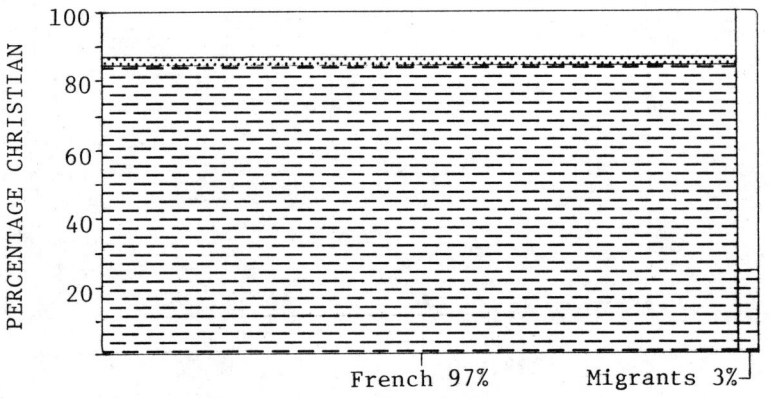

(NOTE: These figures are representative approximations. They should be seen as indications of magnitude, not precise.)

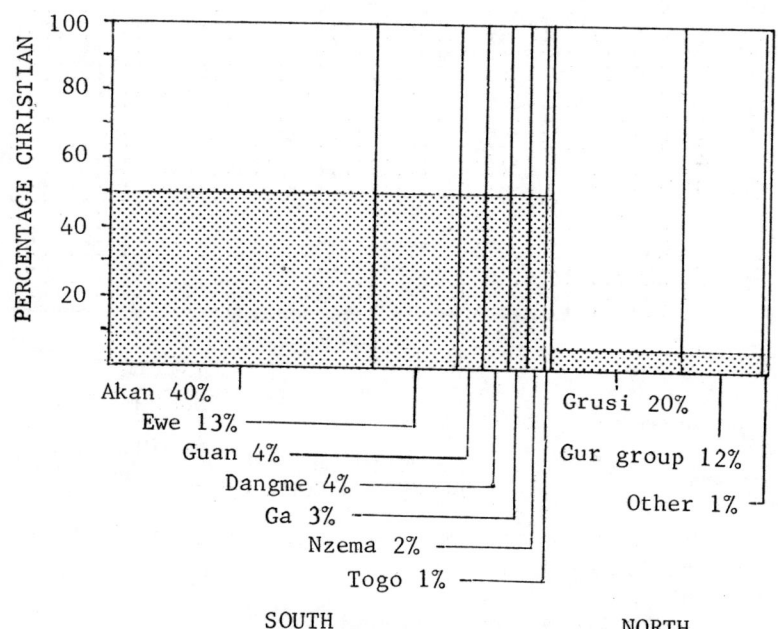

(Note: These figures are representative approximations. They should be seen as indications of magnitude, not precise.)

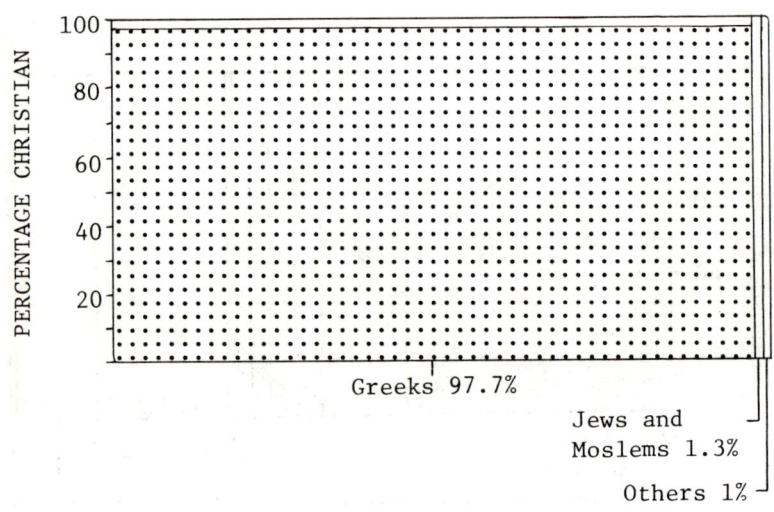

(NOTE: These figures are representative approximations. They should be seen as indications of magnitude, not precise.)

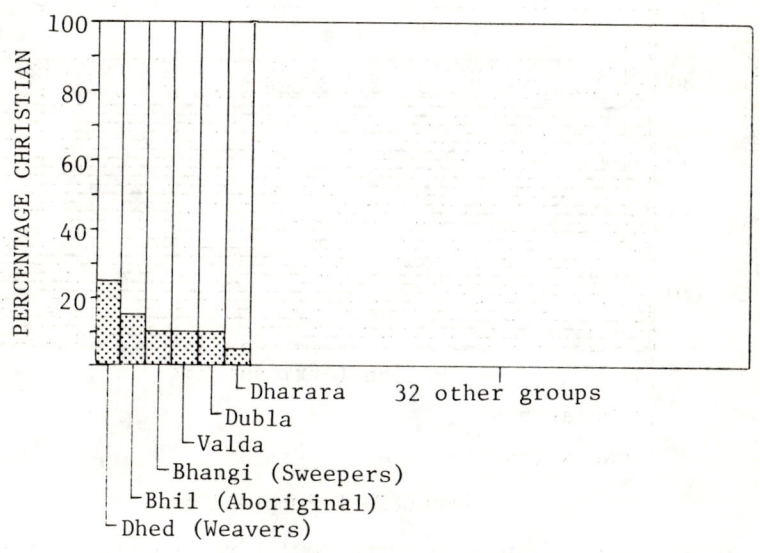

(NOTE: These figures are representative approximations. They should be seen as indications of magnitude, not precise.)

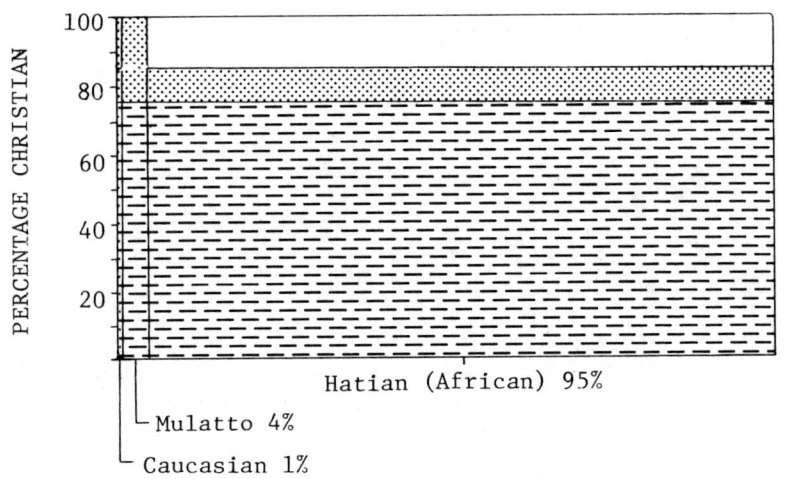

(NOTE: These figures are representative approximations. They should be seen as indications of magnitude, not precise.)

HONG KONG

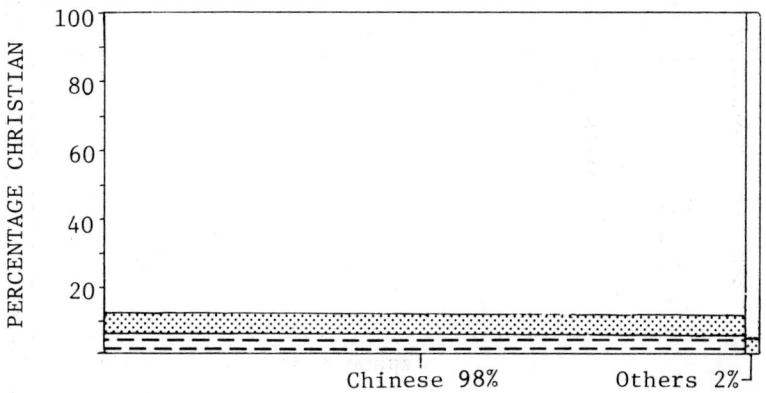

PERCENTAGE POPULATION

(NOTE: These figures are representative approximations. They should be seen as indications of magnitude, not precise.)

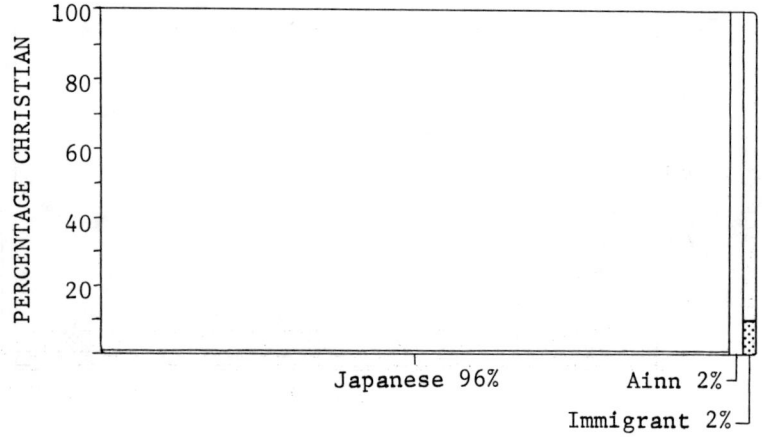

(NOTE: *These figures are representative approximations. They should be seen as indications of magnitudes, not precise.*)

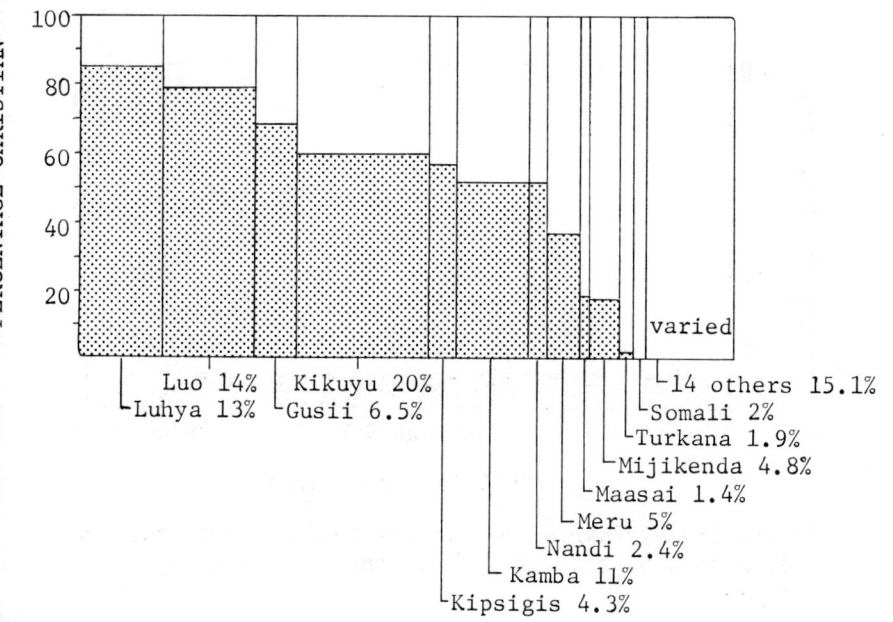

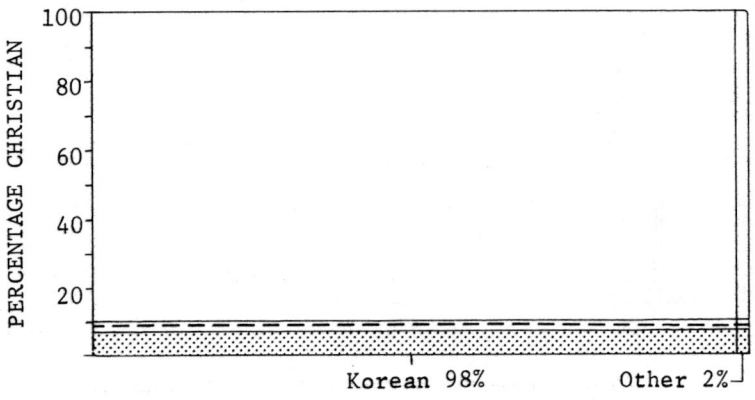

(NOTE: These figures are representative approximations. They should be seen as indications of magnitude, not precise.)

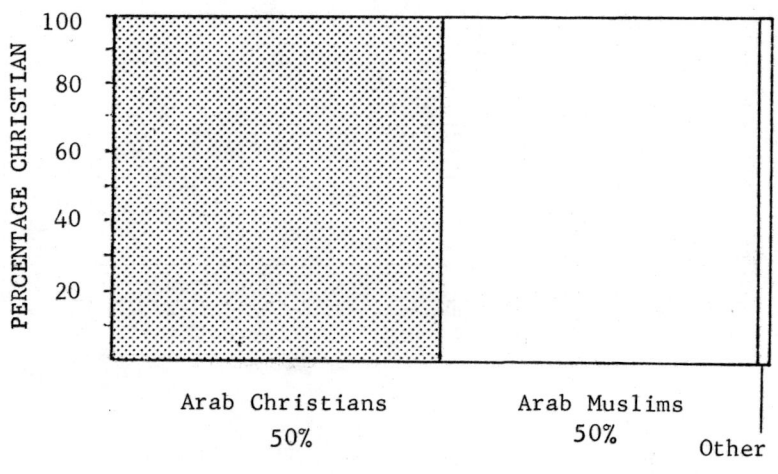

(NOTE: *These figures are representative approximations. They should be seen as indications of magnitude, not precise.*)

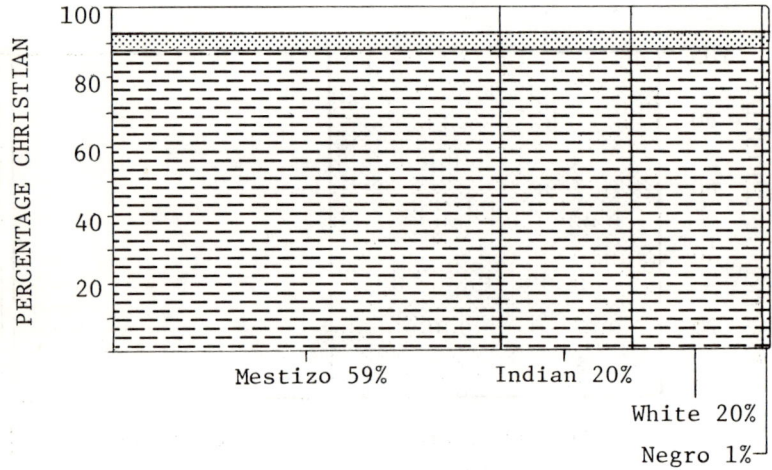

(NOTE: These figures are representative approximations. They should be seen as indications of magnitude, not precise.)

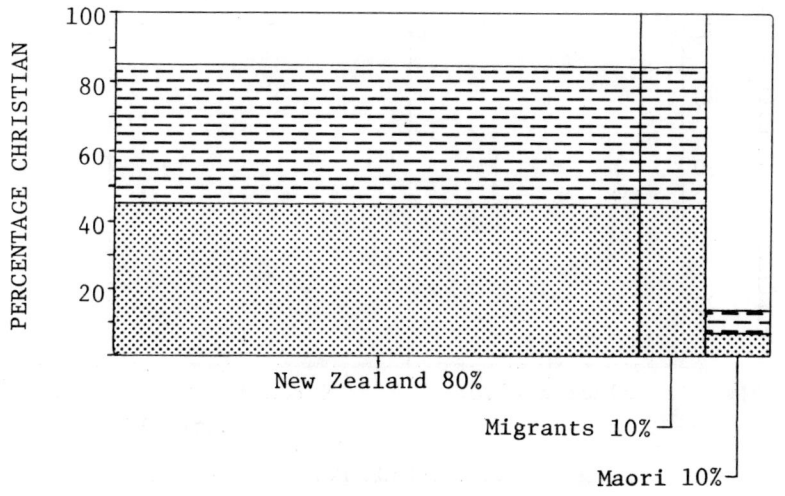

(NOTE: *These figures are representative approximations. They should be seen as indications of magnitude, not precise.*)

NORTH AFRICA

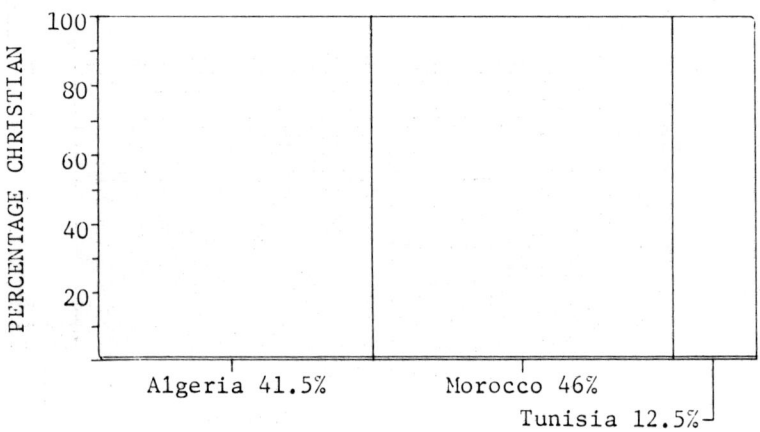

PERCENTAGE POPULATION

(NOTE: These figures are representative approximations. They should be seen as indications of magnitude, not precise.)

NORWAY

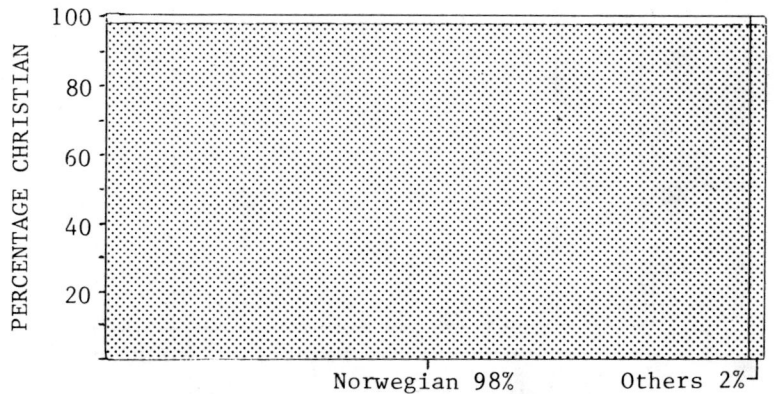

(NOTE: These figures are representative approximations.
They should be seen as indications of magnitude,
not precise.)

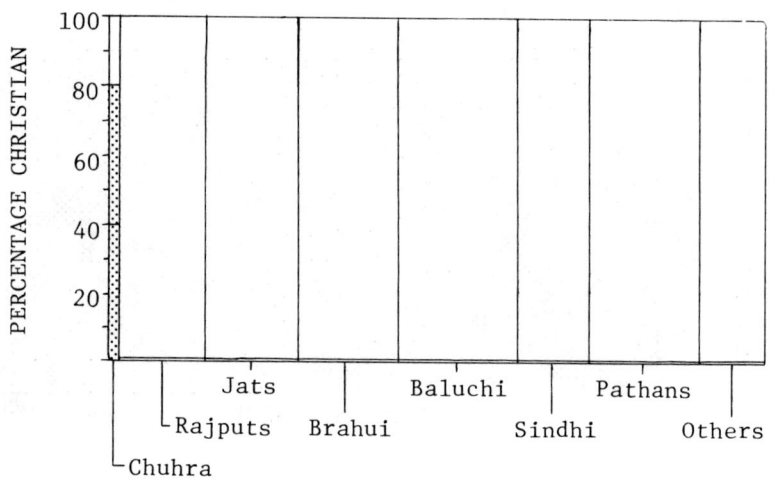

(NOTE: These figures are representative approximations. They should be seen as indications of magnitude, not precise.)

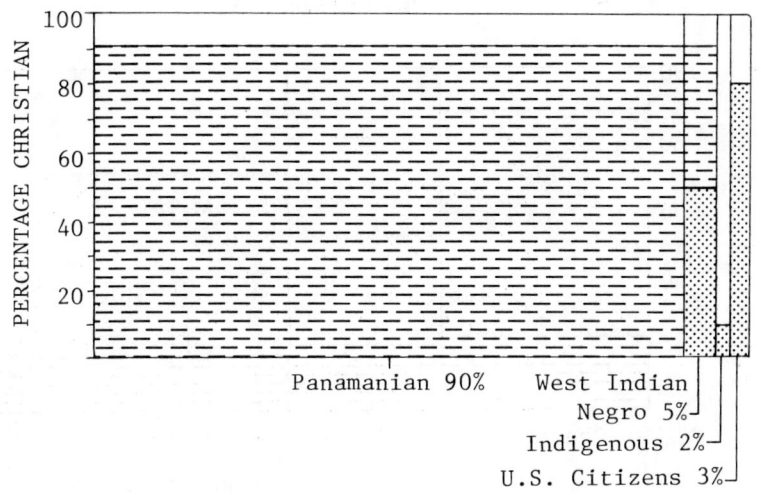

(NOTE: These figures are representative approximations. They should be seen as indications of magnitude, not precise.)

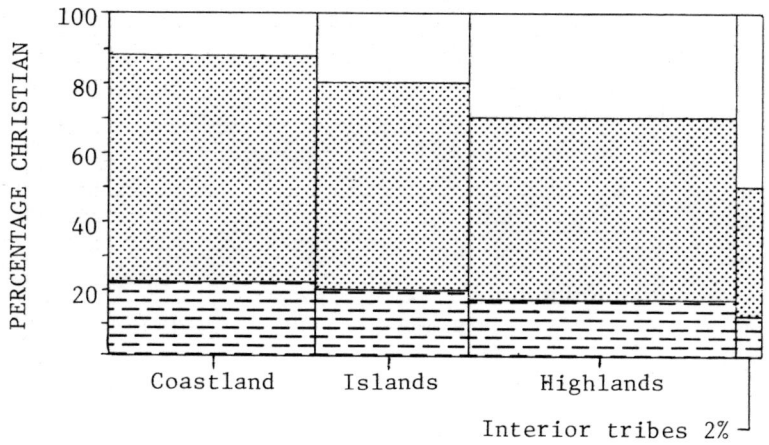

(NOTE: These figures are representative approximations. They should be seen as indications of magnitude, not precise.)

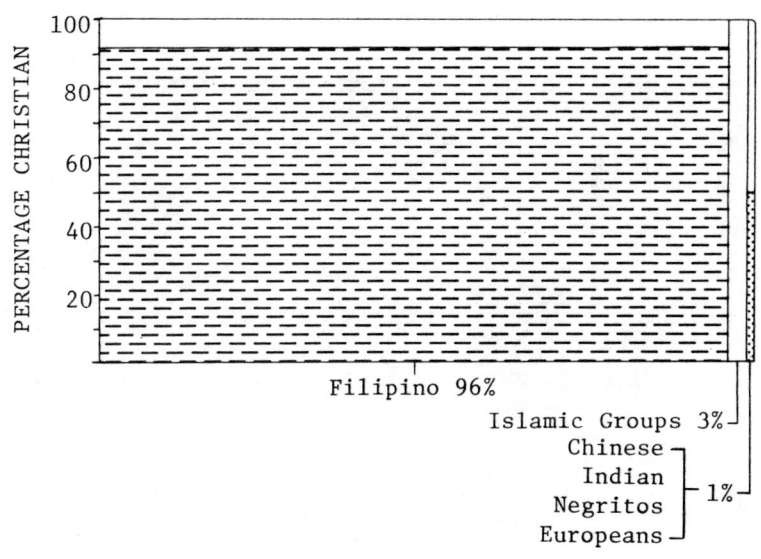

(NOTE: These figures are representative approximations. They should be seen as indications of magnitude, not precise.)

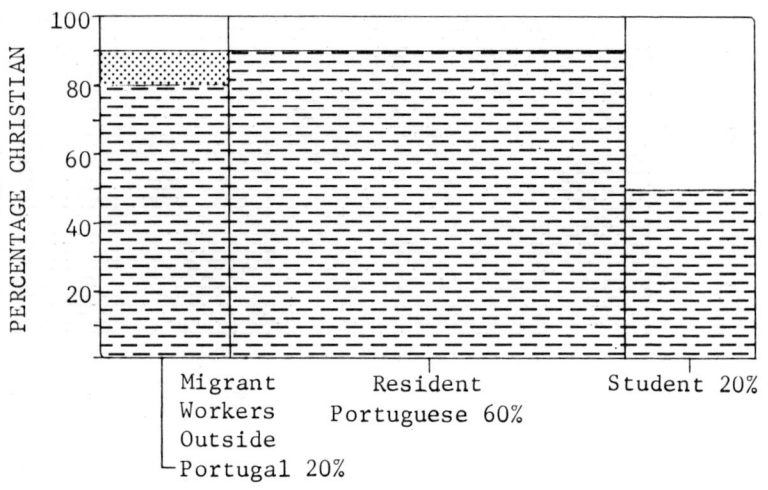

(NOTE: *These figures are representative approximations. They should be seen as indications of magnitude, not precise.*)

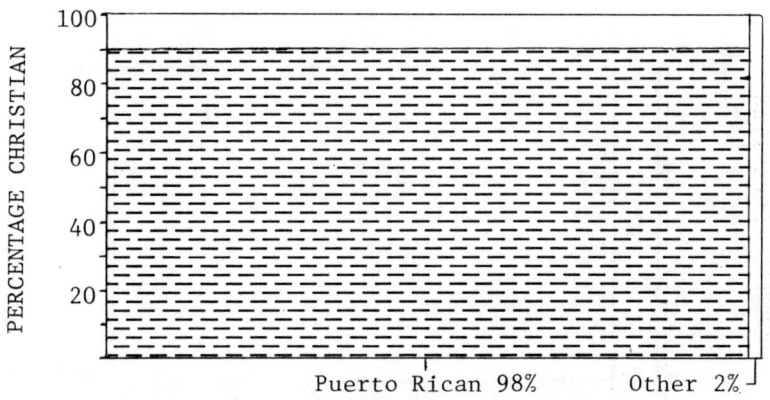

(NOTE: These figures are representative approximations. They should be seen as indications of magnitude, not precise.)

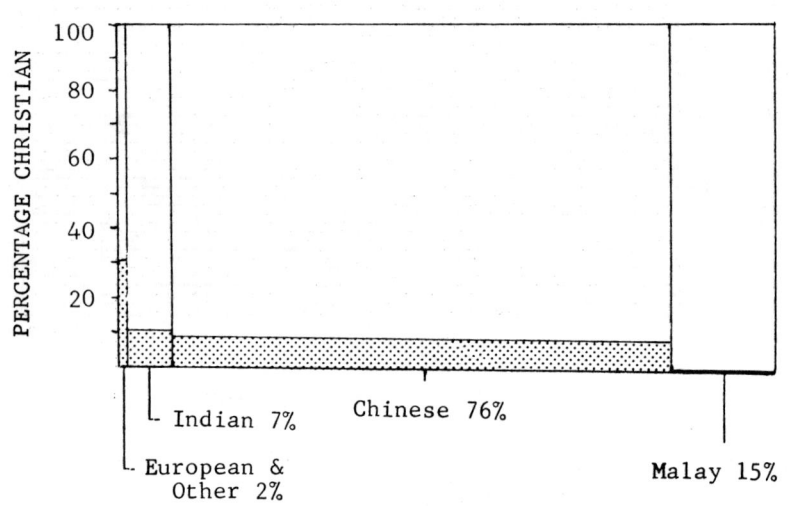

(NOTE: These figures are representative approximations. They should be seen as indications of magnitude, not precise.)

SOUTH AFRICA

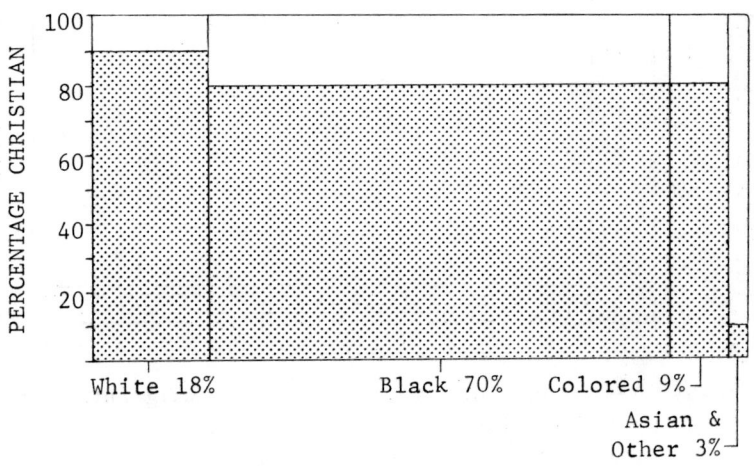

(NOTE: *These figures are representative approximations. They should be seen as indications of magnitude, not precise.*)

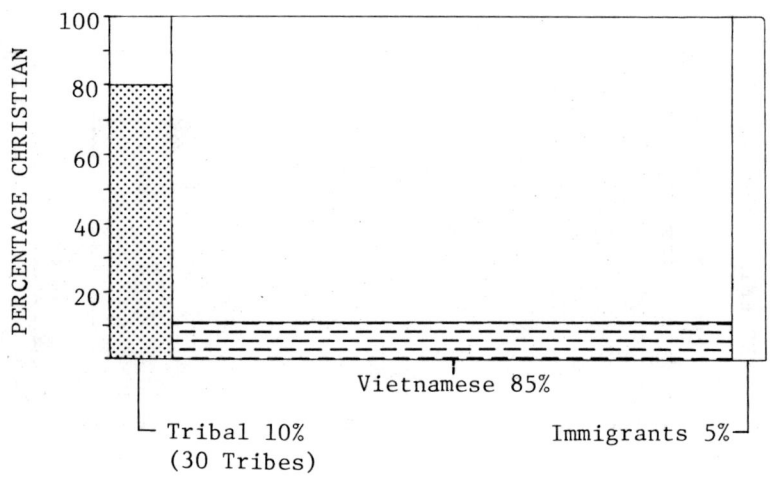

(NOTE: These figures are representative approximations. They should be seen as indications of magnitude, not precise.)

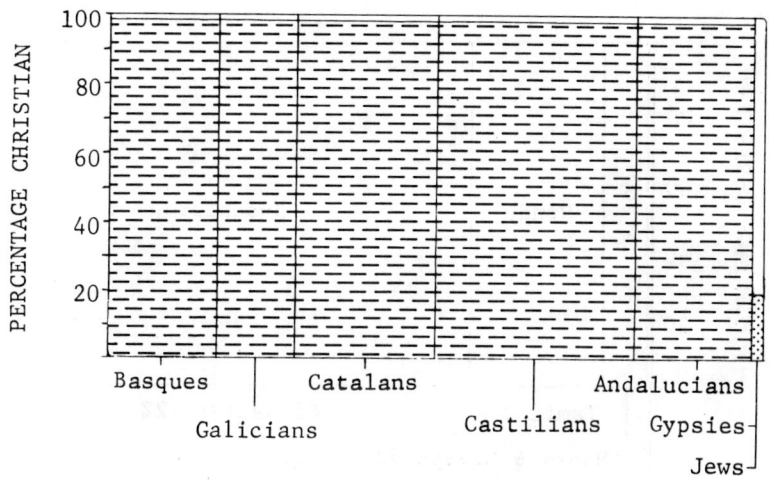

(NOTE: These figures are representative approximations. They should be seen as indications of magnitudes, not precise.)

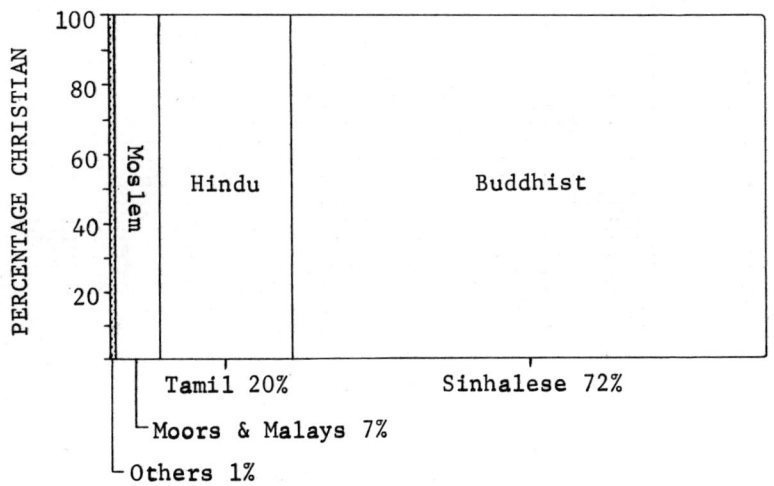

(NOTE: These figures are representative approximations. They should be seen as indications of magnitude, not precise.)

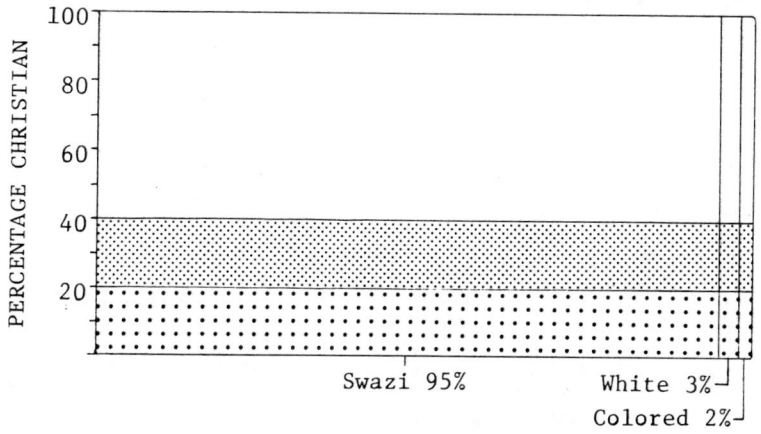

(NOTE: These figures are representative approximations. They should be seen as indications of magnitude, not precise.)

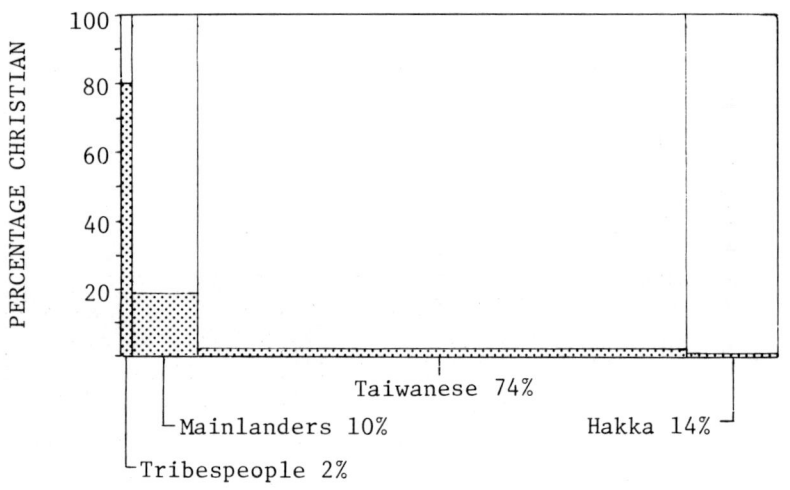

(NOTE: These figures are representative approximations. They should be seen as indications of magnitude, not precise.)

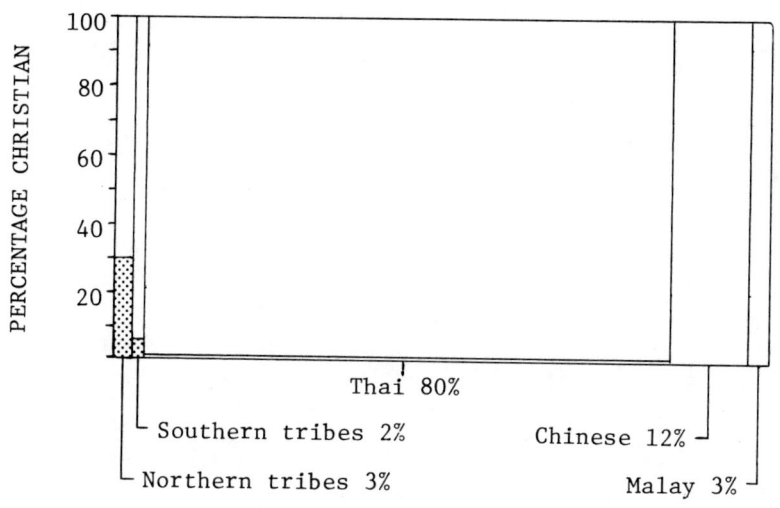

(NOTE: These figures are representative approximations. They should be seen as indications of magnitude, not precise.)

PART II

Section A of this division is a computerized print of the countries of the world, arranged according to size of population, with indication of the percentage of professing Christianity, sub-divided into Protestant, Roman Catholic and other Christian profession. These figures were compiled from various sources, and using different dates of information as available, which means an exact comparison as of any given date is not possible. The information is suggestive, not to be interpreted as authentic.

Section B is a reproduction of the questionnaire which served as a tool for gathering information, with an introductory list of identified unreached peoples, concerning which more information is available in the MARC DATABANK.

Section C is a complete STATUS OF CHRISTIANITY COUNTRY PROFILE of BURMA, as prepared for the INTERNATIONAL CONGRESS ON WORLD EVANGELIZATION, July 16-25, 1974. The complete list of available profiles follows.

Section D is a sampling of the individual people SUMMARY PROFILES, which are available on an increasing number of peoples, as information is made available and incorporated into the DATABANK.

Section E is a sample of the EMPIRICAL DATA which was gathered and used as the working basis for Chapter 8, dealing with PRAGMATICS.

For more information on the aforementioned, please write to:

    MISSIONS ADVANCED RESEARCH AND COMMUNICATIONS CENTER
        919 W. Huntington Drive,
        Monrovia, California
        91016

CODE	COUNTRY	POPULATION	% CHRSTN	PROTESTANT POPULATION	ROMAN CATH POPULATION	OTHER CHRSTN POPULATION
15804	CEYLON-SEE SRI LANKA					
19801	CONGO, D.R. - SEE ZAIRE					
71404	RYUKYU IS. - SEE JAPAN					
63206	NORFOLK I.	1				
93805	VATICAN (HOLY SEE)	1*	99			
95206	WAKE I.	1*				
84606	TOKELAU IS.	2*				
62805	NIUE I.	5*				
71801	ST. HELENA	5*	99			
73202	ST. PIERRE + MIQUELON	5*	99			5 69
57205	NAURU	6*				
87202	TURKS + CAICOS IS.	6*				
11002	BRITISH VIRGIN IS.	9*				
15002	CAYMAN IS.	9*				
95006	WALLIS + FUTUNA IS.	9*	99			9 69
55902	MONTSERRAT	14*				
76005	SAN MARINO	18*	99			18 69
20206	COOK IS.	20*				2 69
48205	LIECHTENSTEIN	20*	98			
03005	ANDORRA	21*	99			
54205	MONACO	24*	99		24 69	
32405	GIBRALTAR	25*	95+		23 69	
80401	SPANISH SAHARA	27*	20			
02606	AMERICAN SAMOA	28*	90			
33602	GREENLAND	43*	92		(50) 70	
27603	FRENCH GUIANA	45*	87	(500) 66	40 69	
07002	BERMUDA	54*	51	22 66	8 69	
32805	GILBERT + ELLICE IS.	55*	45+		25 69	
65202	PANAMA CANAL ZONE	56*				
75601	SEYCHELLES	57	98	4 72	51 72	
72402	ST. KITTS-NEVIS-ANGU.	57*				
74401	SAO TOME + PRINCIPE	60*	95			
03802	ANTIGUA	64*	NA			
23002	DOMINICA	70*				
85006	TONGA	70*	86	54 71	13 70	
92602	U.S. VIRGIN IS.	80	79		19 69	
60206	NEW HEBRIDES	84*			12 69	
34806	GUAM	85	50+			
59406	NEW CALEDONIA	87*	73+		54 69	
73602	ST. VINCENT	91*				
28006	FRENCH POLYNESIA	98*	55±		29 69	
34002	GRENADA	99*				
64006	PACIFIC IS. TRUST TERR.	99*	27			
69804	QATAR	100	-1			
50804	MALDIVE IS.	104	-1			
72802	ST. LUCIA	113*				
09802	BELIZE	122*	87	34 66	64 66	
67206	PITCAIRN I.	(124)*	45			
28801	F.T. OF AFARS + ISSAS	125*	10	5 66	10 69	
96006	WESTERN SAMOA	132*	95+			
11404	BRUNEI	136*				
10606	BRITISH SOLOMON IS.	146*				
05402	BAHAMAS	169*	80	88 66	27 66	
05804	BAHRAIN	200	-1			
38405	ICELAND	200	91	179 66	1 69	
76404	SIKKIM	200				
88204	UNITED ARAB EMIRATES	200	-1			
58402	NETHERLANDS ANTILLES	212*	47		150 69	
06202	BARBADOS	300	98	262 70		

CODE	COUNTRY	POPULATION	% CHRSTN	PROTESTANT POPULATION	ROMAN CATH POPULATION	OTHER CHRSTN POPULATION
14601	CAPE VERDE IS.	300	99		238 69	
24601	EQUATORIAL GUINEA	300	91		221 69	
49004	MACAO	300	15+		37 68	
51605	MALTA	300*	99		310 69	
46602	LEEWARD IS.	324*				
29601	GAMBIA	400	5	6 66	7 69	
34402	GUADELOUPE	400	75+		300 68	
48605	LUXEMBOURG	400	94	6 66	315 69	
52002	MARTINIQUE	400*	95		300 68	
81403	SURINAM	400	36-47	64 66	71 69	
82201	SWAZILAND	400	83		32 69	
29201	GABON	500	96	80 66	241 68	
70201	REUNION	500	95		408 69	
21404	CYPRUS	600	77	1 70	6 70	453 70
26406	FIJI	600	50		43 69	
68601	PORTUGUESE GUINEA	600	9		29 69	
69004	PORTUGUESE TIMOR	600	23+		131 69	
09601	BOTSWANA	700	62	101 66	10 69	
58801	NAMIBIA (S-W AFRICA)	700	84		84 69	
63804	OMAN (INCLUDES MUSCAT)	700	-1			
36003	GUYANA	800	92		104 69	
45604	KUWAIT	800	3		16 69	
07404	BHUTAN	900	-1	(400) 72		
52801	MAURITIUS	900	35	12 66	275 69	H
19401	CONGO (BRAZZAVILLE)	1,000	98	148 66	320 66	
46801	LESOTHO	1,100	87	244 65	365 69	M
8540	TRINIDAD + TOBAGO	1,100	71-76	375 66	300 69	
47201	LIBERIA	1,200	42	120 66	20 69	
52401	MAURITANIA	1,200	-1		6 69	
54604	MONGOLIA	1,400	-1			
96604	YEMEN, DEMOCRATIC	1,400	-1			
15401	CENTRAL AFRICAN REP.	1,600*	90	145 66	213 69	
64802	PANAMA	1,600	86		1,229 69	
20602	COSTA RICA	1,900	81	9 66	1,521 69	
47601	LIBYA	2,000	2	3 66	42 69	
84201	TOGO	2,000	30		319 69	
42802	JAMAICA	2,100	47-57	755 66	154 69	
61002	NICARAGUA	2,200	79		1,698 69	
76804	SINGAPORE	2,200	6-8	25 70	80 70	
01805	ALBANIA	2,300	34		242 69	506 69 B
65606	PAPUA/NEW GUINEA	2,476*	30+		550 59	
44004	JORDAN	2,500	10	7 70	68 70	117 70 G
66003	PARAGUAY	2,600	86	19 66	2,006 69	
22201	DAHOMEY	2,800	20	34 66	374 69	
76001	SIERRA LEONE	2,800	11		29 69	
37202	HONDURAS	2,900	88	57 66	1,500 56	
69402	PUERTO RICO	2,900	93		2,576 69	
77201	SOMALIA	2,900	-1		5 69	
41205	IRELAND	3,000	99		2,673 69	
41604	ISRAEL	3,000	1-5	3 69	12 69	11 69
46404	LEBANON	3,000	59	27 71	652 71	358 71
60606	NEW ZEALAND	3,000	80	1,837 66	369 69	
93603	URUGUAY	3,000	82	40 66	2,250 69	
46004	LAOS	3,100	2	5 68	32 69	
24202	EL SALVADOR	3,700	86	75 66	3,063 69	
12601	BURUNDI	3,800	76	226 66	1,872 69	
71001	RWANDA	3,800	69		822 69	
16201	CHAD	3,900	47	94 67	132 69	
63605	NORWAY	4,000	96		9 69	

CODE	COUNTRY	POPULATION	% CHRSTN	PROTESTANT POPULATION		ROMAN CATH POPULATION		OTHER CHRSTN POPULATION		
35601	GUINEA	4,100	-1	2	66	30	70			
61401	NIGER	4,100	-1			13	69			
75201	SENEGAL	4,100	6			154	69			
37604	HONG KONG	4,400	11-12	206	70	260	73			
42401	IVORY COAST	4,500	25	97	66	484	69			
23402	DOMINICAN REPUBLIC	4,600	87	77	66	3,623	69			
97201	ZAMBIA	4,600	45	810	72	1,375	72			
49801	MALAWI	4,700	53	1,314	72	1,173	72			
26805	FINLAND	4,800	95	4,412	66	3	69			
07803	BOLIVIA	4,900	97	67	66	3,992	69			
22605	DENMARK	5,000	95	4,570	66	26	69			
51201	MALI	5,300	1	7	66	38	69			
35202	GUATEMALA	5,400	93	131	66	4,137	68			
78201	SOUTHERN RHODESIA	5,400	54			525	70			M
86201	TUNISIA	5,400	1			35	69			
36402	HAITI	5,500	75-85	500	69	2,949	68			
93201	UPPER VOLTA	5,600	9	88	68	400	72			
03401	ANGOLA	5,900	83	800	66	2,309	69			
13401	CAMEROON	6,000	52	702	66	950	66			
96404	YEMEN	6,100	-1							
83005	SWITZERLAND	6,400	95	2,990	70	3,100	70			
23803	ECUADOR	6,500	80	19	66	5,016	69			
83404	SYRIA	6,600	10	18	71	141	71	432	71	J
49401	MADAGASCAR (MALAGASY)	7,300	42	1,113	66	1,407	69			
05005	AUSTRIA	7,500*	95	498	66	6,612	68			
13004	CAMBODIA (KHMER REP.)	7,600	-1	4	73	21	73			
56001	MOZAMBIQUE	8,100	34			1,267	69			
74804	SAUDI ARABIA	8,200	-1							
82605	SWEDEN	8,200	97			49	69			
11805	BULGARIA	8,700	85	34	69			7,400	69	B
21002	CUBA	8,700	80	296	66	5,911	68			
33205	GREECE	9,000	98	15	73	46	69	8,800	71	
32001	GHANA	9,600	63	687	66	940	69			M
68005	PORTUGAL	9,700	96	33	66	9,132	69			
06605	BELGIUM	9,800	92	53	66	8,856	68			
16603	CHILE	10,200	90	881	66	7,375	69			
87601	UGANDA	10,332	71	3,202	72	4,132	72			
38005	HUNGARY	10,400	96	26,100	69	6,870	69	2,500	69	B
40804	IRAQ	10,400	4	2	72	221	72	72	72	F
50204	MALAYSIA	11,400	4-5	97	66	220	68			
94003	VENEZUELA	11,500	84	52	66	8,194	69			
57604	NEPAL	11,800	-1							
44401	KENYA	12,091	66	4,606	72	3,397	72	100	70	M
04606	AUSTRALIA	13,000	87	7,550	70	2,800	69	260	69	
80604	SRI LANKA (CEYLON)	13,200	7			829	69			
58005	NETHERLANDS	13,300	75			5,142	69			
83501	TANZANIA	14,002	45	1,960	72	4,340	72			
65403	PERU	14,500	86	128	66	11,783	69			
17404	CHINA (TAIWAN)	14,700	5	168	71	304	69			
44804	KOREA, NORTH	14,700	-1							
21805	CZECHOSLOVAKIA	14,900	70	1,947	66	8,600	69			
02201	ALGERIA	15,000				71	69			
30405	GERMANY, DEM. REP.	16,300	95			1,453	69			B
55401	MOROCCO	16,800	1			235	68			
81001	SUDAN	16,800	16	258	71	420	71	37	71	
01404	AFGHANISTAN	17,900	-1							A
97001	ZAIRE	18,300	86			7,688	69			M
94804	VIETNAM, REP. OF	18,700	11	131	70	1,800	69			
70605	RUMANIA	20,800	94	1,209	66	1,140	69	14,000	66	

CODE	COUNTRY	POPULATION	% CHRSTN	PROTESTANT POPULATION	ROMAN CATH POPULATION	OTHER CHRSTN POPULATION	
96805	YUGOSLAVIA	21,000	72	156 66	6,315 69	8,200 66	
77801	SOUTH AFRICA	21,100	83	6,414 69	1,348 69	3,000 69	M
94404	VIETNAM, NORTH	22,000	4	10 73	1,000 73		
13802	CANADA	22,200	56-81	3,114 70	8,760 70	394 70	
18603	COLOMBIA	22,900	95	254 68	20,126 69		
04203	ARGENTINA	25,000	97	634 69	21,900 69	100 70	L
25001	ETHIOPIA	26,200	51	260 69	134 69	8,027 69	D
12204	BURMA	29,100	4	635 70	250 70		
40404	IRAN	30,200	1	8 70	22 70	154 70	
45204	KOREA, REPUBLIC OF	33,700	10	2,250 71	789 70	(200) 70	
67605	POLAND	33,700	94	464 66	30,641 59		
79205	SPAIN	33,900	97		31,637 69		
24001	EGYPT (U.A.R.)	35,900	12	131 69	122 69	4,017 69	K
86604	TURKEY	37,600	-1	(2600) 69	21 69	137 69	
83804	THAILAND	38,600	-1		140 69		
66804	PHILIPPINES	40,800	88-95	1,300 69	32,460 69	2,050 69	
27205	FRANCE	51,900	83	1,000 69	42,745 69		
53402	MEXICO	54,300	85-90	702 69	39,542 59		
42005	ITALY	54,500	98	100 68	53,025 69		
90005	UNITED KINGDOM	56,600	71		5,036 69		
61801	NIGERIA	58,000	45	2,182 69	2,400 68		M
30805	GERMANY, FED. REP.	59,200	97	29,438 70	27,500 70	20 70	F
64404	PAKISTAN	67,000	1.5				
06004	BANGLADESH	75,000*	-1	90 70	110 70		
09003	BRAZIL	98,400	97	10,000 71	78,283 68	300 70	L
43204	JAPAN	107,000	-1	427 69	343 69	40 70	
39804	INDONESIA	128,700	7-10	6,500 69	2,000 67		
91602	UNITED STATES	209,200	63-91	69,000 71	48,215 71	3,800 71	
88006	USSR (SOVIET UNION)	248,000	24	6,700 69	3,200 69	50,000 69	O
39204	INDIA	584,800	2-3	5,000 69	7,857 69	1,500 69	
17004	CHINA, PEOPLE'S REP.	786,100	-1				C

Unreached Peoples Survey Questionnaire

PURPOSE: The purpose of this questionnaire is to gather information on the unreached/unevangelized peoples of the world which can ultimately lead to their evangelization. This information is to be used at the International Congress on World Evangelization (ICOWE).

PROCEDURES: The ICOWE Research Committee will gather information from all possible sources on unreached/unevangelized peoples. This information will then be compiled into an Unreached Peoples File. The compilation of data will be made available in report form and will further be computer compiled for continuous up-date. It will become the basis for much of the ICOWE discussion.

DEFINITIONS: <u>Homogeneous unit</u> (people or group): A recognizable segment of society having some characteristic(s) in common. The uniting element(s) may be linguistic, ethnic, geographic, socio-economic, political, religious, or any other. Some examples are: *tribal* - Hausa of Nigeria, Auca of Ecuador; *sociological* - university students of Paris, industrial workers of Tokyo, coal miners of West Virginia; *ethnic* - Japanese in Sao Paulo, Brazil.

<u>Unreached/unevangelized</u> people: Those homogeneous units which have not received or responded to the Gospel. This unresponsiveness may be due to lack of opportunity, lack of understanding, or because they have not received sufficient information about the Gospel message within their own language, cultural frame of reference and communication channels to make Christianity a viable option.

For the purpose of this questionnaire, and for the International Congress on World Evangelization for which this initial study is made, we consider that a people is unreached/unevangelized when less than 20% are professing Christians. This assumes that a people has a minority group attitude until that people reaches 15 to 20% of the population. At that point it may move into a recognition of its own self-identity.

INSTRUCTIONS: Please fill in one questionnaire for each homogeneous unit in each country. If the data about a given unit in one country is similar to that of the same unit in another country or area, simply indicate so by responding: "Same as in country XXXXXXXX" and do not take time to fill in all of the details of the additional questionnaire. However if the details are different, then consider the group as a separate homogeneous unit and proceed to give the pertinent information.

Please be assured that we appreciate your answering what you can. It may be that you can give some information and another person may be able to give other. We appreciate your doing what you can.

When you have completed the questionnaire please return to:

        RESEARCH COORDINATOR, ICOWE
        919 West Huntington Drive
        Monrovia, California 91016
        U. S. A.

Select the homogeneous unit to be covered in this questionnaire, and give the following:

1. _____ 2. _____ 3. _____
   Name of unit (people or group)   Population of unit   Country covered by questionnaire

   4. _____ 5. _____
      Population of country   % of population of country

Questionnaire completed by: _____ Date: _____

Organization: _____

Title: _____

Address: _____

_____

_____

(INSTRUCTIONS: If you know further details for this same homogeneous unit in other locations than the one being covered, please mark with "X" ( ) and supply on a separate questionnaire. If you don't know the answer to any question, please leave it blank and go on to the next. An answer to every question is not expected.)

IDENTIFICATION

---

6. Other name(s) by which unit is known:

---

7. What term can best describe the basis for classification of this homogeneous unit? *(Mark only one if possible)*
   ( ) Family   ( ) Racial   ( ) Social class   ( ) Political
   ( ) Tribe   ( ) Linguistic   ( ) Economic class   ( ) Religious
   ( ) Clan   ( ) Geographic   ( ) Occupational group ( ) Other: _____

---

8. In what other ways could you best describe or classify the unit? *(Mark all those that apply)*

URBAN	RURAL	SOCIAL	INCOME
( ) Industrial	( ) Nomadic	( ) Upper class	( ) Upper
( ) Commercial	( ) Semi-nomadic	( ) Upper middle	( ) Upper middle
( ) Professional	( ) Stationary	( ) Middle class	( ) Middle
( ) Student	( ) Agricultural	( ) Lower middle	( ) Lower middle
( ) Other:	( ) Other:	( ) Lower class	( ) Lower

---

9. Is there any other way in which you could classify this homogeneous unit?

---

10. In what other locations is the same unit found, and give the following:

Location	Population of unit in that location	% of population of that location

    a. Source of information: *(For example: census, special studies, etc.)*

    b. How accurate is the information? *(Mark one)*   ( ) High degree   ( ) Fair degree   ( ) Estimate

---

11. Indicate the nature of the geographic distribution of this homogeneous unit within the area being covered:
    (Mark all that apply)   ( ) Rural   ( ) Urban   ( ) Disbursed   ( ) Concentrated.

---

12. Indicate the physical accessibility of this homogeneous unit within the area being covered:
    (Mark one)   ( ) Isolated   ( ) Semi-isolated   ( ) Easily accessible

---

13. Is this unit accessible by: ( ) Trail   ( ) Rail   ( ) Sea
    (Mark all that apply)   ( ) Road   ( ) River ( ) Air

---

14. What communication media are present?   ( ) Postal ( ) Radio ( ) Television ( ) None
    (Mark all that apply)

---

15. What is happening to the size of this homogeneous unit in this country?
    (Mark one)   ( ) Growing   ( ) Stable   ( ) Declining   ( ) Uncertain   ( ) Don't know

---

16. Is this homogeneous unit: ( ) Stable   ( ) Migrating   ( ) Adopting new patterns
    (Mark all that apply)   ( ) Restless   ( ) Resisting change ( ) Other·

---

17. Do members of this homogeneous unit intermarry with other peoples outside of the unit?
    ( ) Yes   ( ) No   ( ) Don't know
    If "yes", are these mixed blood individuals accepted by: ( ) This unit   ( ) Another unit

---

18. Is this unit part of a distinct larger unit?   ( ) Yes   ( ) No   ( ) Don't know
    If "yes", please give name of larger unit:

19. If this unit is a sub-group of a larger one, please give a general description of the larger unit:
    (For example: *social context, ethnic relationship, character, etc.*)

LANGUAGE AND LITERACY

20. What is the common name for the principal (vernacular) language spoken by this unit? _____
    By what other name(s) is this language known? _____ or _____ ( ) None

21. Is there a <u>lingua franca</u> (trade language) used by this unit? ( ) Yes ( ) No ( ) Don't know
    If "yes", name:

22. About what percent of the group members speak other languages, that is, are bi-lingual or multi-lingual?
    _____ _____ _____ _____
    (Language)   (%)   (Language)   (%)

23. About what percent of the group members 15 years of age or older can read and write at least one of the commonly used languages? _____ %

24. What is happening to this literacy rate? ( ) Increasing ( ) No change ( ) Decreasing ( ) Don't know

25. If there are Christians in this homogeneous unit, about what percent of them can read and write? _____ %

RELIGIOUS AFFILIATION

26. What is the predominant religion of this unit in the location being described? _____

27. About what percent of the unit claim this religion? _____ %
    What is the trend of this religion? ( ) Growing ( ) Stationary ( ) Declining ( ) Don't know

28. What religions are practiced among this homogeneous unit? Are they growing or declining?
    a. *(Give all that apply)*   b. *(Mark one for each religion)*

	Percentage of Unit population	Rapid Decline	Slow Decline	Station-ary	Slow Growth	Rapid Growth
Christians (All traditions)	____ %	( )	( )	( )	( )	( )
Animistic, Spirit worship	____ %	( )	( )	( )	( )	( )
Buddhists	____ %	( )	( )	( )	( )	( )
Confucianists	____ %	( )	( )	( )	( )	( )
Hindus	____ %	( )	( )	( )	( )	( )
Jews	____ %	( )	( )	( )	( )	( )
Moslems	____ %	( )	( )	( )	( )	( )
Secularists	____ %	( )	( )	( )	( )	( )
Taoists	____ %	( )	( )	( )	( )	( )
Other: _____	____ %	( )	( )	( )	( )	( )
Other: _____	____ %	( )	( )	( )	( )	( )
	100					

29. Of the Christians, estimate the percentage in each tradition.
    Protestant: _____ %   Roman Catholic: _____ %   Eastern Orthodox: _____ %
    Other(s): _____ _____ % _____ _____ %
              (Name)   (Name)

30. Are there any indigenous or independent Christian churches with members from this unit, founded and led by nationals with no outside support?
    ( ) Yes ( ) No ( ) Don't know. If "yes", please give information concerning.

Name	Number of Congregations	Number of Adherents	Percent of total Christians from this unit
			_____ %

(If additional space is needed, please mark and attach a separate sheet.) ( )

CHRISTIAN WITNESS

31. Is there some form of Christian witness among this homogeneous unit, even if there are no professed Christians? For example: Individual missionaries, mission stations, hospitals, etc.? *(Do not include those listed in Question No. 30)* ( ) Yes   ( ) No   ( ) Don't know

    If "yes", what witness is present?
    (If additional space is needed, please mark and attach a separate sheet.) ( )

32. Are there organized Christian church bodies existing within this area <u>and</u> having members from this homogeneous unit? *(Do not include those listed in Question No. 30)*
    ( ) Yes   ( ) No   ( ) Don't know   If "yes", please give following information if available:

Name of Church group	Year Organized	No. of Adherents from this unit	No. of Total Adherents	"Growing" "Stable" or "Declining"

    (If additional space is needed, please mark and attach a separate sheet.) ( )

33. Are there organized Christian church bodies existing within this area <u>but not</u> having members from this homogeneous unit? *(Do not include those listed in Question 30)*
    ( ) Yes   ( ) No   ( ) Don't know   If "yes", please give following information if available:

Name of Church group	Year Organized	Composed of what unit"	No. of Total Adherents	"Growing" "Stable" or "Declining"

    (If additional space is needed, please mark and attach a separate sheet.) ( )

34. When was the earliest known Christian witness among this unit, and by what group or agency?

    ( ) Don't know

35. In your estimation, is the unit open to any religious change? For example: have there been any revival, renewal or other religious movements, whether Christian or non-Christian, in this homogeneous unit within the last 20 years?   ( ) Yes   ( ) No   ( ) Don't know   If "yes" please describe:

    (If additional space is needed, please mark and attach a separate sheet.) ( )

36. In your estimation, to what extent has this unit had an opportunity to hear a clear presentation of the Gospel?

    ( ) None have heard   ( ) Very few have heard   ( ) 10 to 25 % have heard
    ( ) 25 to 50 % have heard   ( ) 50 to 75 % have heard   ( ) Practically all have heard
                                                              ( ) Don't know

37. What methods have been used to proclaim the Gospel to this unit for the purpose of evangelizing? For example: literature distribution, radio, house visitation, gospel teams, market preaching, Bible studies. *(Indicate effectiveness if possible.)*

    ( ) Don't know
    (If additional space is needed, please mark and attach a separate sheet.) ( )

38. Some groups of Christians may be more effective in communicating with this homogeneous unit. In your estimation which groups, types or categories of Christians <u>within</u> this unit or surrounding geographic area might be most effective in communicating the Gospel to the unreached portion of this society?

    ( ) Don't know

39. Which groups, types or categories of Christians located <u>outside</u> this unit might be most effective in communicating the Gospel to the unreached portion of this society?

40. What factors are likely to <u>encourage</u> the spread or acceptance of Christianity among this unit?

41. What factors are likely to <u>hinder</u> the communication to or acceptance of the Christian faith by this unit?

42. On the following sequence of attitudes toward Christianity, where would you place this unit generally?

( ) Hostile ( ) Strong opposition ( ) Reluctant ( ) Indifferent ( ) Somewhat favorable ( ) Strongly favorable

SCRIPTURE TRANSLATION

43. What Scriptures have been translated and published in this unit's primary language?

	Translated	Date
Entire Bible	( )	
New Testament	( )	
Gospels	( )	
Portions	( )	

44. What Scriptures are now in process of translation or publication?

45. If no Scriptures are published in the primary language, in what other languages can Scriptures be read by members of this homogeneous unit?

46. If Scriptures have been published, are they actually available to the people?

( ) Yes ( ) No ( ) Don't know. Comment:

47. If Scriptures are available, are they readily received? ( ) Yes ( ) No ( ) Don't know

48. In your estimation what Scripture translation or distribution needs exist in this homogeneous unit?

49. In your estimation, what hinders Scripture distribution among this homogeneous unit?

PHOTOGRAPHS

50. Do you have any slides or photographs of this unit which could be made available for the Congress?
Please indicate: ( ) Slides ( ) Color photographs ( ) Black & White ( ) None
(The ICOWE would be happy to purchase up to 5 acceptable photographs of any one homogeneous unit.)

Describe:

INFORMATION SOURCES

51. List any sources, such as studies, surveys or reports which describe this homogeneous unit and Christianity's relation to it. *(Give author, title, year and place of publication where possible.)*

52. List other sources of information on this homogeneous unit. *(Names and addresses of individuals and organizations.)*

COMMENTS

53. Do you have any additional comments about this homogeneous unit, the answers to the questions, this questionnaire or any other related subject? If attaching a separate sheet for comments, please mark here. ( )

Please accept our sincere appreciation for having given what you could on this homogeneous unit. Some items you may have left blank. We appreciate the fact that you have given what you could. Our desire is that the Lord will use the information available to stir others to move out and reach this people with the Gospel.

MARC UNREACHED PEOPLES DATAFILE

SUMMARY LISTING BY GROUP NAME

GROUP NAME	COUNTRY	POPULATION OF GROUP	% OF CTRY	YEAR	PRINCIPAL LANGUAGE	TYPE	MAIN RELIGION	% CHR	SCRIPTURES	ATT
ACHEHNESE	INDONESIA	2,200,000	02	1973	ACHEHNESE	ETH	ISLAM	-1	P	2
ADAMAWA	CAMEROON	380,000	06	1972	FULANI	ETH	ANIMISM	0	NT	5
ADJA	DAHOMEY	250,000	08	1973	GE	ETH	ANIMISM	05	BI	3
AFAR	ETHIOPIA	250,000	.9	1973		REL	ISLAM	.2	NONE	
AFAWA	NIGERIA	10,000	-1	1972	AFAR	ETH	ANIMISM	0	NONE	
AFO	NIGERIA	25,000	-1	1972		ETH	ISLAM	-1	NT	3
AJURAN	KENYA	17,098	.2	1973	SOMALI	ETH	OTHER	-1	NT	5
AKHA	THAILAND	9,916	-1	1973	AKHA	ETH	ISLAM	02	NONE	3
ALABA	ETHIOPIA	200,000	-1	1972	ALABAN	ETH	ANIMISM	-1		
ALAK	LAOS	80,000	03	1973	ALAK	REL	ISLAM	-1	BI	2
ALGERIAN (ARABS)	ALGERIA	8,000,000	51	C1973	ARABIC	ETH	ISLAM	03	BI	
AMBONESE	NETHERLANDS	30,000	-1	1973	AMBONESE	ETH	CHRISTO-PAGAN		PG	5
AMPEELI	PAPUA/NEW GUINEA	1,300	-1	1973	AMPEELI	ETH	ANIMISM		G	
ANKWE	NIGERIA	10,000	-1	1972		ETH	ANIMISM	-1	GNT	
ANUAK	ETHIOPIA	52,000	-1	C1972		ETH	ANIMISM		NT	
ANUAK	SUDAN	30,000	.1	1972		GEO	ANIMISM	04	BI	5
APARTMENT RESIDENTS-SEOUL	KOREA, REPUBLIC OF	87,000	-1	1973	KOREAN	ETH	ANIMISM	15	NTG	
ARUSHA	TANZANIA	110,000	-1	C1973	ARUSHA	ETH	ANIMISM	12	PG	4
ASMAT	INDONESIA	30,000	-1	1973	ASMAT	ETH	ANIMISM	10	NTP	4
ATA OF DAVAO	PHILIPPINES	10,000	-1	C1973	MANUBO	ETH	ANIMISM	05	NTP	4
ATTA	PHILIPPINES	1,000	-1	C1973	ATTA	ETH	ANIMISM	01	GP	6
AZTECA	MEXICO	250,000	.4	C1973	AZTECA	ETH	CHRISTO-PAGAN	02	NONE	
BAGRI	PAKISTAN	20,000	-1	1973	BAGRI	ETH	HINDUISM	-1	NONE	
BAJANIA	PAKISTAN	20,000	-1	C1973	GUJARATI DIALECT	ETH	HINDUISM	0	NTP	
BALANGAO	PHILIPPINES	4,500	-1	C1973	BALANGAO	ETH	CHRISTO-PAGAN	04	NONE	5
BALANTE	PORTUGUESE GUINEA	200,000	33	1972		ETH	ANIMISM	11	NONE	
BALMIKI	PAKISTAN	20,000	-1	1973	HINDUSTANI	OCC	HINDUISM	-1		
BAMBARA	MALI	1,660,000	30	C1972		ETH	ISLAM	02	BI	5
BANAI	BANGLADESH	2,500	-1	1973	BENGALI	ETH	ANIMISM	-1	BI	6
BANARO	PAPUA/NEW GUINEA	2,500	-1	1973	BANARO	ETH		08	NONE	
BANYUN	PORTUGUESE GUINEA	15,000	03	1972		ETH	ANIMISM	08	NONE	6
BAOULE	IVORY COAST	1,200,000	27	1973	BAOULE	ETH	ANIMISM	12	NTOTP	
BARABAIG	TANZANIA	49,000	.3	1972		ETH	ANIMISM	02	NONE	4
BARIBA	DAHOMEY	500,000	19	1973	BARIBA	ETH	ANIMISM	01	NTP	
BASAKOMO	NIGERIA	60,000	.1	1972		ETH	ANIMISM	20	G	
BASARI	TOGO	100,000	05	1972		ETH	ANIMISM	15	NONE	
BASSA	LIBERIA	200,000	17	C1973	BASSA	ETH	ANIMISM	15	OTPNT	4
BHIL	PAKISTAN	200,000	.3	1973	MARWARI	ETH	HINDUISM	.5	P,G	5
BHILS	INDIA	700,000	-1	1973	DANGI	ETH	ANIMISM		BI	5
BIAFADA	PORTUGUESE GUINEA	15,000	03	1972		ETH	ANIMISM	07	NONE	
BIJOGO	PORTUGUESE GUINEA	25,000	04	1972		ETH	ANIMISM	12	NONE	5

Name	Country	Population	Year	Alt Name	Religion		Code	Num
BINGA	CENTRAL AFRICAN REP.	2,000	C1972		ETH	ANIMISM	0	NONE
BLACK CARIBS	HONDURAS	20,000	-7 C1973		ETH	CHRISTO-PAGAN	01	G	5
BLACK CARIBS	GUATEMALA	1,500	-1 C1973		ETH	CHRISTO-PAGAN	01	G	5
BLACK CARIBS	BELIZE	10,000	08 C1973		ETH	CHRISTO-PAGAN	01	G	5
BOBO	MALI	100,000	02 C1972		ETH	ANIMISM	01	GNT	6
BOKO	DAHOMEY	20,000	-6 1973	BOKO	ETH	ANIMISM	0	NTPG	4
BONTOC	PHILIPPINES	20,000	-1 C1973	BONTOC	ETH	ANIMISM	02	NTP	4
BORAN	ETHIOPIA	37,500	-1 1973	BORAN	ETH	ISLAM			
BRAD	BRAZIL	325	-1 1973	BORORO	ETH	ANIMISM	05	P	
BUA	LAOS	80,000	02 1973	BRAD	ETH	ANIMISM	-1	P	4
BUDUGUM	CHAD	20,000	-1 1972		ETH	ANIMISM	0		
BUGIS	CAMEROON	10,000	-1 1972	MASA	ETH	ANIMISM		G	
BUILSA	INDONESIA	300,000	-2 1973	BUGIS	ETH	ISLAM	01	NT	
BUNU	GHANA	80,000	-1 C1972		ETH	ANIMISM		G	
BURUNGI	NIGERIA	150,000	-2 1972		ETH	ANIMISM	10	NONE	2
BUSHMEN	TANZANIA	20,000	-1 1972		ETH	ANIMISM	10	NONE	4
BUTAWA	BOTSWANA	60,000	01 1972		ETH	ANIMISM	10	NONE	2
CAMBODIANS	NIGERIA	20,000	-1 1972		ETH	ANIMISM	0	NONE	
CHUOL SABANILLA	THAILAND	1,000,000	03 1973	NORTHERN CAMBODIAN	ETH	BUDDHISM		P	4
CHAKOSSI	MEXICO	20,000	-1 C1973	CHOL	ETH	CHRISTO-PAGAN	05	NTP	6
CHAKOSSI	GHANA	22,000	-1 1973		ETH	ANIMISM	10	NONE	
CHAM	TOGO	29,000	01 1972		ETH	ANIMISM	10	NONE	
CHAM (WESTERN)	VIETNAM, REP. OF	45,000	-2 1973	CHAM	ETH	HINDUISM	03	NONE	
CHAMULA	CAMBODIA (KHMER REP)	225,000	C1973	CHAM	ETH	ISLAM	.1	PG	2
CHAWAI	MEXICO	50,000	-1 C1973	CHAMULA	ETH	ANIMISM			
CHAYAHUITA	NIGERIA	30,000	-1 1972		ETH	ANIMISM	.6	PG	
CHINESE	PERU	6,000	-1 1973	CHAYAWITA	ETH	CHRISTO-PAGAN	20	GP	5
CHINESE	LAOS	25,000	-8 1973	MANDARIN	ETH	FOLK RELIGION	.5	BI	4
CHINESE	KOREA, REPUBLIC OF	32,000	01 1973	CHINESE	ETH	SECULARISM	03	BI	4
CHINESE	UPPER VOLTA	60,000	01 1973	BUAMU	FTH	ANIMISM	13	PG	5
CHINESE	MALAYSIA	3,555,879	30 1973	CHINESE	ETH	BUDDHISM	10	BI	
CHINESE	THAILAND	409,508	01 1973	CHINESE	FTH	OTHER	-1	BI	
CHINESE REFUGEES	MACAO	10,000	-1 1973	BURMESE	FTH	BUDDHISM	01	BI	4
CHIRIGUANO	ARGENTINA	20,000	-1 1973	GUARANI(BOLIVIAN)	OTH	BUDDHISM	15	NTP	5
CHOKWE & LUNDA	ANGOLA	400,000	06 1973	CHOKWE	ETH	ANIMISM	12		
CHOLA NAICKANS	INDIA	100	-1 1973	CANARESE/MALAYALAM	ETH	ANIMISM	0		
CHRAU	VIETNAM, REP. OF	15,000	-1 1973	CHRAU	ETH	ANIMISM	20	NTP	3
CHUABU	MOZAMBIQUE	250,000	03 1972		ETH	ANIMISM	14	NONE	5
CHUJ OF SAN MATEO IXTATAN	GUATEMALA	17,000	03 C1973	CHUJ	ETH	ANIMISM	20	NT	3
COLOMBIAN INDIANS	COLOMBIA	500,000	02 1973		ETH	ANIMISM	02	PG	5
COMORIANS	COMORO ISLANDS	300,000	99 1973	COMORIAN	FTH	ISLAM	-1		
COREGUAJE	COLOMBIA	500	-1 1973	COREGUAJE	ETH	ANIMISM	-1	NONE	5
COTABOTO MANOBO	PHILIPPINES	10,000	-1 C1973	COTABOTO MANOBO	ETH	ANIMISM	10	NTP	4
CUNA	COLOMBIA	600	-1 1973	CUNA	ETH	ANIMISM			
DAGARI	GHANA	200,000	02 C1972		FTH	ANIMISM		NONE	
DAGOMBA	GHANA	220,000	03 1972		FTH	ISLAM		G	
DAKA	NIGERIA	7,000	-1 1972		FTH	ANIMISM	0	NONE	3
DEGODIA	KENYA	68,667	-6 1973	SOMALI	ETH	ISLAM	0	NT	3
DENDI	DAHOMEY	15,000	-5 1973	DENDI	ETH	ISLAM	0	NONE	2
DIDINGA	SUDAN	30,000	-1 1972		ETH	ANIMISM	0	NONE	

SUMMARY LISTING BY
GROUP NAME

GROUP NAME	COUNTRY	POPULATION OF GROUP	% OF CTRY	YEAR	PRINCIPAL LANGUAGE	TYPE	MAIN RELIGION	% CHR	SCRIP TURES	ATT
DINKA	SUDAN	1,940,000	11	1972		ETH	ANIMISM	04	NT	
DIOLA	SENEGAL	216,000	05	1973		ETH	OTHER	-1	PG	
DIOLA	PORTUGUESE GUINEA	15,000	03	1972	DIOLA	ETH	ISLAM	05	G	
DOGON	MALI	312,000	05	1973		OTH	ANIMISM	10	GN	
DAHOMEY	DAHOMEY	30,000	01	C1972		ETH	ANIMISM	10	G	5
DOMPAGO	CAMEROON	22,300	20	1973		ETH	ANIMISM	20		
DODYAAYO	KENYA	22,300	-2	1973	DODYAAYO	OTH	ANIMISM	01	NONE	
DOROBO	TANZANIA	3,030	-1	1972	NANDI	ETH	ANIMISM	0	NONE	
DOROBO	INDIA	202,218	-1	1973	HADZA	FTH	HINDUISM	04	BI	5
DUBLA	PHILIPPINES	1,000	-1	1973	GUJARATI	FTH	ANIMISM	03	PG	4
DUMAGAT	CAMEROON	20,000	-1	1972	DUMAGAT	ETH	ANIMISM	20	G	
DURU	NIGERIA	80,000	-1	1973	DURU	ETH	ANIMISM	03	NONE	
EGGON	KENYA	1,000	-1	C1972		ETH	ANIMISM	03	G	
EL MOLO	ETHIOPIA	30,000	-1	1973		ETH	JUDAISM	07	BI	
FALASHA	JAPAN	24,988,740	23	1973	JAPANESE	OCC	BUDDHISM	.5	BI	3
FARMERS	GUINEA	1,500,000	37	1973	FULA	FTH	ISLAM	-1	NTP	1
FULA	UPPER VOLTA	300,000	05	1973	FULANI	OCC	ISLAM	-1		2
FULAH	CAMEROON	20,000	-.3	1973	FULANI	ETH	ANIMISM	-1	NONE	3
FULANI	DAHOMEY	70,000	02	C1973	FULANI	ETH	ISLAM	-1	NONE	4
FULANI	PHILIPPINES	5,500	-1	C1973	GA-DANG	ETH	ANIMISM	-1	NONE	3
GA-DANG	NIGERIA	5,000	-1	1972		ETH	ANIMISM	-1	NONE	
GADE	PAKISTAN	40,000	-1	C1973	PUNJABI	FTH	ANIMISM	.5	NT	5
GAGRE	IVORY COAST	25,000	-1	C1972		ETH	ISLAM	10	P	
GAGU	ETHIOPIA	750,000	03	1973	GALLA	ETH	ISLAM	-1	NONE	4
GALLA (BALE)	ETHIOPIA	1,305,400	05	1973	GALLINYA	ETH	ANIMISM	-1	NONE	3
GALLA, HARAR	LAOS	30,500	02	1973	GALLER	ETH	ANIMISM	-1		
GALLER	GUINEA	66,000	02	C1972		ETH	ANIMISM	05	G	
GBANDE	LIBERIA	32,000	03	1973		ETH	ANIMISM	10	G	
GBANDE	NIGERIA	500,000	.8	1973	GBARI	ETH	ANIMISM	0	GNT	
GBARI	DAHOMEY	9,000	-.3	C1973	GBAZANTCHE	ETH	ISLAM	0	NONE	5
GBAZANTCHE	ETHIOPIA	50,000	-.2	C1973	GIMIRA	ETH	ANIMISM	05	NT	
GHIMEERA	LIBERIA	92,000	08	C1973		ETH	ANIMISM	05	BI	
GIO	KENYA	335,900	03	C1972		ETH	ANIMISM	14	NONE	
GIRYAMA	CAMEROON	10,000	-1	1972	MASA	ETH	ANIMISM		P	
GISEI	CAMEROON	30,000	-1	1972	GISIGA	ETH	ANIMISM	01	NONE	6
GISIGA	IVORY COAST	15,000	-.3	1973	GODIE	ETH	ANIMISM	15	NONE	3
GODIE	UPPER VOLTA	300,000	05	C1973	GOURENDI	ETH	ANIMISM	05	NTOTP	5
GOURENCY	IVORY COAST	100,000	04	1973	GOUVO	ETH	ANIMISM	05	NONE	3
GOUVO	THAILAND	100,000	-.2	C1973	THAI	OCC	BUDDHISM	-1	BI	
GOVERNMENT OFFICIALS	GHANA	200,000	02	C1972		ETH	ANIMISM		NONE	
GRUNSHI	COLOMBIA	100,000	.4	1973	GUAJIRO	ETH	ANIMISM	20	PG	4
GUAJIRO	COLOMBIA	1,000	-1	1973	GUANANO	ETH	CHRISTO-PAGAN	01	NTP	4
GUANANO										

Group	Country	Population		Year	Language	Rel	Religion			
GUARANI	BOLIVIA	15,000		03 1973	GUARANI	ETH	ANIMISM	15	PG	6
GUARAYU	BOLIVIA	5,000		.1 1973	GUARAYU	ETH	CHRISTO-PAGAN	-1	GP	3
GUDE	CAMEROON	100,000		20 1972	GUDE	ETH	ANIMISM	0	NONE	
GUGU-YALANJI	AUSTRALIA	500		-1 1973	GUGU-YALANJI	ETH	ANIMISM	0	P	2
GURENSI	GHANA	250,000		03 C1972		ETH	ANIMISM		G	
GURREH	KENYA	54,165		.4 1973	SOMALI	ETH	ISLAM	0	NT	3
GYPSIES	SPAIN				SPANISH	ETH			BI	4
HAJONG	BANGLADESH	17,000		-1 1973	BENGALI	ETH	ANIMISM	-1	BI	5
HAKKA	CHINA (TAIWAN)	1,750,000		12 1973	HAKKA	ETH	BUDDHISM	.3	BI	2
HEIKUM	NAMIBIA (S-W AFRICA)	16,000		02 1972		ETH	ANIMISM	10	NONE	
HIECHWARE	SOUTHERN RHODESIA	1,600		-1 1972		ETH	ANIMISM	10	NONE	
HINDU SINDHIS	INDIA	3,000,000		.5 1973	SINDHI	SOC	HINDUISM	-1	BI	4
HOKKAIDO RESIDENTS	JAPAN	6,000,000		04 C1973	JAPANESE	GEO	ANIMISM	01	BI	3
HOPI	UNITED STATES	6,000		-1 1973	HOPI	ETH	ANIMISM	01	BI	
HUAVE	MEXICO	10,000		-1 C1972	HUAVE	ETH	CHRISTO-PAGAN	03	P,NT	4
HUKKE	ANGOLA	9,000		-1 1972	HUKWE	ETH	ANIMISM	02	NT	3
IBAJI	NIGERIA	20,000		-1 1972		ETH	ANIMISM	05	NONE	5
ICA	COLOMBIA	3,000		-1 1973	ICA	ETH	SECULARISM	18	NONE	
IFUGAO	PHILIPPINES	95,000		06 C1973	IFUGAO	ETH	ANIMISM	10	G	3
IGBIRA	NIGERIA	400,300		.6 1972		ETH	ISLAM	04		4
ILIANEN MANOBO	PHILIPPINES	5,000		-1 1973	ILIANEN MANOBO	ETH	ANIMISM	01	NTP	
IMMIGRANT WORKERS-TURKISH	GERMANY, FED. REP.	1,200,000		02 1973	TURKISH	OCC	ISLAM	0	BI	3
IMMIGRANTS, AMERICAN	ISRAEL	25,797		-8 1973	HEBREW	ETH	JUDAISM	0	BI	4
IMMIGRANTS, ARGENTINE	ISRAEL	17,686		-6 1973	HEBREW	ETH	JUDAISM	0	BI	4
IMMIGRANTS, AUSTRALIAN	ISRAEL	1,257		-1 1973	HEBREW	ETH	JUDAISM	0	BI	4
IMMIGRANTS, BRAZILIAN	ISRAEL	4,005		-1 1973	HEBREW	ETH	JUDAISM	0	BI	4
IMMIGRANTS, MEXICAN	ISRAEL	1,065		-1 1973	HEBREW	ETH	JUDAISM	0	BI	4
IMMIGRANTS, OTHER	ISRAEL	5,520		-2 1973	HEBREW	ETH	JUDAISM	0	BI	4
IMMIGRANTS, URUGUAYAN	ISRAEL	2,720		-1 1973	HEBREW	ETH	JUDAISM	0	BI	4
INDIANS IN RHODESIA	FIJI	265,000		50 1973	HINDUSTANI	ETH	HINDUISM	02	BI	3
INDUST.WORKERS YONGDUNGPO	SOUTHERN RHODESIA	9,600		-1 1973	GUJARATI	ETH	HINDUISM	11	BI	3
INDUSTRY LABURERS	KOREA, REPUBLIC OF	140,000		.4 1973	KOREAN	OCC	SECULARISM	05	BI	3
INGASSANA	JAPAN				JAPANESE	SOC	BUDDHISM	-1	BI	4
IRAQW	SUDAN	35,000		.2 1972	IRAQW	ETH	ANIMISM	0	NONE	
IWAIDJA	TANZANIA	218,000		02 1972	IWAIDJA	FTH	ANIMISM	16	NTP	4
IZI	AUSTRALIA	250		-1 1973	IZI	ETH	ANIMISM		NTOTP	5
JABA	NIGERIA	200,000		-3 C1973		ETH	ANIMISM	15	G	
JAPANESE	NIGERIA	60,000		-1 1972	JAPANESE	ETH	BUDDHISM	20	BI	3
JAPANESE (KAGOSHIMA)	BRAZIL	700,000		.7 C1973	JAPANESE	ETH	SECULARISM	01	BI	4
JAPANESE STUDENTS IN USA	JAPAN	3,500,000		03 1973	JAPANESE	SOC	BUDDHISM	.7	BI	5
JARAWA	UNITED STATES					ETH	ANIMISM		G	
JAVANESE	NIGERIA	150,000		-3 1972	JAVANESE	ETH	ISLAM	20	BI	6
JAVANESE (RURAL)	INDONESIA	70,000,000		53 1973	JAVANESE	ETH	ISLAM	01	BI	5
JAVANESE OF CENTRAL JAVA	INDONESIA	60,000,000		45 1973	JAVANESE	ETH	ISLAM	05	BI	5
JAVANESE OF PEJOAPONGAN	INDONESIA	20,000,000		15 1973	BAHASA JAWA	ETH	ISLAM	10	BI	5
JEMEZ PUEBLO	UNITED STATES	5,000		-1 C1973	TOWA	ETH	CHRISTO-PAGAN	05	BI	2
JENG	LAOS	1,800		-1 1973	JENG	ETH	ANIMISM	0	NONE	
JERAWA	NIGERIA	500		-1 1972		ETH	ANIMISM		G	
JEWS OF MONTREAL	CANADA	120,000		.5 1973	ENGLISH	REL	JUDAISM	-1	BI	3

SUMMARY LISTING BY
GROUP NAME

GROUP NAME	COUNTRY	POPULATION OF GROUP	% OF CTRY	YEAR	PRINCIPAL LANGUAGE	TYPE	MAIN RELIGION	% CHR	SCRIPTURES	ATT
JIYE	UGANDA	34,000	.3	1972	JIYE	ETH	ANIMISM		NONE	
JUKUN	NIGERIA	20,000	-1	1972		ETH	ANIMISM		G	
KABRE	TOGO	273,000	14	1973		ETH	ANIMISM	14	NTG	1
KABYLE	ALGERIA	2,000,000	13	C1973	KABYLE	ETH	ISLAM	.1	NONE	
KADARA	NIGERIA	40,000	-1	1972		ETH	ANIMISM	-1	NONE	4
KAFFA	ETHIOPIA	250,000	.8	C1973	KAFFENYA	ETH	CHRISTO-PAGAN	0	NONE	
KAGORO	MALI	30,000	-1	C1972		ETH	ANIMISM	.3	BIP	5
KAIPENG-KOLOI	INDIA	200,000	-1	1973	KAIPENG	ETH	ANIMISM	-1	NTP	5
KALAGAN	PHILIPPINES	19,000	-1	C1973	KALAGAN	ETH	ANIMISM	01	NONE	3
KALAMIAN TAGBANWA	PHILIPPINES	4,500	-1	C1973	KALAMIAN TAGBANWA	ETH	CHRISTO-PAGAN		NONE	
KAMANTAN	NIGERIA	10,000	-1	1972		ETH	ANIMISM		NONE	
KAMUKU	NIGERIA	40,000	-1	1972		ETH	ANIMISM		NONE	4
KANARESE	INDIA	21,707,000	04	1971	KANNADA	ETH	HINDUISM	12	BI	
KAREN	THAILAND	200,000	.4	1973	SGAW KAREN	ETH	ANIMISM	-1	BI	
KASSENG	LAOS	80,000	-1	1973	KASSENG	ETH	ANIMISM			
KAYAGAR	INDONESIA	9,000	-1	1973	KAYAGAR	ETH	ANIMISM	10	P	3
KEPAS	PAPUA/NEW GUINEA	600	-1	1973	KEWA	ETH	ANIMISM	0		3
KEREWE	TANZANIA	35,000	-1	C1973	KIKEREWE	ETH	ANIMISM		NT	3
KIMYAL	INDONESIA	7,000	-1	1973	KIMYAL	ETH	ANIMISM	06	P	4
KISSI	SIERRA LEONE	43,000	02	1973	KISSI	ETH	ANIMISM	10	NT	4
KISSI	GUINEA	266,000	06	C1972		ETH	ANIMISM	02	GNT	
KITA	MALI	150,000	03	C1972		ETH	ISLAM	02	NONE	
KOALIR	SUDAN	320,000	02	1972		ETH	ANIMISM	10	NONE	
KOCH	BANGLADESH	35,000	-1	1973	BENGALI	ETH	ANIMISM	-1	RI	5
KOLAM	INDIA	60,000	-1	1973	KOLAMI	ETH	ANIMISM	-1	P	5
KOND	INDIA	900,000	.3	1973	KUI	ETH	ANIMISM	03	G	6
KONKOMBA	TOGO	25,000	01	1973	KOM KOMBA	ETH	ANIMISM	-1		4
KONKOMBA	GHANA	80,000	-1	C1972		ETH	ANIMISM	15	NONE	
KONO	SIERRA LEONE	133,000	05	1973		ETH	ANIMISM	05	P	5
KONSO	ETHIOPIA	10,000	-1	C1972		ETH	ANIMISM		NONE	
KORANKO	SIERRA LEONE	103,000	03	1973	KURANKO	ETH	ANIMISM	01	PNT	5
KOREAN PRISONERS	KOREA, REPUBLIC OF	45,000	-1	C1971	KOREAN	ETH	ANIMISM	20	BI	5
KOREANS	JAPAN	600,000	.6	C1971	KOREAN	OTH		10	BI	4
KORKU	INDIA	250,000	-1	1973	KORKU	ETH	ANIMISM	01	PG	4
KORO	NIGERIA	35,000	-1	1972		ETH	ANIMISM		NT	
KOTOKOLI	DAHOMEY	1,000	-1	1973	KOTOKOLI	ETH	ISLAM	0	NONE	3
KOTOPO	CAMEROON	200,000	16	C1972	KOTOPO	ETH	ANIMISM		NONE	
KPELLE	LIBERIA	200,000	16	C1972		ETH	ANIMISM	10	GNT	
KRAHN	LIBERIA	55,000	05	1973	KRAHN	ETH	ANIMISM	10	P	6
KRONGO	SUDAN	121,000	.6	1972		ETH	OTHER	01	NT	
KUI	THAILAND	160,000	.4	1973	KUI	ETH	BUDDHISM	-1	NTPG	4
KULANGO	IVORY COAST	50,000	01	C1972		ETH	ANIMISM	04	G	
KUNG	NAMIBIA (S-W AFRICA)	10,000	01	1972		ETH	ANIMISM	10	NONE	

Name	Country	Language	Population	Year	Religion1	Religion2	Col1	Col2	Col3
KURDS	TURKEY	KURDISH	7,500,000	19 C1973	ETH	ISLAM	0	NONE	4
KURFEI	NIGER		50,000	01 1972	ETH	ANIMISM	0	NONE	
KUTCHI KOHLI	PAKISTAN	GUJARATI	50,000	-1 C1973	ETH	HINDUISM	04	P	5
KWERE	TANZANIA	KWERE	63,000	-1 1972	ETH	ANIMISM	17	NONE	
LAKA	CAMEROON	LAKA	10,000	-1 1973	ETH	ANIMISM	03	P	3
LAMBA	TOGO	LAMBA	29,000	01 1973	ETH	ANIMISM	.5	BI	4
LAO	LAOS	LAO	1,998,600	60 1973	ETH	BUDDHISM	04	NT	3
LAWA	THAILAND	LAWA	10,000	-1 1973	ETH	BUDDHISM	.5	P	5
LEPERS OF NORTHEAST	THAILAND	NORTHEAST THAI	390,000	-1 C1973	OTH	BUDDHISM	0	NONE	
LIGBI	IVORY COAST		20,000	-1 C1972	ETH	ISLAM	05	NT	
LIMBA	SIERRA LEONE		233,000	08 1972	ETH	ANIMISM	0	GNT	
LOBI	IVORY COAST		40,000	-1 C1972	ETH	ANIMISM	-1	NONE	
LOHAR	PAKISTAN	GUJARATI DIALECT			ETH	HINDUISM			
LOHO LOHO	INDONESIA	KOLAKA	10,000	-1 1973	ETH	ANIMISM	0	G	
LOKO	SIERRA LEONE		80,000	03 1972	ETH	ANIMISM	01	G	
LOMA	GUINEA		66,000	02 C1972	ETH	ANIMISM	03	G	
LOMA	LIBERIA		60,000	05 C1972	ETH	ANIMISM			
LOMWE	MOZAMBIQUE		1,000,000	12 1972	ETH	ANIMISM	14	NT	4
LORHON	IVORY COAST	LORHON	4,000	-1 1973	ETH	ANIMISM	-1	NONE	5
LOTUKA	SUDAN	LATUKA	258,000	01 1973	ETH	ANIMISM	06	NT	
LOVEN	LAOS	LOVEN	50,000	-1 C1972	ETH	OTHER	-1		
LUGBARA	ZAIRE		300,000	02 1973	ETH	ANIMISM		BI	
LUNGU	NIGERIA		10,000	-1 1972	ETH	ANIMISM		NONE	
MABA	CHAD	MABA	700,000	17 1973	ETH	ISLAM	-1	NONE	2
MACU	COLOMBIA	MACU	1,000	-1 1973	ETH	ANIMISM	0	NONE	1
MADURESE	INDONESIA	MADURESE	7,000,000	05 1973	ETH	ISLAM	-1	PG	2
MAGINDANAO	PHILIPPINES	MAGINDINAO	450,000	01 C1973	ETH	ISLAM	-1	NTP	1
MAGUZAWA	NIGERIA		100,000	-2 1973	ETH	ANIMISM	0	BI	
MAJI	ETHIOPIA		10,000	-1 C1972	ETH	ANIMISM		NONE	
MAKONDE	TANZANIA		550,000	04 C1973	ETH	ISLAM	08		
MAKONG	LAOS		50,000	02 1973	ETH	ANIMISM	-1		
MAKUA	MOZAMBIQUE		1,200,000	14 1972	ETH	ANIMISM	16		
MALAY	SINGAPORE	MALAY	300,000	13 1973	ETH	ISLAM	0	NTG	3
MAMANWA (MAMANUA)	PHILIPPINES	MIMAMANWA	1,000	-1 C1973	ETH	CHRISTO-PAGAN	03	BIP	5
MAMBILA	CAMEROON	MAMBILA	40,000	-1 C1972	ETH	ANIMISM			
MAMPRUSI	GHANA		80,000	-1 C1972	ETH	ANIMISM		G	
MANDINGO	LIBERIA	MANDINGO	60,000	-1 C1973	ETH	ISLAM	-1	P	2
MANGYAN	PORTUGUESE GUINEA	MANGYAN	80,000	13 1972	ETH	ANIMISM	10	NONE	5
MANJACO	LIBERIA		80,000	07 C1972	ETH	ANIMISM	11	NONE	
MANO	CHILE		400,000	04 1973	ETH	ANIMISM	05	OTPNT	3
MAPUCHE	PHILIPPINES	MAPUCHE	1,000,000	02 C1973	ETH	ISLAM		NT	2
MARANAO	CHAD	MARANAO	80,000	-1 C1972	ETH	ANIMISM	02	GNT	
MASA	KENYA		100,000	-1 1972	ETH	ANIMISM	1C	NT	
MASAI	ETHIOPIA	MASAI	7,000	-1 1973	ETH	ANIMISM	05	NONE	4
MASENGO	CAMEROON	MAJANGIIR	140,000	-2 1972	ETH	ANIMISM	-1	NT	
MATAKAM	TANZANIA	MATAKAM	100,000	-1 1972	ETH	ANIMISM	02	NONE	
MATUMBI	NIGER	MATUMBI	72,000	-1 1972	ETH	ISLAM	15	NONE	
MAURI	ANGOLA		100,000	-1 1972	ETH	ANIMISM	0	NONE	
MBUKUSHU	SUDAN	KUSSO	6,000	-1 1972	ETH	ANIMISM	10	G	
MEBAN	PAKISTAN	MARWARI	130,000	-.6 1972	ETH	ANIMISM	0	NONE	5
MEGHWAR			100,000	-1 1973	ETH	HINDUISM	-1	NONE	

SUMMARY LISTING BY
GROUP NAME

GROUP NAME	COUNTRY	POPULATION OF GROUP	% OF CTRY	YEAR	PRINCIPAL LANGUAGE	TYPE	MAIN RELIGION	% CHR	SCRIPTURES	A T T
MEITEI	INDIA	632,597	.1	1973	MANIPURI	ETH	HINDUISM	.3	NT	4
MENDE	SIERRA LEONE	859,000	30	1972		ETH	ANIMISM	20	BI	5
MEO	THAILAND	29,173	-1	1973	MEO	ETH	ANIMISM	15	NT	5
MILITARY (VIETNAMESE)	VIETNAM, REP. OF	1,100,000	06	1973	VIETNAMESE	OCC	BUDDHISM	10	BI	6
MINANGKABAU	INDONESIA	5,000,000	05	1973	MINANGKABAU	ETH	ISLAM	0	NONE	1
MINIANKA	MALI	300,000	05	C1972		ETH	ANIMISM	0		
MINNAN HOKLU	CHINA (TAIWAN)	11,625,000	77	1973	AMOY DIALECT	ETH	BUDDHISM	04	BI	5
MIXTECO,SAN JUAN MIXTEPIC	MEXICO	15,000	-1	C1973	MIXTECO	ETH	CHRISTO-PAGAN	.1	NTP	4
MOBA	GHANA	80,000	-1	C1972		FTH	ANIMISM	0	G	
MOBA	TOGO	94,000	05	1972		ETH	ANIMISM	12	G	
MOCHA	ETHIOPIA	45,000	.2	1973	MOCHA	ETH	ANIMISM	05	NONE	6
MOKEN	BURMA	5,000	-1	1972	MOKEN	ETH	ANIMISM	-1	NONE	
MOKOLE	DAHOMEY	7,300	.2	1973	MOKOLE	ETH	ANIMISM	-0	NONE	4
MOOR & MALAYS	SRI LANKA (CEYLON)	895,322	.7	1973	TAMIL	REL	ISLAM	0	BI	2
MOSLEM MALAYS	MALAYSIA	5,000,000	42	1973	BAHASA MALAYSIA	REL	ISLAM	-1	G	2
MOSLEM RESIDENTS	UNITED ARAB EMIRATES	202,000	-1	1973	ARABIC	REL	ISLAM	-1	BI	2
MOSLEMS	THAILAND	600,000	-1	C1973	MALAY	ETH	ISLAM	-1	P	2
MOSLEMS	YUGOSLAVIA	2,500,000	11	1973	ALBANIAN	REL	ISLAM		PG	2
MOSLEMS (WEST NILE DIST.)	UGANDA	45,000	.5	1972	LUGBARA	REL	ISLAM	-1	B	2
MOSLEMS OF JORDAN	JORDAN	1,000,000	38	1973	ARABIC	REL	ISLAM	20	BI	2
MOUNTAIN BASOTHO	LESOTHO	70,000	06	C1973	SOUTHERN SESOTHO	GEO	ANIMISM	15	BI	6
MUMUYE	NIGERIA	120,000	.2	1972		ETH	ANIMISM	0	G	2
MURLE	SUDAN	121,000	.6	1972		ETH	ANIMISM	0	G	
MURNGIN (WULAMBA)	AUSTRALIA	3,500	-1	1973	DHUWAL	ETH	ANIMISM		NTPG	4
MURUNG	BANGLADESH	20,000	-1	1973	MURUNG	ETH	ANIMISM	0	NTP,G	3
NAMBIKUARA	BRAZIL	200	-1	1973	NAMBIKUARA	ETH	ANIMISM	03	NONE	
NAMSHI	CAMEROON	30,000	-1	1972	NAMSHI	ETH	ANIMISM	0	NONE	
NGAMO	NIGERIA	10,000	-1	1972		ETH	ANIMISM		NONE	
NGEQ	LAOS	50,000	02	1973	NGEQ	ETH	ANIMISM	05	G	
NGERE	IVORY COAST	150,000	03	C1972		ETH	ANIMISM	0	NONE	
NINGERUM	PAPUA/NEW GUINEA	3,000	-1	1973	NINGERUM BARASANO	FTH	ANIMISM		P	4
NORTHERN BARASANO	COLOMBIA	450	-1	1973	NORTHERN BARASANO	FTH	ANIMISM	03	P	
NORTHERN PAIUTE	UNITED STATES	5,000	-1	1973	NORTHERN PAIUTE	FTH	OTHER	04	P	2
NUER	ETHIOPIA	70,000	-1	C1972		ETH	ANIMISM		GNT	
NUER	SUDAN	844,000	04	1972		ETH	ANIMISM	0	NT	
NUPE	NIGERIA	587,000	-1	1973	NUPE	ETH	ISLAM	02	BI	5
NYAHEUN	LAOS	15,000	.5	1973	NYAHEUN	ETH	ANIMISM	02		
NYAMWEZI	TANZANIA	590,000	04	1972	NYAMWEZI	ETH	ANIMISM	15	NT	
NYANTRUKU	DAHOMEY	4,000	-1	1973	ALEDJO	ETH	ANIMISM	-0	NONE	4
OD	PAKISTAN	40,000	-1	C1973	ODKI	ETH	HINDUISM	-1	NONE	
OGADEN	KENYA	99,129	.8	1973	SOMALI	ETH	ISLAM	-1	PNT	3
OI	LAOS	13,000	.3	1973	OI	ETH	ANIMISM	-1		
OUADDAI	CHAD	750,000	18	1973	MABA	ETH	ISLAM	.3		2

Name	Country	Group	Year	?	Religion Class	Religion	?	Code	?
PALAUNG	BURMA	PALAUNG	150,000	-5 1973	ETH	BUDDHISM	-1	NONE	3
PARKARI KOHLIS	PAKISTAN	GUJARATI	100,000	.1 1973	ETH	HINDUISM	05	P	5
PHU THAI	LAOS	PHU THAI	100,000	03 1973	ETH	ANIMISM	-1	NONE	
PILA	DAHOMEY	PILA-PILA	50,000	01 1973	ETH	ANIMISM	01	OTNTP	5
PODOKWO	CAMEROON	PODOKWO	25,000	-1 1973	ETH	ANIMISM	-1	NONE	
PWO KAREN	THAILAND	PWO KAREN	40,000	.1 1973	ETH	ANIMISM	-1	P	3
PYGMY	ZAIRE	KIBUTI	20,000	-1 1973	ETH	ANIMISM	01	NONE	4
QUECHUA, VALLEY	BOLIVIA	QUECHUA	667,000	15 1972	GEO	CHRISTO-PAGAN	20	NT	5
QUICHE	GUATEMALA	QUICHE	500,000	09 1973	ETH	CHRISTO-PAGAN	07	NT	5
RABINAL-ACHI	GUATEMALA	RABINAL ACHI	21,000	.4 1973	ETH	CHRISTO-PAGAN	05	NTPG	5
RACETRACK RESIDENTS	UNITED STATES	ENGLISH	50,000	-1 1973	OCC	SECULARISM	10	BI	4
RAVA	INDIA	RAVA			ETH	HINDUISM	0		
RESHIAT	ETHIOPIA		10,000	-1 C1972	ETH	ANIMISM	-1	NONE	
RYUKYUAN	JAPAN		1,030,000	01 1973	GEO	BUDDHISM	05		4
SAFWA	TANZANIA	SAFWA	102,000	.7 1972	ETH	ANIMISM	03	NT	
SALUG MANOBO	PHILIPPINES	TIGWA MANOBO	4,000	-1 C1973	ETH	ANIMISM	05	BIP	5
SAMA-BADJAW	PHILIPPINES	SINAMA	400,000	01 1973	ETH	ISLAM	-1	OTNTP	3
SAMAL	PHILIPPINES	SINAMA	600,000	01 1973	ETH	ISLAM	-1	G	2
SAMBURU	KENYA		60,500	-1 C1972	ETH	ANIMISM	03	G	
SAMO-KUBO	PAPUA/NEW GUINEA	SAMO	1,200	-1 1973	ETH	ANIMISM	-1	P	4
SANGIL	PHILIPPINES	SANGIL	7,500	-1 C1973	ETH	ISLAM	-1	NONE	3
SAPO	LIBERIA		30,000	02 C1972	ETH	ANIMISM	20	G	
SAVE	DAHOMEY	SAVE	15,000	.5 1973	ETH	ANIMISM	-1	BI	5
SENUFO	IVORY COAST	SENARI	500,000	11 1973	ETH	ANIMISM	02	PG	3
SHANGA	NIGERIA		5,000	-1 1972	ETH	ANIMISM	0	NONE	
SHANKILLA	ETHIOPIA	SHANKILLA	20,000	-1 1973	ETH	CHRISTO-PAGAN	-1		6
SINHALESE	SRI LANKA (CEYLON)	SINHALA	9,146,679	67 1973	ETH	BUDDHISM	07	BI	3
SO	LAOS	SO	15,000	-1 1953	ETH	ANIMISM	-1		
SOCHI	PAKISTAN				OCC	HINDUISM	-1		
SOKA GAKKAI BELIEVERS	JAPAN	JAPANESE	6,500,000	16 1973	REL	BUDDHISM	0	BI	2
SOMAGAI	INDONESIA	SOMAGAI			ETH	ANIMISM	0	NONE	4
SOMALI	ETHIOPIA	SOMALI	1,000,000	04 C1973	ETH	ISLAM	-1	NTOTP	2
SOMALI	SOMALIA	SOMALI	2,500,000	99 1973	ETH	ISLAM	-1	NTOTP	2
SUMBA	DAHOMEY	SOMBA	60,030	02 1973	FTH	ANIMISM	-1	NONE	5
SONJO	TANZANIA	SONJO	7,400	-1 1972	FTH	ANIMISM	05	NONE	
SORURA	DAHOMEY	SORUBA	5,000	-1 1973	FTH	ANIMISM	-1	NONE	
SOUTHERN BARASANO	COLOMBIA	JANENA	400	.1 1973	ETH	ANIMISM	-1	PG	3
SPIRITISTS	BRAZIL	PORTUGUESE	9,000,000	09 C1973	REL	ANIMISM		BI	2
STUDENTS	JAPAN	JAPANESE	350,000	.3 1973	SOC	BUDDHISM		BI	4
SUBANEN (TUBOY)	PHILIPPINES	SUBANEN	20,000	-1 1973	ETH	ANIMISM	02	G	5
SUK	KENYA		153,200	01 1972	ETH	ANIMISM	12	NT	
SUNDANESE	INDONESIA	SUNDANESE	25,000,000	19 1973	ETH	ISLAM	-1	BI	5
SURI	ETHIOPIA		30,000	-1 C1972	ETH	ANIMISM	-1	NONE	
TA-OI	LAOS	TA-OI	100,000	03 1973	ETH	ANIMISM	-1		
TAIWANESE MAINLANDERS	CHINA (TAIWAN)	MANDARIN	2,010,000	13 1973	ETH	SECULARISM	15	BI	5
TAMIL (CEYLONESE)	SRI LANKA (CEYLON)	TAMIL	1,415,567	10 1973	ETH	HINDUISM	07	BI	3
TAMILS (INDIAN)	MALAYSIA	TAMIL	600,000	05 1973	ETH	HINDUISM	06	BI	4
TAMILS (INDIAN)	SRI LANKA (CEYLON)	TAMIL	1,195,368	09 1973	ETH	HINDUISM	07	BI	5
TATUYO	COLOMBIA	TATUYO		-1 1973	ETH	ANIMISM	-1	P	4
TAUSUG	PHILIPPINES	TAUSUG	300,000	-1 C1973	ETH	ISLAM	-1	BIP	2

SUMMARY LISTING BY
GROUP NAME

GROUP NAME	COUNTRY	POPULATION OF GROUP	% OF CTRY	YEAR	PRINCIPAL LANGUAGE	TYPE	MAIN RELIGION	% CHR	SCRIPTURES	ATT
TBOLI	PHILIPPINES	67,500	-1	C1973	TBOLI	ETH	ANIMISM	03		5
TEM	TOGO	100,000	05	1972		ETH	ISLAM	07	NONE	2
TEMNE	SIERRA LEONE	750,000	27	1973	TEMNE	ETH	ANIMISM	06	NT	5
TENGGER	INDONESIA	400,000	.3	1973	TENGGERESE	ETH	HINDUISM	.1	NONE	3
THARADARI KOHLI	PAKISTAN	40,000	-1	C1973	GUJARATI	ETH	HINDUISM	01	NONE	5
TIGON	CAMEROON	25,000	-1	1972		ETH	ANIMISM		BIP	
TIGWA MANOBO	PHILIPPINES	4,000	-1	C1973	TIGWA MANOBO	ETH	ANIMISM	03	BIP	5
TIN	THAILAND	25,000	-1	1973	TIN	ETH	ANIMISM	-1		3
TOFI	DAHOMEY	33,000	01	C1973	TOFI	ETH	ANIMISM	03	NONE	4
TONGA, GWEMBE VALLEY	ZAMBIA	86,300	02	1973	CI TONGA	ETH	ANIMISM	02	BI	3
TOPOTHA	SUDAN	60,000	.3	1972		ETH	ANIMISM	0	NONE	
TUAREG	NIGER	100,000	02	1973	TAMACHEK	ETH	ISLAM			2
TURKANA	KENYA	224,000	02	1972	TURKANA	ETH	ANIMISM	04	G	3
TURKANA FISHING COMMUNITY	KENYA	20,000	.1	1973	TURKANA	OCC	ANIMISM	04	G	5
TURU	TANZANIA	316,000	02	1973		ETH	ANIMISM	13	NTP	
TWA	BURUNDI	30,000	-1	1972	TWA	ETH	ANIMISM	10	NONE	
UDUK	SUDAN	7,000	-1	1972		ETH	ANIMISM	15	NT	
URBAN BUSINESSMEN	JAPAN	20,000,000	19	1973	JAPANESE	SOC	BUDDHISM	01	BI	4
URBAN WORKERS	CHINA (TAIWAN)				TAIWANESE	ECO	BUDDHISM	-1	BI	4
VAGALA	GHANA	3,000	-1	C1972		ETH	ANIMISM		NONE	
VAGARI	PAKISTAN	30,000	-1	C1973	GUJARATI DIALECT	ETH	HINDUISM	-1	NONE	
VERE	NIGERIA	20,000	-1	1972		ETH	ANIMISM	04	NONE	
VIETNAMESE	LAOS	20,000	.6	1973	VIETNAMESE	ETH	BUDDHISM		BI	5
MADIAKA KOHLI	PAKISTAN	40,000	-1	C1973	GUJARATI	ETH	HINDUISM	01	P	5
MAJITA	TANZANIA	65,000	-5	C1973	KIJITA	ETH	ANIMISM	-1	NT	
WARJAWA	NIGERIA	70,000	-1	1972		ETH	ANIMISM	0	NONE	
MATCHI	TOGO	400,000	20	1973	GE	ETH	ANIMISM	05	BI	3
WESTERN BUKIDNON MANOBO	PHILIPPINES	12,000	-1	1973	MANOBO	ETH	ANIMISM	10	PG	5
WIMBUM	CAMEROON				LIMBUM	ETH				5
MINJI-WINJI	DAHOMEY	5,000	.1	1973	WINJI-WINJI	ETH	ISLAM	0	NONE	3
WOBE	IVORY COAST	40,000	.1	C1972		ETH	ANIMISM	20	NONE	
WOLOF	SENEGAL	1,500,000	36	C1973	WOLOF	ETH	ISLAM	-1	NTP	2
YAKAN	PHILIPPINES	50,000	.1	1973	YAKAN	ETH	ISLAM	-1	PG	3
YALUNKA	SIERRA LEONE	25,000	-8	1973	YALUNKA	ETH	ISLAM	-1	NTP	4
YANOMAM	BRAZIL	2,750	-1	C1973	YANOMAM	ETH	ANIMISM	-1	P	4
YANYULA	AUSTRALIA	150	-1	C1973	YANYULA (YANJULA)	ETH	OTHER	15	NTP	4
YAO	MALAWI	200,000	04	1973	CHIYAO	ETH	ANIMISM	10	BI	3
YAO	MOZAMBIQUE	220,000	02	C1973	YAO	ETH	ISLAM	19	BI	
YAO	THAILAND	19,867	-1	1973	YAO	ETH	ANIMISM	02	NT	5
YAQUIS	MEXICO	14,000	-1	C1973	YAQUI	ETH	CHRISTO-PAGAN		NTP	2
ZARAMO	TANZANIA	296,000	02	1973		ETH	ISLAM	02	G	
ZINACANTECUS	MEXICO	10,000	-1	C1973	TZOTZIL	ETH	CHRISTO-PAGAN	01	GP	2
ZUNI	UNITED STATES	6,000	-1	1973	ZUNI	ETH	ANIMISM	.5	PG	3

STATUS OF CHRISTIANITY
COUNTRY PROFILE

BURMA

INTRODUCTION

This publication is a summary of available information on the status of Christianity in one part of the world. Its purpose is to provide an introduction for those not familiar with Burma, and to increase the overall awareness of Burmese Christians of what God is doing in this country. The emphasis of the material is on Protestant Christianity but relevant information on other Christian traditions is included where available.

As the Church sees herself and the world which surrounds her more clearly, we hope that improved communication will result that will encourage Christians toward the common goal of proclaiming Christ to all men. There are millions upon millions of people in the world who have had little or no contact with the Gospel of Jesus Christ. Within each country there may be unique groups of such unreached peoples. This publication tries to identify unreached peoples within their national setting. Such a setting includes not only the national and social environment, but also the activity of churches and missions.

This is just a beginning, an introduction to the total task of proclaiming Christ to those who have not heard. Hopefully, it will encourage those who are concerned with evangelism to identify unreached peoples and to discover effective means of reaching them with the Gospel.

UNREACHED PEOPLES

The dominant ethnic group is the Burmese, which is comprised of more than 20 million of the total 30 million population and which is largely Buddhist. In Burma's mountainous areas live more than 100 small groups of people speaking different languages and living in relative isolation from others. Communicating the Gospel to some of them has been hindered by this isolation and by language barriers, reinforced in some cases by their adherence to Buddhism.

Among those groups of whom a significant percentage profess to be Christians are the Karen who are found in southern and eastern Burma and number about three million, and the Chin and Kachin in the north and northwest, who together number about one million people. Together these groups form about ten percent of the total population of Burma.

Apart from the Burmese who comprise about 65 percent of the population, other unreached peoples are: the Shans, who number about 1.5 million and are ethnically related to the Thai, living in the eastern plateau region; the Kayah, in the southern Shan plateau; the Mons, scattered in the central south region; the Arakanese, located in the west. These last three groups total about two million people. There are also an estimated 400,000 persons of Chinese origins, and over 100,000 Indians and Pakistanis who are largely non-Christians.

The graph below shows some of the major people groupings of Burma and their response to Christianity. The graph shows both the percentage of the total population that each group represents and the percentage of the individual group that calls itself Christian.

CHRISTIAN POPULATION BY ETHNIC GROUPS

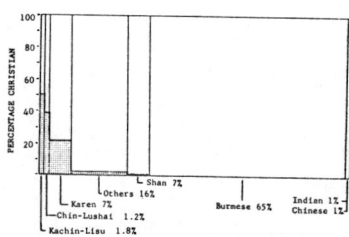

(NOTE: These figures are representative approximations. They should be seen as indications of magnitude, not precise.)

CURRENT STATUS OF CHRISTIANITY

Burma possesses one of the oldest and most impressive Buddhist traditions of Asia, and the Christian faith has come only in recent centuries, being first brought by Portuguese traders in the 16th century. The Roman Catholic Church traces its beginnings in Burma to A.D. 1560, while Protestant Christianity has existed since

---

Prepared for the **INTERNATIONAL CONGRESS ON WORLD EVANGELIZATION**, Lausanne, July 1974

TO PREACH THE GOSPEL TO THE POOR
TO HEAL THE BROKENHEARTED   TO PREACH DELIVERANCE TO THE CAPTIVES
AND RECOVERING OF SIGHT TO THE BLIND   TO SET AT LIBERTY THEM THAT ARE BRUISED

Adoniram Judson baptized U Naw in 1819. Christianity is not considered by most Burmese to be a part of Burmese culture or heritage and the Christian Church tends to be regarded by many as a foreign body, a memory of British colonial rule. Some of the opposition to Christianity therefore is not to the Church as such, but to its foreign nature and relationships.

After three centuries of missions, the total Christian community numbers about one million, or about three percent of the population of 30 million. Protestants are about two and a half times as numerous as Roman Catholics. The government recognizes the right of each person to exercise his religion and churches and temples are open and openly attended. However, the government felt that some restriction on foreign involvement was needed and, in 1966, all Protestant and most of the Catholic foreign missionaries were ordered to leave. Private schools and hospitals (many of them Christian) were nationalized, although theological schools were not affected. For more than a decade, Burmese Christians have found it difficult to gain permission to leave the country to attend conferences or educational institutions in other countries, and visitors from abroad have been restricted in the length of time they could visit and areas in which they could travel.

Although the Burmese government's assumption of responsibility for education and social welfare has taken certain institutions and ministries from the Christian Church, worship services and education continue. Regular church services are permitted, annual meetings and conferences are held, and theological education continues and is even strengthened. Publication of Christian literature is permitted although with some restrictions.

The departure of foreign missionaries and the nationalization of institutions has not paralyzed the Burmese Church. Indeed, there has been renewed vitality in many churches. Evangelistic efforts have been increased and strong church growth has been recorded in several areas. Increased enrollments in formal theological training is one of the encouraging aspects of the present state of the Church in Burma. Despite political and economic difficulties, the Christians of Burma are showing faith, devotion and optimism which give much hope for the future.

The strength of the Christian churches is greatly sapped by emigration. The Indians and Chinese minorities, among whom Christians have been more numerous than among the Burmese, are mistrusted by the Burmese. They stand in a lesser degree of citizenship rights. Some 25,000 Indian and Chinese Christians have emigrated from Rangoon alone in the last few years.

NATIONAL CHURCHES

The last complete government census of Burma was taken in 1931, so that population figures since that time have been estimates. Church statistics too at times are estimates, due to the widespread insurgency of Christianity since World War II which has touched virtually the entire country at one time or another.

Of the estimated population of 29.8 million, the Protestant community numbers slightly over 700,000, or 2.5% of the total population; and Roman Catholics 280,000, or almost 1%. Aside from a small Armenian Church in Rangoon, there are virtually no Orthodox Christians in Burma.

PROTESTANT

Baptists. Protestant missions to Burma began with a brief effort by English Baptists from Serampore in 1807, followed six years later by the arrival of the American Baptist, Adoniram Judson, who laid lasting foundations during his thirty-seven years of service (1813-1850). More than a century and a half of American Baptist efforts, involving a total of 794 missionaries, have contributed to the emergence of a strong Church, the Burma Baptist Convention, with a communicant membership of 276,789 (estimated community of at least 550,000), or 78% of all Protestants.

Baptist efforts to reach the dominant Burmese Buddhists were later paralleled by the sending of missionaries to animistic Karens, Kachins, Chins, Lahus, Was and others, most of them living on the distant hills along the borders. Whereas the Burmese and other Buddhists such as the Mons and the Shans gave minimal response to the Gospel, the animist response, coupled with continued Buddhist resistance, has resulted in a Baptist Church whose membership is roughly 95% animist and 5% Buddhist in background.

The wide linguistic and cultural diversity among Burma Baptists is recognized in the structure of the Burma Baptist Convention, which is composed primarily of language groups such as the Karen Baptist Convention, Pwo Karen Baptist Conference, Kachin Baptist Convention, Zomi (Chin) Baptist Convention, Burma Baptist Churches Union (Burmese speaking), etc. Each of these, in turn, is made up of local congregations using that particular language, regardless of geographical location. Despite the increasing use of Burmese as the *lingua franca* of the country, and the formation of one or two smaller units within the Convention on geographical, rather than linguistic lines, the Burma Baptist Convention basically continues to be composed of language groups, each with its own program in addition to that of the all-Burma organization. These include missionary outreach, publications, youth programs, Bible schools and seminaries.

The Burma Baptist Convention helps to coordinate the efforts of the various language groups, and on a nation-wide basis carries on programs of evangelism, Christian education, youth activities, women's work, and publications. It has primary responsibility for the Burma Divinity School, an English language seminary in which other Protestant denominations share to a limited extent.

Anglicans. The Church of England entered Burma in 1859 through the efforts of the Society for the Propagation of the Gospel, which opened schools in Lower and Central Burma for both Burmese and Karens. In the 1920's, the Bible Churchmen's Missionary Society opened medical centers in the Shan States, the Kachin area, and on the Arakan coast, and emphasized direct evangelism. The departure of British government servants with the granting of political independence in 1948, and of all Anglican missionaries in 1966, placed new responsibilities upon the Anglican Church in Burma. It was a part of the Church of India, Pakistan, Burma and Ceylon until 1970, but now is a separate Province, with its own archbishop and bishops.

Present membership is 26,000, or nearly 4% of the total Protestant community. Anglicans operate three seminaries, with 44 students.

Methodists. American Methodists came to Burma in the 1870's, taking the Gospel primarily to Chinese in Burma, and later working among the Burmese as well. Their efforts have been confined to Lower Burma, in and near Rangoon. An autonomous Church since 1965, Lower Burma Methodists currently number a community of 2,000.

British Methodists began work in Mandalay and other centers in Upper Burma in 1887. Like all missions endeavoring to evangelize Buddhists, they found a very limited response until they came into contact with Lushais, immigrants from India, along the Chindwin River. Comparatively large numbers of these hill people have come into the Methodist Church of Upper Burma, resulting in a present community of 25,000.

All Methodists in Burma now total 27,000 or 4% of the Protestants. The two Methodist groups have been engaged in consultations with a view to church union.

Assemblies of God. The entrance of the Assemblies of God into Burma began with the movement of their Christians of the Lisu tribe from China into the extreme northeastern portion of Burma in the 1930's. That work grew markedly following World War II among both Lisu and Rawang people and a Bible School was established in 1965. Postwar work was begun in Rangoon and vicinity, plus another center in the hills east of Mandalay, in each case with an American missionary initially directing the work. Churches in the Rangoon area have continued to grow, and present Assemblies of God strength in Burma is estimated to be at least 25,000, nearly 4% of all Protestants.

Churches of Christ. Like the Assemblies of God, this mission entered Burma in the 1930's from China, following the movement of the Lisu people. Strong numerical growth and development of the work along agricultural and educational lines was experienced after World War II, encouraged by several missionary families. Converts are from both the Lisu and Rawang tribes. The language of the latter Kachin tribe has been reduced to writing and most of the New Testament translated. Membership is estimated to be at least 25,000.

Other Churches. Smaller denominations include: The Presbyterian Church in the far northwest, made up of Lushai immigrants from India, numbering 14,000; the Lisu Inland Church in the northeast near Lashio, comprised of former China Inland Mission Christians who fled into Burma, with 8,000 members; the Seventh-day Adventist churches, with a membership of 6,000; the Self-Supporting Karen Baptist Churches (independent of the Burma Baptist Convention), numbering 5,000; and other smaller groups totaling about another 20,000.

ROMAN CATHOLIC

The introduction of Roman Catholicism to Burma in the 1550's coincided roughly with the coming of Portuguese and other European mercenaries into Southeast Asia, and the development of commercial relationships between Portugal and numerous native states. Franciscan missionaries in Pegu and Jesuits were followed by others, chiefly Barnabites. However, Catholic missionaries were few in number, only thirty-eight having served in Burma during the two and one-half centuries 1559-1800. Converts were few, chiefly from the Eurasian community which had come into being. Roman Catholic missionary efforts were considerably strengthened after the middle of the nineteenth century, with the arrival of members of the Paris Mission Society and later the Seminary of Milan. Efforts among the Karens brought a number of converts into the Church. In the twentieth century, and especially immediately following World War II, American and Irish missionary orders continued the expansion of the work among Kachins, Chins, Shans, etc. However, the nationalization of schools in 1965-1966 removed from Church control the strong educational work which had been developed.

Recognizing the need for many more national priests, Catholics strengthened the work of their minor seminaries and opened a major seminary during the years after World War II. An archbishop-designate and two or three bishops were chosen from the national priests during the 1960's. Although the government expulsion of missionaries in 1966 affected more than half the Catholic foreign missionaries, a number of the older priests and bishops were permitted to remain, and they have continued, though with dwindling numbers, to the present. Meanwhile, more priests have been trained from among the nationals, strengthening the indigenous nature of the Church.

With schools and hospitals now nationalized, Roman Catholics, like Protestants, are devoting their efforts to local church services, youth work, theological institutions, and publications.

CHRISTIAN COMMUNITY AS PERCENT OF POPULATION

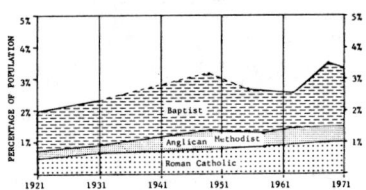

(Note: These figures are representative approximations. They should be seen as indications of magnitude, not precise.)

COOPERATIVE ENTERPRISES

The Burma Christian Council. In its early years, this organization was closely related to the National Christian Council of India and was dominated by missionaries. Political independence and the emergence of more truly national churches have changed this to a marked degree. For more than a decade, Burmese have served as chairmen and secretaries for the Council, although funds to support its work have continued to come from America and Europe. Sponsoring several all-Burma Pastors' Conferences arranged by World Vision has been a positive contribution of the Council to a greater sense of Christian unity among the various denominations.

Relief projects, especially to meet refugee needs, have received considerable attention. Aside from the two Methodist bodies, none of the denominations has seriously considered possible church union.

MAJOR CHRISTIAN PROGRAMS AND ACTIVITIES

The following descriptions are intended to make the readers aware of the potential for various types of ministries. Not all church agencies are specifically mentioned.

EVANGELISM

There is renewed concern for evangelistic outreach in many of the churches. Evangelistic campaigns, including mass rallies, have been held in widely scattered areas in the country.

BROADCASTING

Through the arrangements of the Audio-Visual Center of the Burma Christian Council, a daily broadcast, alternating between Burmese and Sgaw Karen, is aired from the stations of the Far East Broadcasting Company in the Philippines. Similar programs are beamed to Burma from the South East Asia Radio Voice of the National Christian Council of the Philippines. Except for an occasional special program at Christmas or Easter, the government-controlled Burma Broadcasting Station does not permit religious broadcasting on its station.

LITERATURE

The Christian Literature Society is the interdenominational publishing society of Burma. In addition, the various denominations have their own publishing programs, including (especially among the Baptists) presses which have been established by the different language groups. Paper shortages and government censorship have made Christian publishing difficult but not impossible.

BIBLE TRANSLATION AND DISTRIBUTION

The entire Bible has been translated into Burmese, Sgaw Karen, Pwo Karen, Shan, Kachin/Jinghpaw, Man and Lisu. Some nine other Burma languages have the entire New Testament, with portions available in 12 other languages. Thus, a total of about 28 of the 126 languages and major dialects of the country possess some part of God's word.

Translation is presently being carried on in six languages, three of them (Burmese, Shan, and Falam Chin) in popular style. Translators' conferences and workshops are held at times, occasionally with a translations expert from abroad assisting.

Revision of some older translations, plus the completion of the Pa-O New Testament and the Lahu Old Testament are among the more urgent needs still unmet.

The Bible Society of Burma, for many years the Burma Agency of the British and Foreign Bible Society, has been an independent Bible Society since 1965. The last permit to import Scriptures in Burman languages printed abroad (available from London) was granted in 1969, so that stocks of Bibles and New Testaments are now virtually exhausted. Portions and Selections from the Scriptures are being printed in Burma, and plans are being made to print New Testaments and Bibles in several languages—a monumental task in view of paper shortages and existing restrictions.

Scripture distribution through the Bible Society in 1972 totaled:

Bibles	2,628
New Testaments	4,156
Portions	37,952
Selections	195,867
Total	240,607

EDUCATION

Although private schools, including several hundred Christian institutions, were nationalized in 1965-1966, this order did not apply to theological schools, many of which have continued with enlarged enrollments (see Table 2). These institutions vary from one or two-year vernacular Bible schools to the Burma Divinity School and the Roman Catholic Major Seminary, each with a curriculum of at least four or five years, with English the medium of instruction.

SOCIAL CONCERN

Considerable financial assistance has been given to Burma each year for relief and rehabilitation through the World Council of Churches and Church World Service. This has been used primarily to assist refugees (those who have fled into Burma from China, and those dispossessed by insurgent action within the country), plus victims of fire, flood, and famine. Blankets, used clothing, medical supplies and the like were also sent to Burma and distributed widely during the years before governmental restrictions rendered this largely impossible.

Disasters in other countries, such as cyclones and floods in East Pakistan in the 1960's, prompted many churches in Burma to contribute to Christian relief efforts, comparatively sizeable sums being raised for such needs.

THE NATION AND ITS PEOPLE

POPULATION

Burma's population in 1973 was estimated as 29.8 million, most of whom live in towns and villages. Rangoon (1,500,000), Mandalay (350,000), and Moulmein (200,000) are the largest cities. The Burmese people constitute 65 to 70% of the total population, followed by much smaller ethnic groups of Karens, Shans, Kachins, Chins and others, many of them quite small in numbers.

LITERACY AND LANGUAGES

There are 126 languages and major dialects spoken in Burma. Burmese is increasingly becoming the *lingua franca* of the land. Approximately 60% of the people are literate.

RELIGION

The state religion of Burma is Buddhism though right of religious profession is guaranteed. 85% of the population profess Buddhism, while 11.5% practice some animistic or other form, and about 3.5% profess Christianity.

The graph following presents the relative distribution of the religious professions.

ESTIMATED RELIGIOUS AFFILIATIONS

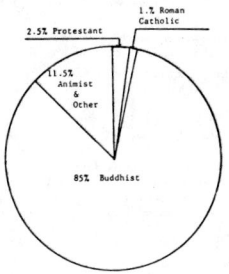

GEOGRAPHY AND CLIMATE

Burma, a country roughly the size of the state of Texas, or of France, Belgium, Netherlands and Denmark combined, lies between China and India, the world's two most populated nations. Through the centuries, this land has not been absorbed by either of its big neighbors, due primarily to the great horsehoe of mountains that protects it on three sides. Large sections of Burma's boundry with its neighbors follow the crest of these mountainous ridges. The flat land lies in the center and south of the country, drained by the Irrawaddy River system, with the rich soil of the delta one of the great rice-producing areas of the world.

The climate is controlled by monsoons, blowing from the southwest from May to October bringing rains, and from the northeast from October to May bringing dry and cooler air.

HISTORY

Until 1826, the political history of Burma involved the rise and fall of numerous kingdoms in the south and central portions of the country. Conflicts between these kingdoms, and with Thailand and Assam, occupied much of the time and interest of the Buddhist monarchs--Mon, Shan, and Burmese--who ruled during the centuries preceding the nineteenth.

British expansion from India, met by Burmese opposition, lay back of the First Anglo-Burmese War, 1824-1826, by which the British took over the coastal areas of Arakan and Tenasserim. All of Lower Burma as far north as Toungoo and Prome fell to the British in 1852, and the remainder fell in 1885. Burma became a part of British India and continued so until 1937, when it came under separate administration, with its own British governor and separate legislative body, which was given limited powers.

World War II brought the Japanese invasion of Burma. In the end, the people revolted against this, and cooperated with the re-invading British and American forces. At the end of the war, they demanded complete independence. This was achieved on January 4, 1948, and Burma, unlike most former British colonies, severed all political ties with the Commonwealth.

Political instability and lawlessness, evidenced in the assassination of Burma's popular freedom-fighter, General Aung San, and several other cabinet members in 1947, continued in the years following independence. Both leftist groups (Communist and others) and rightists (nationalistic Karens and others) waged open and covert warfare against the parliamentary democracy which had been established. At one time or another, most sections of the country came under insurgent control.

In March 1962, the Burma armed forces under General Ne Win assumed power, set up the Revolutionary Government of the Union of Burma, and have controlled the country since then. No political opposition has been permitted. Nationalization of the economy and social services of all kinds has taken place, including that of private schools and hospitals during 1965-1966. All Protestant foreign missionaries and more than half the Roman Catholics were ordered out by the Burma Government in 1966. Visits by foreigners have been severely restricted, a visa presently being valid for a maximum of one week.

ECONOMY

Burma is predominantly agricultural, rice being its chief crop and major export. It is a leading exporter of teak. Silver, lead, zinc and wolfram are its mineral exports, along with some rubber. The average per capita income of Burma is 388 Kyat (U.S. $80).

Table 1

THE CHRISTIAN POPULATION, CLERGY
AND THEOLOGICAL INSTITUTIONS OF BURMA

	Size of Community	Ordained Ministers	Seminaries and Bible Schools	Students
Baptists	550,000	718	26	874
Roman Catholics	280,000	175	6	480
Anglicans	26,000		3	44
Methodists, Upper Burma	25,000	10+	1	7
Assemblies of God	25,000	40	1	25
Churches of Christ	25,000			
Presbyterian Church	14,000	15		
Lisu Inland Church	8,000			
Mara Christians	8,000			
Seventh-day Adventists	6,000	30	2	60
Self-Supporting Karen Baptists	5,000			
Methodists, Lower Burma	2,000	13		
Lutherans	400			
Salvation Army	300			
St. Gabriel's Church	200			
Other Christian Groups	12,000			
	986,900			

(Figures are for the total Christian community.)
Source: *Secretary, Burma Christian Council, 1973.*

Table 2

CHRISTIAN POPULATION BY ETHNIC GROUPS -- BURMA 1971

Ethnic Group	Total Population	Percent of Burma Pop.	Christian[1] Community	Percent of Ethnic Population	Percent of Christian Population
Burmese	18,200,000[2]	65.0%[2]	20,000[4]	.1%	2.0%
Karen	2,000,000[3]	7.0%	450,000[4]	23.0%	45.0%
Shan	2,000,000[3]	7.0%	10,000[4]	.5%	1.0%
Kachin-Lisu	500,000[3]	1.8%	250,000[4]	50.0%	25.0%
Chin-Lushai	400,000[4]	1.4%	150,000[4]	38.0%	15.0%
Others	4,900,000	18.0%	120,000[4]	2.0%	12.0%
	28,000,000[5]		1,000,000		

Note: *There has been no nation-wide census of Burma since 1931.*

[1] *Includes Protestant and Roman Catholic communities.*
[2] *Based on latest census (1931) figure, indicating 65% of population was Burmese.*
[3] *Estimates of the Secretary, Burma Christian Council.*
[4] *Estimates, based on estimates of Secy., Burma Christian Council, and statistics from Agenzia Internazionale Fides, Rome, plus compiler's background as Field Secy., Burma Baptist Missionary Fellowship, Rangoon, 1961-1966.*
[5] *Extrapolation from U.N. estimate (1970) of 27,584,000.*

SELECTED BIBLIOGRAPHY AND INFORMATION SOURCES

The sources listed below are to help the reader find additional information on this country and Christian ministries there. This list does not try to be comprehensive or complete.

DOCUMENTS

American University Field Staff, Area Handbook for Burma, DA Pam. 550-61, Washington, D. C., U. S. Government Printing Office.

Cady, John F., Thailand, Burma, Laos, Cambodia. Englewood Cliffs, New Jersey, Prentice-Hall, 1966.

Kane, J. Herbert, A Global View of Christian Missions. Grand Rapids, Baker Book House, 1971.

Lebar, Frank M., Hickey, Gerald C., and Musgrave, John K., Ethnic Groups of Mainland Southeast Asia. New Haven, Connecticut, Human Relations Area Files Press, 1964.

Shwe Wa and Sowards, Burma Baptist Chronicle. Rangoon, Burma, Baptist Convention, 1963.

Tegenfeldt, Herman G., Through Deep Waters. Valley Forge, Pennsylvania, American Baptist Foreign Mission Society, 1968.

Trager, Frank N., Burma: From Kingdom to Republic. New York, Praeger, 1966.

ORGANIZATIONS

Burma Christian Council, 20, Signal Pagoda Road, Rangoon, Burma.

ACKNOWLEDGEMENTS

The information in this profile was taken from many sources which were the best available to the editors at the time of preparation. However, the accuracy of the information cannot be guaranteed. Views expressed or implied in this profile are not necessarily those of the ICOWE convenors or planning staff. The editors have tried to present the ministries of various organizations in an objective manner, without undue bias or emphasis. Where we have failed, we apologize for erroneous impressions that may result and request that comments and corrections be sent to MARC, 919 W. Huntington Drive, Monrovia, California, USA, 91016. We appreciate and acknowledge the comments and contributions of various organizations and individuals in the preparation of this profile, with special recognition to Dr. Herman Tegenfeldt.

Copyright © 1974* International Congress on World Evangelization. Reproduction of this document is permitted if appropriate credit is given.

(Printed in the U.S.A.)

STATUS OF CHRISTIANITY PROFILE SERIES

Andhra Pradesh
Argentina
Arunachal Pradesh
Assam
Australia
Bangladesh
Bolivia
Brazil
Burma
Cambodia
Canada
Colombia
Ecuador
Egypt
Ethiopia
Fiji Indians
Finland
France
Ghana
Greece
Gujarat
Haiti
Hawaii
Hong Kong
India
Indonesia
Japan

Karen People
Kenya
Korea
Laos
Lebanon
Malaysia
Mexico
New Zealand
North Africa
Norway
Oceania
Pakistan
Panama
Papua New Guinea
Philippines
Portugal
Puerto Rico
Singapore
South Africa
Spain
Sri Lanka
Swaziland
Taiwan
Thailand
U. S. A.
Vietnam

Available through:

Missions Advanced Research & Communications Center
919 W. Huntington Drive
Monrovia, Cal. 91016

William Carey Library

04/22/74

MARC UNREACHED PEOPLES DATA FILE

GROUP NAME: ADJA   COUNTRY: DAHOMEY

GROUP TYPE: ETHNO-LING

GROUP POPULATION: 250,000 DATE: 1973 % OF NATION: 08 GROUP TREND: GROWING
MURDOCK CODE: FA18   MARC ID: 423S

OTHER LOCATIONS: TOGO

PRIMARY LANGUAGES: GE   FON (YORUBA)

LITERACY: GENERAL-20%. CHRISTIAN-20%

MAIN RELIGION: ANIMISM   % OF GROUP: 95   TREND: STABLE

OTHER RELIGIONS	% OF GROUP	GROWTH TREND	CHRISTIAN COMMUNITY	% OF GROUP
CHRISTIANITY	05	GROWING	PROTESTANT	02
ANIMISM	95	STABLE	ROMAN CATHOLIC	03

CHURCHES & MISSIONS (LARGER)	TRAD	YEAR BEGUN	ADHERENTS FROM GROUP	GROWTH TREND	TOTAL ADHERENTS IN COUNTRY
METHODIST CH. IN DAHOMEY-TOGO	PRO	1930	3,000	GROWING	45,000
PENTECOSTAL CHURCH	PRO	1950	2,000	STABLE	10,000
ROMAN CATHOLIC CH. IN DAHOMEY	RCC	1930	4,500	GROWING	1,500,000

FIRST CHRISTIAN WITNESS: 1930'S ROMAN CATHOLIC & METHODIST CHURCH.

OPEN TO CHANGE: YES   % HEARING GOSPEL: 25-50   ATTITUDE: FAVORABLE
SCRIPTURE AVAILABILITY: BIBLE IN EWE 1900; N.T. IN MINA 1940.

COMMENT: ADJA ARE A TRIBAL GROUP OF AGRICULTURAL WORKERS IN LOWER SOCIO-ECONOMIC CLASS. SEMI-ISOLATED WITH POSTAL & RADIO MEDIA. A SUB-GROUP OF BENIN TRIBE. EFFECTIVE EVANGELISTS ARE LOCAL PREACHERS, NATIONAL CHRISTIAN TEAMS & FOREIGN MISSIONARIES LEARNING LANGUAGE & CULTURE. CHRISTIANITY WOULD BE ENCOURAGED BY GOSPEL LITERATURE RELATING TO THEIR LIVES & MODERN REVISION OF SCRIPTURE IN GE (A MIXTURE OF EWE & MINA). HINDRANCES ARE PRICE OF SCRIPTURE & INFLUENCE OF RELIGIOUS SECTS.

INFORMATION SOURCES: H.HENRY,METH.CH.IN DAHOMEY-TOGO,B.P.34,COTONOU,DAHOMEY
REV.J.PERRY,40,PEMBERTON RD.,E.MOLESEY,SURREY,ENGLAND.

TOTAL ORIGINAL SOURCES: 1   ORIGIN DATE: 2/74   LATEST ENTRY DATE: 2/74

04/22/74

MARC UNREACHED PEOPLES DATA FILE

GROUP NAME: AFAR   COUNTRY: ETHIOPIA

OTHER NAMES: DANAKIL, ADAL, TSELTAL   GROUP TYPE: RELIGIOUS

GROUP POPULATION: 250,000 DATE: 1973 % OF NATION: .9 GROUP TREND: STABLE
OTHER LOCATIONS: F.T. OF AFARS+ISSAS   MARC ID: 21S

PRIMARY LANGUAGES: AFAR   ARABIC

LINGUA FRANCA: ARABIC   LITERACY: GENERAL-08%. CHRISTIAN-20%

MAIN RELIGION: ISLAM   % OF GROUP: 99   TREND: STABLE

OTHER RELIGIONS	% OF GROUP	GROWTH TREND	CHRISTIAN COMMUNITY	% OF GROUP
CHRISTIANITY	.2	STABLE	PROTESTANT	.1
ISLAM	99	STABLE	ROMAN CATHOLIC	.1
ANIMISM	50	DECLINE		

CHURCHES & MISSIONS(LARGER)	TRAD	YEAR BEGUN	ADHERENTS FROM GROUP	GROWTH TREND	TOTAL ADHERENTS IN COUNTRY
ROMAN CATHOLIC CHURCH	RCC		250		

FIRST CHRISTIAN WITNESS: 1956 RED SEA MISSION TEAM

OPEN TO CHANGE: NO   % HEARING GOSPEL: -10 ATTITUDE: RELUCTANT
SCRIPTURE AVAILABILITY: GOSPEL OF JOHN TRANSLATED BUT NOT YET PUBLISHED.

COMMENT: AFAR ARE A TRIBAL, RELIGIOUS GROUP, MOSTLY SEMI-NOMADIC LOWER CLASS: A FEW ARE PROFESSIONALS & STUDENTS. IN DESERT, LOWLANDS & E. COAST OF ETHIOPIA. THEY ARE SEMI-ISOLATED HAVING A STABLE GROWTH IN POPULATION. VERY LITTLE RESPONSE FROM EVANGELISTIC METHODS. AFARS & FOREIGNERS OVERLOOKING CULTURE DIFFERENCES WOULD BE EFFECTIVE EVANGELISTS. SCRIPTURE IN VERNACULAR, CHRISTIANS MEETING PEOPLE ON THEIR LEVEL WOULD ENCOURAGE CHRISTIANITY. HINDRANCES ARE ILLITERACY, LACK OF WORKERS & OTHER CULTURES.

INFORMATION SOURCES: MISS E.M. PARKER, INSTITUTE OF ETHIOPIAN STUDIES, BOX 30730, ADDIS ABABA, ETHIOPIA; ALSO LIST OF BOOKS GIVEN.

TOTAL ORIGINAL SOURCES: 1   ORIGIN DATE: 10/73 LATEST ENTRY DATE: 10/73

04/22/74

MARC UNREACHED PEOPLES DATA FILE

GROUP NAME: ALAK　　　　　COUNTRY: LAOS

GROUP TYPE: ETHNO-LING

GROUP POPULATION: 80,000　DATE: 1973　% OF NATION: 03　GROUP TREND: DECLINE

MARC ID: 1125

PRIMARY LANGUAGES: ALAK

LINGUA FRANCA: LAO　　　　LITERACY: GENERAL-10%.

MAIN RELIGION: ANIMISM　　% OF GROUP: 99

OTHER RELIGIONS	% OF GROUP	GROWTH TREND	CHRISTIAN COMMUNITY	% OF GROUP
CHRISTIANITY	-1			
ANIMISM	99			

CHURCHES & MISSIONS (LARGER)	TRAD	YEAR BEGUN	ADHERENTS FROM GROUP	GROWTH TREND	TOTAL ADHERENTS IN COUNTRY

FIRST CHRISTIAN WITNESS: 1957-61

OPEN TO CHANGE: NO　　% HEARING GOSPEL: -10
SCRIPTURE AVAILABILITY: NO TRANSLATION HAS BEEN DONE.

COMMENT: ALAK ARE AN ETHNO-LINGUISTIC GROUP OF AGRICULTURAL WORKERS. SEMI-ISOLATED, THEY ARE WITHOUT COMMUNICATION MEDIA. MANY ARE REFUGEES FROM THIS UNIT. LITERACY RATE IS PROBABLY UNDER 10%. LESS THAN 10 CHRISTIANS ARE AMONG THIS GROUP WITH NO CHURCHES REPORTED. SCRIPTURE TRANSLATION AND DISTRIBUTION ARE NEEDED.

INFORMATION SOURCES: OVERSEAS MISSIONARY FELLOWSHIP, PO BOX 55, SAVANNAKHET, LAOS.

TOTAL ORIGINAL SOURCES: 1　ORIGIN DATE: 11/73　LATEST ENTRY DATE: 11/73

04/22/74

MARC UNREACHED PEOPLES DATA FILE

GROUP NAME: AMBONESE   COUNTRY: NETHERLANDS
OTHER NAMES: AMBON MALAY   GROUP TYPE: ETHNO-LING
GROUP POPULATION: 30,000 DATE: 1973 % OF NATION: -1 GROUP TREND:GROWING
                                  MURDOCK CODE: OH4   MARC ID: 67N
OTHER LOCATIONS: INDONESIA
PRIMARY LANGUAGES: AMBONESE   DUTCH

MAIN RELIGION: ANIMISM   % OF GROUP: 70 TREND: STABLE

OTHER RELIGIONS	% OF GROUP	GROWTH TREND	CHRISTIAN COMMUNITY	% OF GROUP
CHRISTIANITY	03	GROWING	PROTESTANT	01
ANIMISM	70	STABLE	ROMAN CATHOLIC	01

CHURCHES & MISSIONS(LARGER)	TRAD YEAR BEGUN	ADHERENTS FROM GROUP	GROWTH TREND	TOTAL ADHERENTS IN COUNTRY

SCRIPTURE AVAILABILITY: BIBLE IN DUTCH. NO SCRIPTURE IN AMBON.

COMMENT: AN IMMIGRANT GROUP FROM AMBON ISLAND,INDONESIA, CLANNISH IN OUT-
LOOK,NOT INTERMARRYING, AND LIVING IN RURAL AND URBAN AREAS. MOST FOLLOW
SPIRITISM. WITNESS IS LIMITED TO A FEW CHRISTIAN AMBONESE, INDONESIANS,
AND DUTCH. JESUS PEOPLE HAVE RECENTLY HAD SOME IMPACT ON YOUTH. SOME
GOSPEL TEAMS USED;ALSO CORRESPONDENCE COURSES IN DUTCH. REACHING YOUTH
AND YOUNGER LEADERS CAN ENCOURAGE SPREAD OF GOSPEL. INDONESIAN EVANGEL-
ISTS, ESPECIALLY AMBONESE, CAN BE EFFECTIVE.

INFORMATION SOURCES: DAVID RICHARDS, PRESIDENT, CENTRAL PENTECOSTAL BIBLE
COLLEGE, THE HAGUE, SCHEVENINGSEWEG 11.

TOTAL ORIGINAL SOURCES: 1   ORIGIN DATE: 11/73 LATEST ENTRY DATE: 11/73

04/22/74

MARC UNREACHED PEOPLES DATA FILE

GROUP NAME: ARUSHA   COUNTRY: TANZANIA

OTHER NAMES: AGRICULTURAL MAASAI   GROUP TYPE: ETHNO-LING

GROUP POPULATION: 110,000 DATE:C1973 % OF NATION: -1

MARC ID: 142B

OTHER LOCATIONS: KENYA

PRIMARY LANGUAGES: ARUSHA

MAIN RELIGION: ANIMISM   % OF GROUP: 88   TREND: STABLE

OTHER RELIGIONS	% OF GROUP	GROWTH TREND	CHRISTIAN COMMUNITY	% OF GROUP
CHRISTIANITY	12	GROWING		
ANIMISM	88	STABLE		

CHURCHES & MISSIONS(LARGER)	TRAD	YEAR BEGUN	ADHERENTS FROM GROUP	GROWTH TREND	TOTAL ADHERENTS IN COUNTRY
LUTHERAN	PRO		7,000		
CATHOLIC	RCC	1921			
ASSEMBLY OF GOD	PRO				
SEVENTH-DAY ADVENTIST	PRO				
BAPTIST	PRO				

FIRST CHRISTIAN WITNESS: POSSIBLY LIEPZIG MISSION IN 1904.

OPEN TO CHANGE: YES   % HEARING GOSPEL: 10-25
SCRIPTURE AVAILABILITY: NEW TESTAMENT IN 1922,GOSPELS IN 1904.DETAILS UNK

COMMENT: INDIGENOUS TRIBAL UNIT,NOMADIC AND SEMI-ISOLATED.SUBGROUP OF
BANTU UNIT.ARUSHAS ALSO RESEMBLE,LIVE WITH,AND SHARE THE LANGUAGE OF THE
NILOTIC MAASAI.THERE WAS RAPID GROWTH OF THE LUTHERAN CHURCH FROM 1950-60
WHEN MEMBERSHIP INCREASED FROM 3000 TO 7000 IN A SHORT PERIOD OF TIME.
THERE ARE NOW SIX AGENCIES WORKING WITH ARUSHAS.

INFORMATION SOURCES: DAVID BARRETT'S SURVEY REPORT ON AFRICA. DAVID BARRETT
UNIT OF RESEARCH,P.O.BOX 40230, NAIROBI, KENYA

TOTAL ORIGINAL SOURCES: 1   ORIGIN DATE: 11/73 LATEST ENTRY DATE: 11/73

04/22/74

MARC UNREACHED PEOPLES DATA FILE

GROUP NAME: APARTMENT RESIDENTS-SEOUL   COUNTRY: KOREA, REPUBLIC OF

GROUP TYPE: GEOGRAPHIC

GROUP POPULATION: 87,000 DATE: 1973 % OF NATION: -1 GROUP TREND: GROWING

MARC ID: 301N

PRIMARY LANGUAGES: KOREAN

LITERACY: GENERAL-99%. CHRISTIAN-99%

MAIN RELIGION: ANIMISM   % OF GROUP: 50

OTHER RELIGIONS	% OF GROUP	GROWTH TREND	CHRISTIAN COMMUNITY	% OF GROUP
CHRISTIANITY	15	GROWING	PROTESTANT	11
ANIMISM	50		ROMAN CATHOLIC	04
BUDDHISM	09	GROWING		
CONFUCIANISM	01	STABLE		

CHURCHES & MISSIONS (LARGER)	TRAD	YEAR BEGUN	ADHERENTS FROM GROUP	GROWTH TREND	TOTAL ADHERENTS IN COUNTRY
KOREAN APARTMENT EVANG. SOC.	PRO	1972	8,000		
ASSEMBLIES OF GOD	PRO				
BAPTISTS	PRO				

FIRST CHRISTIAN WITNESS: CA. 1965 WHEN APARTMENTS FIRST BUILT.

OPEN TO CHANGE: YES   % HEARING GOSPEL: 25-50   ATTITUDE: FAVORABLE
SCRIPTURE AVAILABILITY: BIBLE IN KOREAN

COMMENT: AN URBAN SOCIO-ECONOMIC GROUP FOUND IN APARTMENT COMPLEXES OF SEOUL. SIMILAR GROUPS FOUND IN OTHER URBAN AREAS. EASILY ACCESSIBLE AND GROWING IN SIZE. MOST ARE OF LOWER MIDDLE CLASS. 40-50% FOLLOW ANIMISM OR SHAMANISM. SOME KOREAN 'NEW RELIGIONS'. SOME OPENNESS TO GOSPEL. SYSTEMATIC VISITATION IS EFFECTIVE. SEVERAL CHURCHES HAVE WITNESS TO THIS GROUP. ABOUT 20% OF THOSE APPROACHED IN DOOR-TO-DOOR VISTS BY APART. EVANG. SOC. MAKE DECISIONS FOR CHRIST.

INFORMATION SOURCES: KOREAN APARTMENT EVANGELISM SOCIETY, 3/35 CHOONG CHONG RO, SUDAIMON-KU, SEOUL.

TOTAL ORIGINAL SOURCES: 1   ORIGIN DATE: 1/74 LATEST ENTRY DATE: 1/74

EMPIRICAL DATA FORM

One of the interesting findings that I have come up with in the study of unreached peoples, is the fact that apparently there are some signs that can be read as indicators of a people readiness for change. This means that if they were presented the Gospel at such a time in a way that was acceptable, they might be ready to accept Christ.

I am looking for more information to try this out in test cases, and wonder if you will assist me by providing simple information from your experience.

Consider one group of people that you know best, a homogeneous unit. Confine your information to that group. Then think how you would rate the following factors as they influence the group. This should be done by thinking in terms of a scale analysis, working within the range of 1 to 5. "1" would be very low activity, and "5" would be very high activity. In this pattern, would you supply the following information?

Name of unit: _SGAW KAREN TRIBE_   Country: _THAILAND_

	Low High
Is there much cultural change taking place?	2
Is there much political change taking place?	1
Is there much economic change taking place?	2
Is there much religious change taking place?	3
Has the Scripture been introduced or translated recently?	5
Are migratory patterns becoming evident?	1
Is the image of Christianity low or high?	4
What degree of Christian witness has reached the group?	3
How would you rate its receptivity to Christianity?	4

EMPIRICAL DATA FORM

One of the interesting findings that I have come up with in the study of unreached peoples, is the fact that apparently there are some signs that can be read as indicators of a people readiness for change. This means that if they were presented the Gospel at such a time in a way that was acceptable, they might be ready to accept Christ.

I am looking for more information to try this out in test cases, and wonder if you will assist me by providing simple information from your experience.

Consider one group of people that you know best, a homogeneous unit. Confine your information to that group. Then think how you would rate the following factors as they influence the group. This should be done by thinking in terms of a scale analysis, working within the range of 1 to 5. "1" would be very low activity, and "5" would be very high activity. In this pattern, would you supply the following information?

Name of unit: _____ *HIGI* _____   Country: *NIGERIA*

	Low — High
Is there much cultural change taking place?	3 - 4
Is there much political change taking place?	3 - 4
Is there much economic change taking place?	3
Is there much religious change taking place?	3 - 4
Has the Scripture been introduced or translated recently?	*N. T. COMING OFF PRESS IN 1974*
Are migratory patterns becoming evident?	2 - 3
Is the image of Christianity low or high?	3 - 4
What degree of Christian witness has reached the group?	2 (?)
How would you rate its receptivity to Christianity?	4

EMPIRICAL DATA FORM

One of the interesting findings that I have come up with in the study of unreached peoples, is the fact that apparently there are some signs that can be read as indicators of a people readiness for change. This means that if they were presented the Gospel at such a time in a way that was acceptable, they might be ready to accept Christ.

I am looking for more information to try this out in test cases, and wonder if you will assist me by providing simple information from your experience.

Consider one group of people that you know best, a homogeneous unit. Confine your information to that group. Then think how you would rate the following factors as they influence the group. This should be done by thinking in terms of a scale analysis, working within the range of 1 to 5. "1" would be very low activity, and "5" would be very high activity. In this pattern, would you supply the following information?

Name of unit: _RURAL TAIWANESE_   Country: _S. TAINAN_

	Low	High
Is there much cultural change taking place?	2	
Is there much political change taking place?	1	
Is there much economic change taking place?		3
Is there much religious change taking place?	2	
Has the Scripture been introduced or translated recently?	1	
Are migratory patterns becoming evident?	(OUT)	5
Is the image of Christianity low or high?	2	
What degree of Christian witness has reached the group?	2	
How would you rate its receptivity to Christianity?	2	

ABOUT THE AUTHOR

Edward C. Pentecost served as representative of the International Fellowship of Evangelical Students in Mexico, which resulted in the formation of the Compañerismo Estudiantil Evangelico Mexicano with its own board. During the time of service there he also saw the initiation of indigenous churches whose ministries continue. Upon completion of the assignment of work in Mexico he accepted a teaching position at Philadelphia College of Bible, where he also served as Chairman of the Department of Missions and Director of the Bible Missions Major. During that time he served as Secretary-Treasurer of the Association of Evangelical Professors of Missions.

In 1971 he entered the School of World Mission of Fuller Theological Seminary to pursue the program leading to the Doctor of Missiology. Fulfilling this program and working in cooperation with Missions Advanced Research and Communications Center, he spent the year 1973-74 as Research Coordinator for the International Congress on World Evangelization, which gave the opportunity to study more in depth the unreached peoples of the world, and produce the foregoing.

His ministry has included serving as visiting professor at the Central American Mission Bible Institute and Seminary in Guatemala, and as invited Bible expositor at the annual meeting of ALERTA in Argentina.

He holds the Th.M. degree from Dallas Theological Seminary, the M.A. in Spanish from the National University of Mexico, the M.A. and D.Miss. from the School of World Mission of Fuller Theological Seminary.